THE TRAIN
KEPT A-ROLLIN'

First published in Great Britain in 2016 by Soundcheck Books LLP, 88 Northchurch Road, London, N1 3NY.

Copyright © Spencer Vignes 2016

ISBN: 978-0-9932120-9-3

Every effort has been made to contact copyright holders of photographic and other resource material used in this book. Some were unreachable. If they contact the publishers we will endeavour to credit them in reprints and future editions.

A CIP record for this book is available from the British Library

Book design: Benn Linfield (www.bennlinfield.com)

Printed by: Bell & Bain Ltd, Glasgow

THE TRAIN
KEPT A-ROLLIN'
HOW THE TRAIN SONG CHANGED
THE FACE OF POPULAR MUSIC

SPENCER VIGNES

soundcheck books

the stories behind the sounds

For Jane, who loves the music and tolerates the trains

"There's nothing that stirs my imagination like a steam locomotive,
that lonesome whistle cutting through the night and that
column of black smoke and steam throwing shadows across the land.
When I was a boy the trains ran right past my house and
they carried with them that promise that somewhere down
the track anything would be possible."

Johnny Cash

"Trains are percussive. Trains sing. If you don't like trains,
you probably don't like music either."

Peggy Seeger

CONTENTS

INTRODUCTION

In January 1997, while working as a Los Angeles-based journalist for a wire agency providing entertainment news, I was fortunate enough to interview Carl Perkins, the man once dubbed the King of Rockabilly, whose song "Blue Suede Shoes" helped propel Elvis Presley onto the global stage. Perkins had just released what would be his last album, *Go Cat Go!* and the press officer from the record label behind it wanted me to focus my questions on that rather than Elvis. Needless to say, those in charge at my agency's headquarters back in London had stressed they wanted Presley stories – and plenty of them. Desperate to open the interview with anything other than "So, Carl, tell me about Elvis then…" I spent the moments prior to our introduction dredging my mind for something fitting yet slightly offbeat to set the ball rolling.

Then it came to me from out of nowhere. Growing up, I had loved trains. Deep down, I still did. Carl Perkins, so I'd been told, also liked trains. In fact my earliest memory of Perkins had been watching him perform "This Train Is Bound For Glory" on television with Roy Orbison, and I told him so. "I don't think you can come from where I come from and not have a deep affection for the railroads," Perkins said in his rich Tennessee accent. "It's that sound, that rhythm. And it's what they mean – love, loss, hope, escape, even death because that's what the train is in the gospel sense. It's the train that's gonna take you to heaven if you've been good or some place else if you ain't. Roy, Bill Monroe, Sister Rosetta Tharpe, John. Everyone's got their train song because everyone loves a train."

Back then the names Bill Monroe and Sister Rosetta Tharpe meant nothing to me. As for John? Well Johnny Cash never needed any introduction. Ultimately it was Perkins who brought Elvis into our conversation by saying how much he admired Presley's recording of the song "Mystery Train". And that was it. We were away and London declared itself happy.

Many years later I was driving along the M62 motorway in northern England, with my daughter for company, when Elvis came on the car radio singing "Mystery Train". Rhiannon, who was 10 at the time, had never heard it before and seemed entranced. Up went the volume and we sat in silence taking it all in until the fade out, at which point Rhiannon turned to me and said:

"Daddy, why are there so many songs about trains?"

As we consumed the miles I tried, and failed, to conjure one of those authority-on-everything answers that dads are supposed to give inquisitive children. I recalled how Carl Perkins had nailed the relationship between railways and music that day in Los Angeles. The problem was I couldn't remember exactly what he had said. Fortunately I'd kept a transcript of the interview located in a brown folder at the back of an old filing cabinet. It made for fascinating reading and that last line – "Everyone's got their train song because everyone loves a train" – stirred me to enter the words "train songs" into an internet search engine. Up came a web page containing a list of approximately 1,000 songs featuring trains in the lyrics or, in the case of instrumentals, embedded in the sound. Many old familiars were there – "Rock Island Line", "Last Train To Clarksville", "Homeward Bound", "Midnight Train To Georgia", "Folsom Prison Blues", "Smokestack Lightning", "Freight Train" – yet the closer I looked the more I began to notice the ones which were missing.

Some omissions were understandable; the apocalyptic "Runaway Train Driver" by punk rock singer songwriter TV Smith is to my ears sublime, but I've never once heard it on a radio. However, where was "Train In Vain" by The Clash which, while carrying no mention of trains in the lyrics, has its foundations set in the core rhythm of a steam locomotive chugging down the tracks? Where was "Waterloo Sunset" by The Kinks, "White Room" by Cream and a cluster of other well-known songs using railways as location settings for broader stories? I'm not especially fond of "You're Beautiful" by James Blunt but who am I to argue with the multitudes seduced by the poignant tale of a man coming face to face with an ex-girlfriend and her new beau while trapped inside the confines of a London Underground train carriage?

Singers, musicians and songwriters are inspired by what is around them. For almost 200 years, trains have played an integral part in our lives. They have taken us to work. They have taken us on holiday. They have taken us to visit loved ones. They have separated us from loved ones. They have symbolised escape and freedom, even fear and oppression. They changed the social and economic landscapes of entire countries including Britain and the United States Of America which would become the engine rooms of the entertainment world. Small wonder trains and railways feature so prominently in music. Tune your radio to any station playing country, blues, jazz, soul, folk or rock'n'roll and it won't be long before a train makes its way through the lyrics or tempo of a song. If there was such a thing as Skiffle FM then pretty much everything on the playlist would contain a train.

This is the story of how some of those songs came to be and what it is, or perhaps was, about the railways that seduced generations of musical talent from Birmingham, England, to Birmingham, Alabama. I decided to write it having looked for a book on the subject in the wake of that car journey with my daughter only to discover no such thing existed. That made me want to go out and capture the stories behind the songs before any further members of the assembly line passed away. Johnny Cash, Lonnie Donegan and Ewan MacColl, to name just three, had already caught their last trains bound for glory. Pete Seeger would die during the research process before I had a chance to speak to him. Fortunately the lyrics of many train songs performed by the late greats speak for themselves while their legacies continue to be a major influence on other living performers with a soft spot for railroads, something which helped my cause during the research process.

Dear reader, a few words of warning – if you are searching for a scholarly tome on the history of railways or indeed modern music, then you've come to the wrong place. This is a book about how those two subjects became intrinsically linked, with some history thrown in. If that sounds like your cup of tea, keep reading.

Cards on the table, I embarked on this book with a hunch that the ever-changing face of western society, not to mention the music industry, had sounded the death knell for the train song. I wanted to believe there was still a place for lonely platforms and midnight specials in the hearts and minds of young singers, musicians and songwriters, but I wasn't holding my breath. At the time of writing, elder statesmen such as Ray Davies, Bryan Ferry and Ralph McTell continue to look to the railways to stir their creative juices. Bruce Springsteen is as likely to name-check railroads in his latter day work as Cadillacs and chrome fenders. By contrast, I can't remember the last time I heard a fresh-faced 20-something sing about a train on any Saturday night TV talent show.

"I'm constantly disappointed by train journeys in a way that I never used to be," admitted the singer and songwriter Chris Difford as he recalled the significant part played by railways in his own childhood. It was a sentiment echoed by others to whom I spoke. In the words of Jethro

Tull's Ian Anderson, "Trains will be with us for a long time to come. It's just they don't really look like trains anymore."

But it wasn't always like this. Not by a long stretch.

1

ONCE I BUILT
A RAILROAD

It may have been September, it may have been October. Neither John Lennon nor Paul McCartney could ever quite remember. But the year was definitely 1957 and the place 20 Forthlin Road in the relatively comfortable Liverpool suburb of Allerton. Introduced to one another for the first time by a mutual friend at a church fête that July, the like-minded teenagers had started playing truant from their respective seats of learning, preferring instead to write songs together. Back to McCartney's house they would go in the early afternoon while his Father was at work, sitting opposite each other in the living room practising guitar chords and scribbling lyrics until it was time to clean up whatever mess had been created and make their escape.

At the time, Britain's skiffle epidemic was in full swing and just about every band, whether professional or amateur, had at least one train song in its repertoire. Those that weren't about trains still tended to sound like them, the tea-chest bass and clickety-clack of a washboard creating a driving repetitive rhythm similar to that of a steam locomotive pounding over the rails. Lonnie Donegan had "Rock Island Line". Johnny Duncan had "Last Train To San Fernando". Chas McDevitt and Nancy Whiskey had "Freight Train". And so Lennon decided he wanted one as well.

"One After 909" was the bare bones of a story about a girl who takes a train ride. Written at Forthlin Road in 1957, and recorded by The Beatles six years later, it finally saw the light of day in 1970 with the release of *Let It Be*, having failed to make the cut on earlier albums. McCartney later described "One After 909" as a homage to British Rail, the much-maligned body which ran the United Kingdom's railways from 1948 until the arrival of privatisation in 1994. His tongue had, of course, been firmly in cheek. "One After 909" was in no way related to signal failures in the Wimbledon area or buffet cars awash with stale sandwiches bound for

1

Bognor Regis. It was about Streamliners, Zephyrs, Cannonball Expresses and Flyers…

…The United States Of America, in other words.

The railways as we know them, designed to carry passengers and freight over long distances, began appearing on either side of the Atlantic Ocean almost simultaneously during the third decade of the 19th century. There the similarities end. In Britain they had to be shoehorned into a landscape already colonised by towns, cities, industry, agriculture and landowners. In the USA and Canada the scenario couldn't have been more different. Conceived by pioneers and explorers, the railroads opened up the whole country. First came the rails, then the settlements. Streets were arranged parallel and at right angles to the railroad tracks which became demarcation lines separating commerce from industry and wealthy living areas from the not so wealthy. As America's economic fortunes ebbed and flowed over the years that followed, occasionally those lines became blurred. "I could say we lived on the wrong side of the tracks, but in those days in Tupelo there wasn't really a right side of the tracks," Elvis Presley would recall of the Mississippi city in which he spent the first 13 years of his life.

Right from the get-go, America's railroads were being immortalised in music. In fact the earliest known train song pre-dated the railroad it was written about by almost two years. Composed in June 1828 by Arthur Clifton (born Philip Antony Corri in Edinburgh, Scotland, but who changed his name on emigrating to the USA), "The Carrollton March" celebrated the start of construction work on the Baltimore & Ohio Railroad. Within days another song marking the same event called "The Rail Road March" was unveiled by the German-born pianist and composer Charles Meineke, who had moved to the USA in 1800 at the age of 18.

Once the American Civil War ended in 1865, so the railroad boom went into overdrive particularly in the west of the country. Men came from far and wide to build, run and rob the trains that ran on them. Gamblers and women of the night swarmed to the busy railheads rising up out of the land, eager to relieve navvies of their hard earned pay. It was a colourful, exhilarating, often dangerous new world and the players at the centre of it all were ripe for celebrating in stories and songs. Which is how the legend of John Henry was born.

Despite almost certainly being a fictional character, John Henry has come to embody the physical strength and endurance required of the men who built the American railroads. Henry, so the story goes, is a "steel driver" who hammers a drill into rock creating holes for explosives to blast a path for the iron road. When his superiors make clear their plans to replace him with a steam-powered drill, this African American ex-slave with biceps the size of Montana challenges the machine to a race. He wins only to drop down dead of exhaustion, hammer still in his hands.

Henry may have been a creation (or, what is more likely, an amalgamation of several men) but it is believed such a race did occur near Talcott, West Virginia, during the construction of Big Bend Tunnel on the Chesapeake & Ohio Railway in the early 1870s, and that the traditional song "John Henry" was spawned by this event. It has since been recorded in various guises by over 100 artists including Jerry Lee Lewis, Lonnie Donegan and Bruce Springsteen, the majority favouring the upbeat narrative ballad describing the race, Henry's death and the stoic reaction of his wife. Braver souls, such as the singer, actor and civil rights activist Paul Robeson, have instead leaned towards a slower interpretation performed in the style of a work song, almost as if they themselves are laying down railroad tracks. The song's enduring popularity in the USA, regardless of lyrics and tempo which vary from version to version, has cemented John Henry's place at the heart of the North American labour movement, continuing to inspire musicians with a finger on the working man's pulse.

"It was in my Dad's repertoire and that of many singers on the folk scene as I was making my way up," says blues singer songwriter Eric Bibb, son of folk musician Leon Bibb and godson of Paul Robeson, who recorded his own version of "John Henry" for the 2011 album *Blues, Ballads & Work Songs*. "He competes against the steam drill and beats it but pays the ultimate price. I just loved the song, always have, in particular the million different verses that you get telling the story, like when his wife takes over from him after he's died and carries on hammering the steel drill in his place. People have been playing that song for over 100 years and they'll be playing it another 100 more. It is part of American folklore and because of that it won't ever go away."

tmmttmmttmm

By 1900, men in the mould of John Henry had laid approximately 200,000 miles of track throughout the USA being traversed by around 40,000 steam locomotives. With every passing year the older, smaller engines were taken out of service and replaced by larger more powerful ones needed to satisfy the ever increasing demands being placed on the railway system. That demand meant trains, in particular the ones carrying freight, grew significantly in length. The noise as one of these giant locomotives powered its way through a neighbourhood – whistle blowing, smoke belching out across the rooftops, boxcars rattling in its wake – permeated every corner, something the popular American grid street system only served to amplify.

"You couldn't fail to hear them," says Tom Johnston, founder member and original lead singer with The Doobie Brothers, recalling his childhood years in Visalia, California. "Whenever a train came through you would hear that whistle, no matter where you were. And you know what? It always sounded different according to what time of the day it was. At night time you would hear it and it used to sound mournful, sad. Then in the daytime you would hear it and it sounded like excitement, like adventure. But you were always hearing it. That for me is the single biggest reason why trains get written about so much in songs. A lot of us grew up in towns like that, my generation of songwriters and the ones before, and we grew up listening to trains. You couldn't always see them, but you were always aware of them."

In her 2015 autobiography, *Reckless*, Chrissie Hynde – another singer and songwriter of Johnston's generation – recalls her student days in Kent, Ohio, where the trains ran right through the middle of town behind the bars on Water Street, and the effect their presence had on her. "The sound of the train whistle always had an underlying feeling of promise to it: 'Come away'. There is no other sound like it, haunting and imploring and mysterious. 'Come away'".

For others, the railroad provided something far more important than a soundtrack to their lives. It meant bread on the table. In 1920, approximately two million United States citizens were employed directly by the railways, a number that had fallen to 1.66 million by 1929 and a still far from insignificant 793,071 in 1960. Those figures don't include thousands more working in hotels, cafes, shops and other businesses adjacent to the tracks whose very existence depended on trade generated by trains. They say every musician in the USA of blue collar origin, regardless of colour, has at least one person in their family tree who worked on the railroads. A father, a brother, an uncle, a cousin or, like Dennis Locorriere, a grandparent.

"When I was young I lived with my grandfather and grandmother on my mum's side, Ralph and Angelina Mantovani, because my mum was only 19 when she had me and had other things going on in her life," says Locorriere, the former lead singer with Dr. Hook And The Medicine Show. "We lived in Union City, New Jersey, and my grandfather worked on the Erie Lackawanna Railroad. Every morning he would get up at four o'clock and put his uniform on with these heavy canvass pants and a brakeman cap like the one Donovan used to wear. He'd have his flashlight with him. It would be pitch black outside and he was going to work on the railroad. That kind of stuff sticks with you."

Like Ralph Mantovani, John Luther Jones looked to the rails for his livelihood. Born in 1863 and raised in Cayce, Kentucky, Jones worked as an engine driver on the Illinois Central Railroad. During the late 19th century so many railroad employees carried the same surnames that nicknames based on home towns became commonplace. Jones thus became "Cayce" which when written down morphed into "Casey".

Train drivers often gained hero status in the communities they served. Renowned for his punctuality and trademark pull on a steam locomotive's whistle, Jones was no exception. If the engine's call began softly and rose to a scream before dying away slowly, then people knew it was "Casey" at the controls. Jones was a master of his craft and the kind of man who would go out of his way to help a colleague, which is how he came to be working on the night of Sunday 29 April 1900. When another engine driver reported sick, Jones deputised and took the delayed Cannonball Express out of Memphis bound for Canton, Mississippi, 188 miles away to the south. The weather was foggy but the load was light and Jones had an exceptional fireman in Simeon Webb for company. Consequently the train managed to make up time and after 178 miles was almost back on schedule having left Memphis 95 minutes late.

Steaming round a bend just before the town of Vaughan, Webb spotted a red light ahead hanging from the rear of a stationary freight train parked on the same stretch of track. He shouted a warning and Jones slammed on the brakes, reversed the locomotive's throttle and told the fireman to jump. Webb leapt from the cab whereas Jones continued wrestling with the doomed Express managing to reduce his train's speed from 75 to 35 miles per hour at the point of impact. As a result his was the only life lost in the crash. "Casey" made the ultimate sacrifice and in return the whole country made him a hero.

It was Wallace Saunders, a locomotive cleaner and friend of Jones from Canton, who initially came up with a song documenting the events surrounding the driver's death. Other railroad workers soon picked up on it including William Leighton whose two brothers, Frank and Burt, had their own vaudeville act touring the southern states of the USA. They incorporated the song into their shows but never bothered copywriting it. Spotting a potentially lucrative opportunity, another pair of vaudeville entertainers, T Lawrence Seibert and Eddie Newton, jumped in and published "Casey Jones, The Brave Engineer" as their own in 1909. At which point the floodgates opened. It is impossible to say how many acts have subsequently recorded or performed the song known today as "The Ballad Of Casey Jones" or simply "Casey Jones" but the list includes Sidney Bechet, Pete Seeger, Tex Ritter and Mississippi John Hurt. Like "John Henry", the lyrics and tempo tend to vary between recordings but the underlying message always remains the same – Casey was a brave engineer who gave his life so that others could live.

In 1957, the US television station KTTV commissioned a children's series called *Casey Jones* based on the fictional exploits of an engine driver called Casey (played by actor Alan Hale Jr.) and the crew of the Cannonball Express, using a version of "The Ballad Of Casey Jones" (sung by Burl Ives) as its theme tune. Broadcast during 1957 and 1958 in the USA, the 32 episodes shot in black and white were screened at regular intervals over the next 20 years, not only in the States but as far afield as Britain and Australia, becoming must-see-TV for millions of children (mainly boys, it has to be said) who lapped up the glamour associated with driving an American railroad engine.

"I just loved that show as a kid," says Dave Pirner of the American rock band Soul Asylum. "There was this guy who was a railroad engineer and his name was Casey Jones and I wanted to be him. Growing up in Minneapolis my life used to stop when that show came on. When I wrote 'Runaway Train' [Soul Asylum's Grammy-award winning 1993 global hit] I was having more or less a nervous breakdown because I thought I was losing my hearing and was getting pretty hysterical about it. During this period of soul searching the lyrics sort of came to me in an evening. I already had the tune in my head but I thought back to when I was a kid, like when I used to watch *Casey Jones* on television, and the words just poured out. That show had a huge impact on how 'Runaway Train' came about." Of which more later.

═══════════

Besides being a major source of employment, the railroads also gave the less well off in American society a life-changing opportunity to better themselves. Suddenly people were free to travel, providing they could afford a ticket, and the mass migrations particularly from the southern farms to the northern cities began. "People would be out there in them fields, working hard, and they would see the train come through, and they would hope that one day they could save enough for the train fare to the northern states where they felt there was a better life than working in the cotton fields or whatever," says Jimmy "Duck" Holmes, the veteran blues musician, who as a child watched legions of African-Americans boarding passenger trains out of his native Bentonia, Mississippi, in search of new urban lives; a fair percentage of the men with guitars strapped across their backs. "People caught the train from Mississippi to the north in search of a factory job where you got paid by the hour rather than a field job where you got paid by the day. It was a way out of poverty, the main source of transportation from hard times to good times. And they took their music with them to the streets of the cities."

Not that Jimmy ever felt like joining the exodus. His parents, Carey and Mary Holmes, were sharecroppers in Bentonia who in 1948 sank their hard earned savings into opening the Blue Front Café serving groceries, fish, moonshine whiskey and live blues music. In 1970 Jimmy took over ownership, since when this tiny venue has developed a worldwide reputation for delivering authentic blues in a suitably rustic, non-pretentious setting. Situated no more than 50 yards from Bentonia's railroad tracks, when a train comes thundering past you hear it, no matter how loud the entertainment is. "There's something special about the trains and the railroads," adds Jimmy. "Some people have had bad experiences with the trains because at some point the girlfriends or the wives have left them, the train has carried their baby away and so forth. It's not always a happy story but they are important. They are part of the blues and they are part of the Blue Front Café, oh yeah."

For those unable to afford a ticket there was always another, albeit, riskier way of riding the rails. During the Great Depression of the 1930s, jumping aboard a freight train without paying became a way of life for thousands of men criss-crossing the USA in search of work. As far as they were concerned, the railroads weren't so much a way out of poverty as a means of survival, their plight encapsulated in the mournful finality of the words *Once I built a railroad, now it's done* from the song "Brother, Can You Spare A Dime?" written by the lyricist Edgar Yipsel "Yip" Harburg for the 1932 musical *Americana*.

It sounds romantic, watching America rolling by from the open door of a boxcar, and during the warm summer months it probably could be. But there were a number of perils associated with living the life of a hobo.

Being caught by the "checkers" and "car knockers" tasked with ridding the freight trains of unwanted stowaways was the least of their worries. If that happened, a hobo would probably be searched for money and forced to buy a ticket for as far down the line as his pennies would take him. Far worse was the fate that befell those who dared fall asleep while perched precariously over the wheels of a long line of wagons. When the bodies were found there was usually no way of telling who they were, either through disfigurement or lack of identification. Getting locked inside a boxcar, particularly an "ice car" used to transport refrigerated goods, was also tantamount to a death sentence. It could be days or even weeks before a corpse was discovered.

▥▥▥▥▥▥▥

Jimmie Rodgers was someone who empathised with the hobos' plight. Born in 1897, exact location unknown, Rodgers got a job on the railroads aged 13 as a water boy, fetching and carrying refreshment for the men working around him. By 20, he had graduated to become a brakeman, responsible for applying the brakes on individual freight train wagons as well as ensuring that the couplings between each car were set properly. Taught to play the guitar from a young age by rail workers and hobos, Rodgers mixed with gangs of men known as "gandy dancers" who sang and chanted in a call-and-response style while maintaining the tracks. Although tuberculosis put an end to his railroad career in 1927, Rodgers turned misfortune on its head by realising his dreams of becoming a musician. Dubbed "The Singing Brakeman" and renowned for his distinctive yodelling technique, he went on to record some of the definitive songs of the early Depression years, including one described by the late country and western singer Merle Haggard as "the most heartbreaking thing you're ever likely to hear." That song was "Hobo Bill's Last Ride".

Written by a Texas farm boy with a flair for poetry and writing called Waldo O'Neal, "Hobo Bill's Last Ride" tells the story of a man at death's door. Hobo Bill is riding through the night on an eastbound freight train battling its way through the wind and rain. He is cold and has no means of keeping warm. Passing in and out of consciousness, Bill's only crumb of comfort comes from the familiar blast of the steam locomotive's whistle which sends him to eternal rest with a smile on his face.

Recorded by Rodgers just weeks after the Wall Street Crash of October 1929, the lyrics to "Hobo Bill's Last Ride" would prove to be horribly prophetic as the Great Depression ripped chunks out of the social and economic fabric of North America. Men like Bill had existed before the Crash but for a decade after it the linesides and freight yards of the USA's railroad system crawled with them. Most survived to tell the tale, some perished, and one subsequently wrote songs and a best-selling autobiography inspired by his own experiences riding in boxcars. Regarded today as the father of American folk music, Woody Guthrie's *Bound For Glory* continues to put money into bookshop tills. Yet contrary to popular belief, the song that gave the book its title was not one of his own creations.

"This Train", or "This Train Is Bound For Glory", as it is often known, is a traditional American gospel song dating back to the 1920s. Exactly who wrote it has never been established, but a religious group called Wood's Famous Blind Jubilee Singers made the inaugural recording in 1925, 14 years before Sister Rosetta Tharpe – the first acknowledged performer to blend gospel music with primitive forms of rock and soul – brought it to the attention of a wider audience with her own version (which she continued playing live until suffering a stroke in 1970, three years prior to her death aged 58). "That's a powerful song coming from a lady who made history," Carl Perkins said of Tharpe when I interviewed him in Los Angeles in 1997. "It really inspired me as a young man and so did she. People say if there were no Carl Perkins then there would never have been no Beatles. I don't know about that, but I do know if there had been no Sister Rosetta Tharpe then there might never have been no Carl Perkins."

Guthrie had intended calling his autobiography *Boomchasers* but was persuaded to change it by the woman assigned to be his editor, Joy Doerflinger. She preferred *Bound For Glory*, lifting the phrase from the song "This Train Is Bound For Glory", which Guthrie describes singing to a boxcar full of men in the book's opening and closing chapters accompanied by his trusty guitar. The author wasn't so sure, believing the revised title gave the impression that *he* was bound for glory, not the common man as Guthrie had intended. The ambiguity over who exactly is bound for glory, and what in fact glory is, continues to this day. For some the song is about the emancipation of the people, something the railways played a major part in not just across North America but much of the world. Others, pointing to its gospel origins, are of the opinion that there is a message involved – live a clean, honest life and you will get to go to heaven.

The Train Kept A-Rollin'

This train is bound for glory, this train
This train is bound for glory, this train
This train is bound for glory
Don't ride nothin' but the righteous and the holy
This train is bound for glory, this train

This train don't carry no gamblers, this train
This train don't carry no gamblers, this train
This train don't carry no gamblers
No hypocrites, no midnight ramblers
This train is bound for glory, this train

... and so on through numerous verses in which the lyrics, as with "John Henry" and "The Ballad Of Casey Jones", are nearly always altered by whoever is performing the song, an artistic licence Pete Seeger once wonderfully referred to as "the folk process."

"I always thought it was God's train, but I suppose it means whatever you want it to mean," was Carl Perkins' interpretation of "This Train Is Bound For Glory". Which is as good an explanation as you're likely to get.

The Great Depression marked a watershed moment in the history of music and the train song. It inspired lyrics and sounds that had never been written or heard before, the former more brutal and honest, the latter frequently resembling the actual noises made by trains. Jimmie Rodgers punctuated his songs with "*Whoo whoo!*" locomotive cries, while Woody Guthrie, accustomed to the wide variety of unique sounds created by steam engines and freight wagons as they rolled over the rails, began channelling the beats and rhythms that he heard through his guitar. The music they and other artists created reached a younger audience via radio stations springing up across the country. In Dyess, Arkansas, little Johnny Cash tuned into his family's brand new radio for the very first time and heard Jimmie Rodgers singing "Hobo Bill's Last Ride". Before long, he would develop his own distinctive sound, a boom-chicka-boom-chicka-boom resembling a train moving at speed over joints in the track. Pete Seeger, from an altogether more privileged background than Cash, found himself drawn to Guthrie's folk leanings and the portal that the railroads provided into the hard knocks life of the working man, citing his first teenage hearing of "John Henry" as "a light bulb moment."

For this next generation of singers, musicians and songwriters – the generation that would invent rock'n'roll, soul and skiffle music while championing other existing forms such as jazz, folk, country and rhythm & blues – the railroads were a goldmine of colossal proportions, providing not only a wealth of material to write about but also a soundtrack to accompany it.

2

JAIL, MAMA, TRAINS... AND CASH

As a snapshot of American life during the years of the Great Depression, *Bound For Glory* has few rivals. True, some have questioned the extent to which Woody Guthrie embellished his tales of riding the boxcars. The English folk singer Ralph McTell, a self-confessed Guthrie "junkie", is far from alone in believing that *Bound For Glory* is "more of a novel than an autobiography." Yet regardless of how much fiction might have been involved, Guthrie's stab at capturing the USA's trials during arguably the most testing time in its post-Civil War history struck a loud chord. His words and music continue to resonate and inspire. "That," adds McTell, "is what matters."

On the other hand, Johnny Cash never really needed to rely on fiction, certainly not when it came to the railroads. They were as good as in his DNA.

John R. Cash was born on 26 February 1932 at the height of the Great Depression's destructive powers. Home was a shotgun shack beside a railway line just outside Kingsland, Arkansas, that shook to its foundations whenever a train went by. One of John's earliest memories was of his father, Ray Cash, leaping from a moving boxcar as it levelled with their house having been away in search of work. His mother Carrie's favourite song was "Life's Railway To Heaven" written by Baptist preacher M. E. Abbey and Baptist preacher's son Charles Davis Tillman which John, amongst many others, would later record. Shaken to the core as a child by the song on the radio about Hobo Bill taking his last ride, he even made what was technically his first record at a railway station in Munich while serving abroad with the US Air Force, paying one Deutsche Mark to perform Carl Smith's "Darlin' Am I The One" in a do-it-yourself acetate booth.

By the time he turned 22, Cash had set his heart on becoming a professional musician. He'd heard all about Elvis Presley's fledgling success at Sun Records in Memphis and so began hustling Sam Phillips, the label's founder, into giving him an audition. Phillips eventually relented and Cash performed a number of cover versions for consideration. The songs didn't really do much for Phillips, but the voice was something else. Did Cash have anything self-penned that he'd like to sing? And so the rookie launched into "Hey Porter", the story of a traveller itching to get back to Tennessee riding an overnight passenger train. Phillips was impressed and asked him to return the following day and record it. "Hey Porter'" became Johnny Cash's first single, released in July 1955.

That very same month, on 11 July to be exact, Elvis Presley had been in the studio at Sun with his guitarist Scotty Moore and bass player Bill Black. At some point, the trio hit upon the lick from "Mystery Train", a song written and recorded two years previously by Phillips together with the blues musician Junior Parker. The original had been a slow, mournful number mimicking the lumbering movement of a freight train moving steadily across the landscape. The version Elvis, Scotty and Bill came up with was more akin to a fast moving express. Phillips had always loved the song particularly the lyrics which described a feeling so many people had experienced, that of putting a loved one on a train at a station and the questions such a scenario poses. Where are they going? For how long? When will I see them again? Will I *ever* see them again? Parker originally wanted to make the train 50 coaches long but Phillips insisted 16 were enough. Enthralled by the spin that Elvis, Scotty and Bill put on his "Mystery Train", Phillips (who later described their take as "a fucking masterpiece") knew straight away that it had to be released as a single.

All these years later there's still an electricity about Presley's "Mystery Train" capable of stopping you dead in your tracks. This is Elvis on the cusp of something huge, just before fame consumed him. It's the pre-Colonel Tom Parker Elvis – no sycophants, no overblown string arrangements, no white jump suits, just three men performing a gripping stripped down version of a song dealing with a subject that anyone can relate to.

"That song is so evocative with the train rhythm and the way it describes the actual train itself," says John Illsley, co-founder member and bass player with the group Dire Straits. "The train is setting off on a journey, but of course there's more to it than that because we know Elvis is at the beginning of his own musical journey, something that gives it this extra buzz."

"It's the first, or one of the very first, rockabilly songs," says the guitarist, singer and songwriter Brian Setzer who has covered "Mystery

Train" both as a member of the Stray Cats and his own band, the Brian Setzer Orchestra. "It's almost like Elvis told Scotty 'I want to do this song called "Mystery Train"' and then Scotty came up with that guitar which doubles as a train. If you picture a train chugging along, back in the day, that's what Scotty is playing. It's so simple and timeless. That ('Mystery Train') is like the gold standard. When you look back at rockabilly, that's right there at the top."

Within six months of recording "Mystery Train", Presley had left the innocence of Sun and its cottage industry existence for RCA records, destined to become the label's biggest selling recording artist ever. "It was the greatest thing I ever did on Elvis," Sam Phillips would say of "Mystery Train" while reflecting on his relatively brief yet hugely important union with Presley. Not that the Sun Records impresario was overly distraught at the defection of his best known act. Waiting in the wings, Phillips had two singers with dynamite singles cocked and aimed at an unsuspecting public. One was Carl Perkins and his song "Blue Suede Shoes". The other was Johnny Cash singing one of the most iconic train anthems ever recorded.

"There's an old story I once heard that goes something like this," says Bobby Hart, one half of the prolific songwriting duo Boyce and Hart, along with the late Tommy Boyce. "Two songwriters are sitting in a bar. One says to the other 'I think I've written the perfect country song'. And he goes ahead and sings him the song. The other songwriter shakes his head and says 'It can't be the perfect country song unless it mentions jail, mama or trains'. And so the first songwriter goes off for a few minutes before coming back. He starts singing and of course he's thrown the whole lot in – 'I robbed the train and went to jail, miss my mama, hurts like hell'. I love that story. Some might say it's not so far from the truth!"

"Folsom Prison Blues" has the jail, the train, and mama.

Folsom State Prison is the second oldest prison in the state of California, built in 1880 and located approximately 20 miles north east of Sacramento, the state capital. It was, and indeed remains, a maximum security prison designed to house dangerous and disruptive detainees of the kind that might try escaping. In "Folsom Prison Blues", Cash tells the story of a man incarcerated for shooting another man in Reno, Nevada, just for the hell of it. The sound of the trains passing within earshot of the prisoner's cell serve as a piercing reminder of the circumstances he finds himself in as a result of his crime. Thinking about what the passengers are free to do on those trains – eat dinner in the dining car, drink coffee, smoke cigars – tortures him to the point of madness. That, in itself, is punishment enough.

"Folsom Prison Blues" peaked at number five on the American Billboard charts in 1956. Twelve years later, on 13 January 1968, Cash recorded a live album inside the prison itself called *At Folsom Prison*. The accompanying live single release of "Folsom Prison Blues" went to number one that summer and remains for many the definitive version of the song, accompanied as it is by the charged response from a captive yet appreciative audience.

No doubt about it, going inside proved to be an astute career move but his concern and empathy for those who found themselves behind bars was genuine. Cash never lost sight of the fact that in desperate times good people often find themselves doing desperate things. For him, railroads represented the kind of freedom that enabled his father and thousands of others to scour the land looking for work during the Great Depression, breaking the law in the process by riding freight trains instead of passenger ones, which cost money they didn't have. To be denied that freedom, like the prisoner in "Folsom Prison Blues", was tantamount to stripping a human being of all dignity and hope, irrespective of the crime committed.

"The culture of 1,000 years is shattered with the clanging of the cell door behind you," wrote Cash in the original liner notes to *At Folsom Prison*. "Life outside, behind you, immediately becomes unreal, you begin not to care that it exists. All you have with you in the cell is your bare animal instincts. I speak partly from experience. I have been behind bars a few times, sometimes of my own volition, sometimes involuntarily. Each time I felt the same feeling of kinship with my fellow prisoners."

Thirty four years before Cash played Folsom Prison, the musician Huddie William Ledbetter, better known as Lead Belly, recorded a version of the traditional American folk song "Midnight Special" at Angola Prison in Louisiana. Believed to have originated among prisoners in the deep south, common consensus has it that the "Midnight Special" in question is a train providing an escape route from an unspecified jail by way of salvation ("*Let the Midnight Special shine her light on me, let the Midnight Special shine her ever-loving light on me*" goes the song's refrain). As far as "Folsom Prison Blues" is concerned there is no such ambiguity. The attention to detail and heartfelt delivery is such that Cash was frequently asked why he'd served time. The truth was he never had. The occasional night behind bars recovering from the effects of amphetamines, yes, but a lengthy stretch, no. The song's brutal honesty gives it a power that will last as long as society has prisons that people long to escape from.

"I love the idea of being literally 'stuck' in prison, a place where time is frozen, and the sound of the rushing train that is literally tearing the narrator apart," says the Australian musician and songwriter Nick Cave of "Folsom Prison Blues". "And the sound of the whistle reminding him of his terrible, nihilistic deed. A wonderful song."

With Johnny Cash, there really was no escaping trains. In 1973, CBS released a six-record box set of his work divided into themes – *Johnny's Big Hits, Johnny On The Railroad, Johnny Down West, Johnny In Love, Johnny On Sunday* and *Johnny In Jail*. Only religion ended up being spared at least one train song. His popular networked television show, commissioned by ABC following the success of *At Folsom Prison*, included a segment in each episode called "Ride This Train" in which Cash, sometimes accompanied by guests, performed songs about America as seen through the eyes of people watching the landscape roll by from railway carriages, boxcars or locomotive footplates. His live shows not only featured railroad songs but back projections of film footage depicting trains, the on-screen collision between two steam engines at the climax of "Orange Blossom Special" becoming something of an in-concert highlight.

The Orange Blossom Special had been a luxury passenger train that ran between New York City and Miami during the winter months at a time when development in Florida was booming. The song of the same name, a homage to the train, was written in 1938 by 21-year-old Ervin T. Rouse who, for much of his life, led a frugal, almost hermit-like existence in the Florida Everglades. In 1942, Bill Monroe, widely regarded as the father of bluegrass music, enjoyed a hit with the song which would become known on both sides of the Atlantic Ocean simply as "The Special". Often performed at breakneck speed and a particular favourite with fiddlers, Cash's 1965 album, *Orange Blossom Special*, included a cover version of the track on which the fiddle parts were replaced by a harmonica and saxophone. Fun to play live, it became an integral part of his shows for many years with a chance encounter at a concert in Florida adding an extra dimension to Cash's appreciation of the song.

"This gentleman walked quietly into our dressing room during intermission at our show in Miami," wrote Cash, fastidious as ever in the album's liner notes. "He had the kind of magnetism that makes you turn around and look, and everyone did. After I stood up and introduced myself, I was very embarrassed when he called me 'Mr Cash'. I usually can cover my embarrassment by replying 'Mr Cash is my daddy' but this time I was afraid it might sound disrespectful. His name, he said, was Ervin Rouse and he hesitatingly went on to say that a few years ago he had written a few songs himself, but that I had probably never heard of them. I felt the name should ring a bell and, offering him a chair, I asked what songs he had written. He honestly tried to avoid answering by saying they were just a bunch of old tunes. I asked him again what songs he had written and he replied in a beautiful southern seaboard dialect that a southerner such as myself enjoys hearing. Evidently people had not believed him in the past when he mentioned his songwriting, so he reluctantly said 'Well, I guess my biggest one was 'The Special...'" The pair remained in contact until Rouse's death in 1981.

≡≡≡≡≡≡≡≡

Prior to becoming a successful session musician drumming with the likes of Chris Rea and David Coverdale, the late Ian Naisbitt earned a living driving lorries for Edwin Shirley Trucking, the first dedicated rock'n'roll haulage firm in Europe (company slogan – "You rock, we roll"). One particular assignment during 1975 saw him behind the wheel on a Johnny Cash European tour. "That was one of the best tours I ever did," recalled Naisbitt, just three months before his death in February 2014. Raised in the north east of England, and a railway enthusiast since childhood, he remembered how, "All we did was talk trains all the time. He would talk about the American steamers that I didn't know much about, and I would tell him about British steam trains like the Pacifics and the A4s and A3s which he wanted to know more about. There's me, an absolute train nut, listening to songs like 'Orange Blossom Special' and 'Folsom Prison Blues' every night and getting to talk trains with Johnny Cash. For anyone who loves trains and music life doesn't really get any better than that!"

Though few realised it at the time, by 1955 – the year of "Mystery Train" and "Hey Porter" – North America's railroads had already experienced their glory days. The creeping onset of the jet age and increasing car ownership meant the number of passengers travelling by train would steadily dwindle. Steam engines began making way for modern diesel locomotives which, while being more efficient, lacked the romance of their predecessors. As far as American singers, musicians and songwriters were concerned this gradual change in transportation trends and technology bore little significance. For them the attraction of the railroads was what they continued to represent: freedom, hope, love, adventure, escape, the overwhelming sense that, in the words of Johnny Cash, "Somewhere down the track anything would be possible." Young people in the America of the mid-1950s were starting to want to break free – from the shadow of the Second World War, from parental control, from the small towns where a life of conformity and drudgery awaited. The majority of them didn't own a car or have enough money to buy an air ticket. Instead it was the railroads that offered a realistic get out clause from the birth, school, work, death template they so dreaded, something songwriters were quick to jump on and exploit. The songs that would pour forth over the ensuing years ensured that the railroads continued to occupy a prominent place in American popular culture, with those old enough to remember the glory days tapping into their own memory banks for material.

"When I was about six or seven years old my mum took me from Phoenix where I lived to see her father, my grandfather, in Ohio, and for part of the way we took the 'Sunset Limited' train which was such a brilliant experience," says Bobby Hart. "The feel of the seats, the look of the stainless steel coaches, the views from the window as the country rolled by. It was just magical. This would have been just after the Second World War. At some point I thought I would go to the bathroom, so I got up and left the Pullman car and went to the men's room, and it was much louder out there, the noise of the wheels on the tracks. And this rhythm just entranced me. Immediately I started making up a song to the rhythm and the sounds I was hearing. I didn't write it down. I don't think I even got a title. But it was the first song I ever made up and it was all down to the sounds and feel of that train."

The next song Hart wrote about a train did get a title. Not only that, "Last Train To Clarksville" would make it to number one on the *Billboard* chart.

"We didn't take a lot of trips by train, but the thrill of seeing that huff-huff puff-puff chuff-chuff coming into the station when we did was absolutely wonderful," adds the folk singer, songwriter and activist Peggy Seeger. "American trains were bigger than the ones in Britain and Europe. Don't get me wrong – European trains were glorious. But in America they were just huge. The engineer and the fireman would be further up away from you, almost on a pedestal. The posh dining cars – and they really were posh – had these little slots where you put your wine glass so it wouldn't move. No coffee cup was ever filled full because the train rocked. And the stations were like cathedrals! I remember Grand Central Station from when I was 16 or 17, meeting my mother in this big, high wonderful hall and going to eat at the oyster bar that was there. I mean, it had an oyster bar! Doesn't that just say it all?"

Having Pete Seeger as an older half-brother only enhanced Peggy's appreciation of all things to do with the railroads. Pete, a folk icon, was also good friends with Woody Guthrie. The pair's repertoires were littered with songs featuring trains and people whose lives revolved around them. One in particular called "Gamblin' Man", written by Guthrie and later adapted by other folk artists including Pete Seeger, emerged as one of Peggy's favourites. "It's actually about a girl who falls in love with a gambler. And she says *'I wouldn't marry a farmer, he's always in the rain, I'd rather marry that gamblin' man who wears a big old chain. I wouldn't marry a doctor, he's always away from home, I'd rather marry that gamblin' man who wouldn't leave me alone. And I wouldn't marry a railroad man, I'll tell you the reason why, I never knew a railroad man who wouldn't tell his wife a lie'*. So they didn't always have a good press. The railroads represented all the places that men could get away from, for whatever reason, and not have to socialise. It was a way of running away quick to somewhere distant, whether you worked on the railroads, rode the rails as a hobo, or whatever. Trains could get them [men] away from their responsibilities."

This darker side of the railroads proved especially alluring for some songwriters. Forget about the romance so often associated with trains; cold reality could be far more interesting or even dangerous, as one of Peggy Seeger's earliest memories as a child illustrates. "We were living at Silver Spring in Maryland which is now just a suburb of Washington, D.C. I was gotten up in the middle of the night by my father who took me and my brother and my mother to see a train wreck. I remember sitting on his shoulders so that I could see over the crowds. The engine had fallen down the bank and the cars were all draped behind it back up to the track. Whether anyone had died, I don't know, but for some reason everyone came to see, the way that people are drawn to something bad that's happened. I remember the fire in the steam engine's cab was still glowing. The engine was still puffing, puffing, puffing even though it was just lying there on its side. That would have been in about 1937 and it's still there in my head as clear as the day it happened."

Twenty years later, Peggy joined forces with her husband-to-be Ewan MacColl to record "The Ballad Of John Axon", the first in a series of what became known as *Radio Ballads*, produced for the BBC, telling the true story of a train driver from Stockport, England, who remained at the controls of his runaway steam locomotive and perished in the ensuing crash. While making it, the image of that stricken engine lying at the bottom of a bank in Silver Spring would never be far from her mind. "It did leave an impression," she admits. "But, hey, accidents happen. Since then I've got to appreciate that there's far more to trains than them coming off the tracks. Trains are percussive. Trains sing. If you don't like trains, you probably don't like music either."

Like Peggy Seeger, Chester Arthur Burnett also found himself drawn to childhood memories of trains, albeit ones running upright on rails rather than lying sideways off them. Born in June 1910 in White Station, Mississippi, a blink and you miss it railroad halt between the cities of Aberdeen and West Point, Burnett spent the first 13 years of his life rubbing shoulders with trains as they rolled through the tiny community he called home, bound for passenger stations and freight yards across the south and in the distant north. A big admirer of Jimmie "The Singing Brakeman" Rodgers and his yodelling technique, Burnett's father gave him a guitar at the age of 17 and he never looked back, filling concert halls across America and the UK for decades with his powerful, raw voice and 6' 3", 270 lb frame. By that time, the world beyond White Station knew him as Howlin' Wolf and the song audiences longed to hear more than any other was "Smokestack Lightning".

Wolf had been playing variations of "Smokestack Lightning" for years prior to recording it for Chess Records in January 1956. The song delved back to his youth in White Station yet could have applied to any community adjacent to a railroad track during the days when steam locomotives still ruled in the USA. "We used to sit out in the country and see the trains go by, watch the sparks come out of the smokestack," Wolf told one interviewer about observing steam locomotives at night time. "That was smokestack lightning."

With other railroad-themed songs such as "Mystery Train" and "Hey Porter" coming into the public domain, Wolf resurrected what he had originally recorded in 1951 as "Crying At Daybreak" only this time reworking some of the lyrics and calling it "Smokestack Lightning". Punctuated throughout by Wolf's "*Whoo hoo*" train-like moans, evoking the spirit of Jimmie Rodgers, "Smokestack Lightning" is built around a distinctive guitar line played by Hubert Sumlin (Wolf's long-time band member) which winds its way through the song like a steam locomotive chugging relentlessly in search of a destination, sparks showering from its smokestack (or chimney, depending which side of the Atlantic you're listening on). The lyrics refer to a woman, although what exactly she's done to make Wolf cry is unclear, some kind of betrayal being hinted at. But it's the train that takes centre stage. Regularly listed as one of the greatest songs of all time, "Smokestack Lightning" is the blues number which helped shape rock'n'roll, as the extensive head count of acts who have covered it (from The Animals to The Yardbirds) testifies.

"Whenever you hear it you think straight away of the old blues people, guys like Howlin' Wolf and Lead Belly, out in the country hearing the trains go by," says Ray Davies who borrowed the distinctive "Smokestack Lighting" guitar riff to underpin his own "Last Of The Steam-Powered Trains" recorded by The Kinks in 1968. "It takes you right there. You're no longer in Finchley or Neasden. You're in Louisiana or Mississippi. And you're not in the modern world anymore. You're in a bygone era."

Adored equally by black and white audiences at a time when racial segregation in many US states was part of day-to-day life, Howlin' Wolf's "Smokestack Lightning" served as a reminder of the important social and economic role played by trains in black American culture. By the 1950s, the railroads were far more than just a way out of poverty and the cotton fields. Those smokestacks belching cinders of gold (or, as was more likely by 1956, a brand new powerful shiny diesel engine) represented not just a gateway into another world but also decent employment prospects to boot.

"With African-Americans the trains played a big role providing lucrative employment for many families," says Eric Bibb. "They took people to places they might never have otherwise seen. An African-American porter on the railroads would come back home and tell stories of cities that were like fabled places. They were there in what was still just about the golden era of trains, when the actual appointments – the buildings, the décor, the woodwork, the uniforms – were just beautiful. To be a part of that showed that you were someone, that you had made something out of your life."

"Smokestack Lightning" and those childhood memories of trains certainly helped make Howlin' Wolf. Contrary to traditional blues stereotypes he didn't die penniless, drunk or broken hearted. In later life Chester Arthur Burnett (so named after the 21st President of the USA, Chester A. Arthur) became a respectable middle-class family man who volunteered for his local fire department, enjoyed fishing and even joined the Masons. As one of the most influential blues singers of all time there's plenty to admire in Wolf's canon, but "Smokestack Lighting" remains his calling card. He was 45 years old when it was released and audiences at his live shows subsequently soared. Wolf wasn't exactly an overnight sensation, but from 1956 onwards life for this giant of a man would never quite be the same again.

Approximately 4,000 miles due east from Wolf's adopted Chicago, a primitive form of music thought to have originated in the Windy City was making 1956 equally memorable for legions of British teenagers. And once again railroads, or rather railways, were proving to be the driving force behind many of the songs being heard.

3

RULE BRITANNIA

Nobody knows where skiffle came from – the USA, for sure, but exactly what part is anyone's guess. Some say it developed from New Orleans jazz. Others believe its origins can be traced back to jug bands which were popular across the southern states of America during the early 20th century. These involved people coming together and playing songs on utensils such as jugs, combs, washboards and cigar box fiddles as well as more traditional instruments like banjos and acoustic guitars. The music was first recorded in Chicago during the 1920s by the likes of Jimmy O'Bryant and his band the Chicago Skifflers, "skiffle" being a slang word for a rent party featuring musicians where a small entry charge was paid by guests to help the tenant satisfy their landlord. It didn't last. Within 20 years the word skiffle had disappeared completely from the American musical lexicon. That, so it seemed, was that.

Fast forward a decade to Britain in the late 1950s. Estimates bend under the sheer number of bands, but it can safely be said that anything up to 50,000 skiffle groups were kicking up a racket across the country in various forms, some making money out of their music, the vast majority just having fun. They were everywhere: school halls, town halls, village fêtes, jamborees, bedrooms, street corners, carnivals, parties, wedding receptions and ultimately on television, the skiffle-inspired BBC programme *Six-Five Special* becoming in 1957 the first ever youth TV music show in the United Kingdom. There were even local competitions purely for skiffle bands.

Bizarre or what?

There are several reasons why skiffle proved to be so popular in Britain. To be honest, there wasn't a lot else around musically to float the younger generation's boat. Elvis and Bill Haley had started to break, but the likes of Buddy Holly, Eddie Cochran and Cliff Richard were all yet to happen. Money was scarce particularly among the working classes. Skiffle wasn't about expensive instruments, so that took care of that. Skiffle didn't require high levels of musical expertise either. It was do-it-yourself stuff you could play with your mates, comprising of washboards, tea-chest basses and anything that made a semi-decent sound. Anyone could do it. And, so it seemed, pretty much anyone did.

Yet quite how skiffle managed to climb off the mortician's slab stateside and embed itself in British youth culture is something else altogether. It just so happens that traditional jazz was starting to replace swing music in people's affections on the eastern shores of the Atlantic, creating a fertile new jazz scene led by bands such as Ken Colyer's Jazzmen. Playing guitar, banjo and supplying vocals in the Jazzmen was a Scots-born singer and instrumentalist in his mid-twenties called Anthony Donegan, going by the name of Lonnie Donegan (in honour of the blues musician Lonnie Johnson). During intervals at shows, Donegan and other members of the Jazzmen would put on what they called "skiffle breaks". Encouraged by the positive reaction from audiences, he went ahead and recorded a speeded up version of an American blues/folk song popularised by Lead Belly called "Rock Island Line" featuring a washboard. Released as a single in the UK towards the end of 1955 (with a cover of "John Henry" on the flip side), "Rock Island Line" went on to sell truckloads of records throughout the early part of 1956, almost single-handedly launching the British skiffle phenomenon in the process.

"Rock Island Line" is a song about the Chicago, Rock Island & Pacific Railroad which, until its dissolution in 1980, covered approximately 7,000 miles of track, linking a number of major American cities including Chicago, Denver, Houston and Kansas City. It tells the story of a train driver who lies about his load to avoid paying a toll charge, telling the man on the gate outside New Orleans that he's carrying livestock when his freight wagons are in fact full of pig iron. Hardly seems like the essence of teen spirit, does it?

But then "Rock Island Line" was never really about the lyrics. It was the sound that grabbed people's attention, a bizarre hybrid of blues, folk and jazz that actually resembled a train. Donegan set the scene with a long spoken introduction over a gently strummed guitar and stroked cymbal. Close your eyes and you can almost touch this filthy great steam locomotive of the mind sat impatiently waiting to go. Seventy five seconds in, the signalman gives the right away and the song takes off down the "*mighty good road*" in a blur of smoke and pistons, steadily upping its speed to breakneck proportions before finally running dry on coal and water.

A precedent had been set. Skiffle and trains went together and, in the wake of Donegan's "Rock Island Line", a whole heap of railroad related songs – usually old American folk, bluegrass, blues or jazz numbers – were picked up in the UK, dusted off and given the skiffle treatment. "There's the rhythm of the train for a start which lent itself typically to a washboard sound," explains leading light in the UK skiffle movement Chas McDevitt, of the close relationship between skiffle and railways. "When you hear a washboard player, it sounds just like the clickety-clack of a train going over the joints in the track. Visually, trains look great as well, so I think there was always that in the back of our minds. But it was also what these songs were about. You didn't tend to get story songs in the charts in those days. It was all lovey-dovey stuff, 'I love you, you love me'. These were songs that had stories in them. They could be very impersonal and sometimes had double meanings. They were about escape, jails, what it was like to be a train driver, wanting to be somewhere else, even sex if you looked deep enough. Trains lend themselves easily to stories and people liked that."

"I was 9 years old, I had some Christmas or birthday money, and I went into Woolworths at the end of Princes Street in Edinburgh to buy the first gramophone record that I ever purchased on my own," recalls Ian Anderson, creative force behind the band Jethro Tull, of a defining moment in his life during 1957. "It was Johnny Duncan and the Blue Grass Boys singing 'Last Train To San Fernando'. I suppose it was bluegrass, but it was what was known as skiffle. It was more or less the real deal because he was American, a serving soldier in the US who had been drafted to the UK, met a girl and stayed. It was born out of this wonderful bit of reverse engineering where Irish and Scottish emigrants to the USA had taken elements of their folk music with them which had developed in America, then found their way back into British popular culture as skiffle, thanks to people like Johnny Duncan and Lonnie Donegan. That absurd introduction to 'Rock Island Line' that he [Donegan] does in a sort of fake hillbilly voice to disguise his Glaswegian tones! However, we bought it literally hook, line and sinker."

Although "Rock Island Line" and "Last Train To San Fernando" sold like hot cakes, arguably the most enduring song from the skiffle period proved to be "Freight Train" by the Chas McDevitt Skiffle Group featuring Nancy Whiskey. Like Donegan, McDevitt was born in Scotland but raised south of the border in the London suburbs. He'd heard versions of "Freight Train" being played around the London jazz clubs. Unsure of the song's origins but aware that it had no copyright, McDevitt added some new words and made a recording for Oriole Records featuring guest vocals by the folk singer Nancy Whiskey at the suggestion of his manager, Bill Varley.

"We had a demo record that we played for Oriole Records consisting of 'Freight Train' and a song called 'Giddy Up A Ding Dong' which, had they chosen that, would have sent us on a completely different route entirely," says McDevitt. "Thankfully they didn't and 'Freight Train' struck a chord with people. We were controlled by American influences because that's what we were hearing in the blues and folk songs that came our way. The funny thing was that skiffle ended up being very, very popular in America. We did *The Ed Sullivan Show* seven years before The Beatles. Although they had 73 million viewers we had 45 million. When you consider that fewer people had television sets when we went on, that's just staggering. We played 'Freight Train' and in the background there was this lovely, big backcloth of a freight train on the wall. After that everybody seemed to give it ['Freight Train'] a go. Rusty Draper [the American country singer] tried it and it actually did better in the [American *Billboard*] charts than ours did."

"I must have been about 7 years old when the Chas McDevitt and Nancy Whiskey version of 'Freight Train' came out and I was completely mesmerised," says guitarist and songwriter Jeremy Spencer, one of the original members of Fleetwood Mac. "Even now, whenever I hear it, it's like 'Wow!' It can't fail to move you. The whole thing about travelling and moving has been my life so there's something in that song that really gets to me. I'm sure I'm far from alone in feeling that."

<hr>

It was only after the skiffle-era resurrection of "Freight Train" that the truth about the song's origins became known. It had been written at the age of 11 by Elizabeth Nevills, later to become Elizabeth Cotten, a self-taught guitar player born in 1893. Lying in bed at night, she listened to the sound of freight trains hauled by steam locomotives passing through her home town of Chapel Hill, North Carolina. Hey presto, a song. It really was as simple as that. Except at some point she put her guitar down and only really began playing it again decades later while working as a domestic servant for Charles Seeger and his wife Ruth Crawford Seeger, parents to four children including the young Peggy Seeger.

"My mother was a very busy woman, teaching piano for virtually 12 hours a day, six days a week," says Peggy. "She had four children. Father went off to work in Washington, D.C. The people who came to work in homes were almost all black, coming up from the south. The folklore in the family is that I got lost as a little girl in Lansburgh's Department Store [in Washington D.C.] and that 'Libba', as we came to call Elizabeth, found me. She stayed with me until my mother turned up. And when my mother turned up there was an immediate connection between the two of them. Libba was looking for work and my mother was looking for someone that she could really get along with, so Libba came to work on Saturdays and she mostly did cooking, cleaning and some ironing. She'd been there about five years when one of us walked in the kitchen one day and found her playing the guitar that always hung on the wall. We just had no idea so, yes, it was quite a surprise. She played it what you would call backwards. She didn't re-string it, which most left handed people do. She just turned it around so that the index finger did what normally the thumb would do."

Over time in the Seeger household the songs, including "Freight Train", began pouring out of Elizabeth. Both Peggy and her brother Mike learned to play the guitar like her, using the index finger to pick rather than the thumb to strum. When Mike started performing for a living he would drive Elizabeth to concerts in his car and appear as her opening act. With the Seeger family's musical stamp of approval and practical support, Cotten was able to resurrect her career and continued recording and playing concerts into her eighties. She died in 1987, aged 94.

Cotten's re-emergence almost inevitably sparked controversy over the copyright of "Freight Train". As the man behind the best known of many cover versions, McDevitt found himself caught in the crossfire, his defence against accusations of theft being that copyright simply hadn't existed prior to him releasing his 1957 interpretation. How can you steal something that doesn't have an owner? "That was a big bone of contention and it went to court, but was finally settled out of court and we all became part-authors," says McDevitt. "But it wasn't a nice experience to go through, no."

Regardless of the controversy over copyright, we can count ourselves fortunate that Cotten got to experience her Indian summer as a performer. If she hadn't, then "Freight Train", as it was originally written and intended, would have been lost forever. Her recordings and public performances of the song during later life inspired younger generations all the way from her adopted Syracuse, New York, to Surrey in England, home of Croydon-born and raised Ralph McTell. "The best version of it is by the lady that wrote it," he acknowledges. "She played finger style guitar and was one of my teachers, although she never knew that. I listened to her guitar playing and absolutely loved it. That song, sung in her quivery voice, has an authenticity that can't be beaten."

Besides the similarity in sound between trains and skiffle bands, plus the way in which stories involving railways made good lyrical material for songs, there was another much simpler reason why train songs were all the rage in the UK. During the late 1950s one of the most popular hobbies, pastimes – call it what you will – among young boys and teenage males was trainspotting. This involved physically going in search of trains, writing down the numbers of the ones that you saw, and then underlining those numbers in a book listing every single locomotive in the country.

Today trainspotters are an endangered species, the result of easy-on-the-eye steam trains and the space-age diesels that replaced them being ousted by what amount to functional tubes on wheels. But in the days of skiffle railway station platforms the length and breadth of the land were crammed with people writing down numbers. It was, for reasons no one has ever really been able to put their finger on, a very British pursuit which retained its popularity right up until the 1980s before steadily declining in appeal to the point where it's now regarded as almost the height of madness. Back in 1957, it was *the* thing to do, almost as popular among young men and boys as soccer. Just like skiffle, trainspotting was cheap, fun, something you could do with your mates. They went together like Lennon and McCartney or, come to think of it, Chas & Dave.

"I followed on from all the other kids with trainspotting," says Chas Hodges, the former session musician who went on to become one half of Chas & Dave, performing an enduring mix of folk, pop and boogie-woogie style piano. "I thought 'Well that doesn't sound very interesting' but once I got into it, well, I was really impressed. We'd be standing on a bridge or wherever and some of the cleverer kids could tell what they were a mile off. They'd say 'That's a Sandringham class'. I'd be like 'How do you know from that distance?' and they'd be like 'Well, you get to know'. The Britannia class were probably my favourites with exotic names like Hereward The Wake and Clive Of India – we [Chas & Dave] even did a song called 'Clive Of India' as a tribute because that was the first Britannia class that I ever saw. My younger days was all fishing and trainspotting and there was one place where I could actually do both which was magical. I still love trains. It's nice to see them now in a museum but it's nothing compared to seeing them in steam. They really come alive. That's what it is about them old trains – they're alive."

Many of those who weren't into trainspotting nevertheless found themselves falling under the spell that trains radiated. "I must have been about four years old, standing on the platform at Dunfermline station in Fifeshire, Scotland," adds Ian Anderson. "My father took me down to the train station which he used to commute from into Edinburgh to see the big, scary, thundering steam locomotives and it's one of my first childhood memories. I actually found them very frightening. Consequently, unlike most children of a pre-teen vintage, I did not want to be an engine driver. I thought I might just have a more sedate or genteel occupation ahead of me, like being a jet pilot or a platoon infantryman. However, it left an indelible imprint on my mind."

"When I was very young I used to be able to hear the trains coming out of Forest Hill station from our house," says Francis Rossi of Status Quo, remembering his formative years in south London. "There was something romantic about it. I don't mean romantic in a kissy sense, but in that 'Ah, I wonder where it's going? Is it travelling somewhere nice?' way. Even now at night, when I hear a train in the distance, I still have those same kind of feelings. It always struck me as quite a lonely sound. You know subliminally that the train is probably empty, travelling back to rest somewhere after its last trip of the day, but it brings out all sorts of emotions in you, really weird shit that is kind of inexplicable."

One of those trains in the distance from Rossi's childhood could well have been the "Golden Arrow" luxury Pullman car service which ran between London and the port of Dover from 1929 until 1972. "It seemed to be parked permanently in a station then, most probably [London] Victoria where it was in service for many years taking people to the coast to catch the ferry across to France," remembers the punk and new wave forefather Graham Parker, who found himself seduced at first sight by the steam locomotive attached to the front of the train. "This would have been about 1954 as I was born in 1950. It's one of my earliest memories. I can still see this massive, brutal and beautiful piece of machinery in my mind's eye. My Dad talked about it and I was entranced, and so he took me to see it."

<hr>

For the untold thousands into trains and skiffle, February 1957 must have seemed like all their Christmases had arrived at once. Inwardly stuffy yet conscious of having to move with the times, the BBC commissioned a ground-breaking music television programme showcasing skiffle bands and some of the other acts that were starting to blow away the post-war British cobwebs. Called *Six-Five Special* and produced by something of an entertainment and theatrical all-rounder, Jack Good, the show (which was recorded live) helped plug a gap in the schedule created by the abolition of what was known as the "Toddlers' Truce". This increasingly antiquated piece of television scheduling required transmissions on the BBC and recently launched ITV to cease between 6 p.m. and 7 p.m. so that parents could put their young children to bed.

On the very night that the "Toddlers' Truce" bit the dust, Saturday 16 February 1957, the first episode of *Six-Five Special* was screened. The opening credits said it all – a railway signal turning to green, the piercing whistle of a steam engine, an aerial shot of a London Midland & Scottish Railway Coronation class locomotive streaking its way through the countryside, all to the accompaniment of a catchy skiffle-style theme tune performed by Don Lang And His Frantic Five. Cut to the presenter, more often than not disc jockey Pete Murray, who would deliver the line which prefaced every one of the 96 episodes broadcast at 6.05 p.m. on Saturdays – "It's time to jive on the old Six-Five". For those already drunk on the heady mix of skiffle and trainspotting, *Six-Five Special* amounted to an unadulterated form of TV heaven.

"Saturday evenings, five past six – '*Over the points, over the points, over the points, the Six-Five Special's steaming down the line, the Six-Five Special's right on time. It's time to jive on the old Six-Five!*' That's what we lived for," remembers Ray Davies of a television programme that hit the buffers after 22 months when Good, frustrated by the stuffy production restrictions placed on him by the BBC, defected to ITV to create the rival music show *Oh Boy!* "Everything stopped for the *Six-Five Special*. Trains, music, that theme tune, girls, it had it all."

A little too much, so it would seem, for some train-obsessed small boys. "I used to watch the *Six-Five Special* on TV," says session drummer Ian Naisbitt recalling his formative Saturday evenings at home in Stockton-On-Tees. "I watched it thinking it was going to be about trains. I was like 'This is going to be great!' not realising of course that it was a music show. I'd be sitting there, waiting for my trains, wondering why all these people were singing and playing instruments. I honestly felt like I'd been conned. It was all one big lie as far as I was concerned!"

And so by the summer of 1957 Britain, you'd be forgiven for thinking, was a land crawling with trainspotters and skiffle groups. The vast majority of the latter were amateur outfits such as The Quarrymen featuring John Lennon and some of his mates from Quarry Bank Grammar School in Allerton, Liverpool, guys (and, credit where credit's due, the occasional girl) giving old American songs the skiffle treatment and occasionally trying their hands at something original often built around railroads (such as "One After 909" written at 20 Forthlin Road by Lennon and his new friend Paul McCartney). Railways were something that Lennon, Chas Hodges, Ian Anderson, Francis Rossi and countless others could identify with. Just like in the USA, Britain's railways represented real life. The men employed on them were regarded as *bona fide* working class heroes. What's more, trains were as much about the emancipation of the people in the UK as they were in North America, something that resonated with aspiring Woody Guthries from Essex living parallel lives, at least inside their heads, in Memphis.

"That's something people really underestimate compared to America, how much the railways changed the lives of people in Britain," says Paul Simmonds, songwriter and guitarist in the punk/folk band The Men They Couldn't Hang. "In Britain, the railways freed people to travel. Before that people didn't really leave their villages. In America it was slightly different because of the social and economic issues going on – freeing the slaves so that they could travel from the south to the north, enabling people to travel and bum rides during the Depression. But otherwise it was just the same. People in Britain suddenly had the ability to travel, to go to the cities, to migrate, just like in America. It was almost like the emancipation of the peasants really."

"My family, when you go back through the Difford family tree, used to live in Somerset," says singer and songwriter Chris Difford who, like Francis Rossi, was also raised in the southern suburbs of the English capital. "Some of the men became workers building the train line to London, and when the train line was built they hopped on a train, went to London, and never came back. They built that journey which brought our family tree to London. In America people would get on trains and travel across the country to places that would enlighten them like Chicago and New York, places that would give them a fresh start. My family were no different really, coming up from Somerset with its fields and hills to London and all the opportunities it presented them."

Hugely influential, remarkably short-lived. That was the UK's skiffle craze. Come January 1959 *Six-Five Special* was a thing of the past and the hits had dried up for the likes of Chas McDevitt and Johnny Duncan, although Lonnie Donegan remained at large into the 1960s releasing singles such as "My Old Man's A Dustman" appealing to an older, wider audience. However, a fuse had been lit and continued, out of sight, to burn. The majority of those who had played in skiffle bands abandoned their instruments once the craze was over, trading making music for the harsh realities of having to work for a living. Yet for a sizeable minority reared on the sounds of Donegan, Duncan, McDevitt and Nancy Whiskey, skiffle – with its do-it-yourself attitude, catchy rhythms and songs containing actual stories in the lyrics – was only the beginning. They'd seen the future and it had nothing to do with working in an office, factory or even for that matter becoming a train driver, the dream occupation of many a young male.

Within a few years, many of these ex-skifflers were taking on the world with their brand of blues, folk and rock'n'roll. There wouldn't be a jug, washboard or tea-chest bass in sight. But the trains, they kept on rolling.

4

FROM WIDNES TO WATERLOO

It's the evening of Monday 23 October 2000. On stage at the Hammersmith Apollo in west London, better known for years as the Hammersmith Odeon, Paul Simon is performing songs spanning four decades as a solo artist and one half of Simon & Garfunkel. To the delight of the packed hall he plays "Homeward Bound", the ultimate paean to being somewhere alien, soulless, alone, when you'd far rather be in more familiar surroundings, preferably in the arms of a loved one. The applause as he finishes comes in a rush, the way it does at a concert after a crowd favourite gets an airing. Simon waits patiently for the noise to die down, then stares menacingly at the rows of faces looking up at him. "A word to the person who has stolen the plaque from the platform at Widnes station," he says. "He'd better return it as soon as possible." It gets a big laugh. After all, everyone seems to know the story of how "Homeward Bound" came to be written on a humble railway station platform in north west England.

Or do they?

One evening in August 1965 Geoff Speed received a phone call at the house he shared with his father, Arthur, and mother, Joyce, in Widnes, an industrial town on the banks of the River Mersey approximately 13 miles east of Liverpool. Speed, who was 23 at the time, helped run a local folk club called The Howff, a Scottish Gaelic term for a friendly meeting place. On the line was a contact of his from London wanting to know if The Howff would be interested in booking a young American singer piecing together a tour of northern England. Speed said yes and agreed to cover the £12 fee the singer was asking for, a considerable sum at the time for a complete unknown.

A couple of weeks later Paul Simon – suitcase in one hand, guitar in the other – arrived on the doorstep of the Speed family home at 123 Coroners Lane, Widnes. "We got on very well," Speed recalls. "We put him up for an entire week and I drove him around to various folk clubs that had arranged to book him in places like Liverpool, Birkenhead, Chester and Warrington. On the evenings when he wasn't busy we went down to Liverpool. He wanted to go and have a look at the Cavern, which was still the original Cavern at the time, smelling of apples and oranges and things because of all the fruit that used to get stored there. And of course he made his appearance for us one night at The Howff."

At that time Speed was working as a buyer for his grandfather's electrical engineering company, Speeds of Widnes, leaving Simon to his own devices during the days. Legend has it that he wrote "Homeward Bound" while standing on the platform at Widnes station waiting for the early morning milk train back to London. Simon was depressed, homesick and missing his girlfriend, Kathy Chitty, who he had met at a folk club in Brentwood, Essex, shortly after arriving in England from the USA. Speed, perhaps not surprisingly, remembers things a little differently.

"On the last day he was there, a Friday, I went to work and told Paul to give me a call when he wanted to move on. He was going over to Hull to play in a folk club there run by the Watersons, who were a well-known group of people on the folk circuit. At some point the phone went and he said 'Geoff, I think I'm ready to go down to the station now'. So I went in my car to pick him up and dropped him off at Widnes station which in those days was called Farnworth station. The train was almost in the station by the time we got there. We only had a few minutes to say our goodbyes and for him to book himself in and get onto the platform. Now, if he managed to write that song in such a short space of time then he's a miracle worker. I would suggest that he started to write it at my home in Widnes and finished it on the train, but I don't think anyone's going to find out now."

Simon, famously a man of few words outside his songs, declined to be interviewed for this book, so Speed might just be right about that.

"Homeward Bound" paints a grim picture of England as seen through Simon's eyes, a treadmill of factories, strange faces and gigs in towns which all look the same. How does Speed feel about that considering the hospitality he and his parents extended the American for an entire week back in 1965? "I take a great amount of pride in the fact that perhaps he wrote it at my house, although when someone's been staying with you and they write a song like 'Homeward Bound' it makes you think perhaps they didn't enjoy it as much as you thought! But it's a delightful song and it means a lot to people. As far as I'm concerned that's what's important."

Speed does, however, have one gripe with the man who went on to become a multi-millionaire global superstar. "I actually recorded Paul's performance at our club. Afterwards he took it with him and promised to return it, but he never did. He did send a postcard though with 'Do not shoot!' written on it apologising for not being in touch. That was the last time I heard from him, so I don't think I'm going to get it back now!"

While Simon went down the mainstream career route, Speed stayed true to his roots. For 47 years he presented a folk show on BBC Radio Merseyside, ill health forcing him reluctantly into retirement in 2014. Farnworth station subsequently became Widnes North station before being re-christened Widnes. In 1990, a plaque was unveiled commemorating the location's place in rock'n'roll history. It was stolen, replaced, then stolen again much to Simon's mock horror, prompting him to issue his "threat" from the Hammersmith Apollo stage that night in 2000.

⫘⫘⫘⫘⫘⫘⫘

Swinging London, if you believe popular folklore, was the place to be in 1965, so it is perhaps unsurprising that Simon longed to be back there. However, it's easy to forget just how much artistic creativity existed in the British regions at that time. Widnes may have lacked star quality, but nearby Liverpool had been a fixture on the pop music map for some years (though most of the city's top acts still ended up disappearing south to London once the hits started coming). The folk revival was also in full swing bringing musicians to a myriad of clubs from Aberdeen to St Albans to Cardiff, often literally located on the wrong side of the tracks as Peggy Seeger recalls of one shadowy Caledonian venue where she appeared with Ewan MacColl.

"We were singing somewhere in Scotland in a club that was right up against the railway tracks. If that sounds romantic, then this was a little too close. There we are, and we started to do 'The Iron Road' (more commonly known as 'Song Of The Iron Road') which has this excellent rhythm. I just loved playing the banjo on it. Ewan sings a couple of verses, then I start in on the break. Suddenly we hear 'Woo hoo' and an express train runs through, right as I'm doing the break. And by the end of the break, it's gone. And Ewan goes 'Yup, it was on time!'"

Then there was Manchester and neighbouring Salford, the "Dirty Old Town" MacColl had sung about where the sparks from steam trains set the night on fire amid the grey surroundings of factories and seemingly

35

endless rows of terraced houses. It's often said that urban decay lends itself to the arts – witness the London squats of the 1970s that helped give birth to punk music, or the artists and photographers drawn to downtrodden early 21st century Detroit – and the bleak, industrial Manchester environs proved similarly inspirational during the 1950s and 1960s with its flourishing folk, jazz, blues and pop scenes. It was also an important media hub (most of Britain's national newspapers had offices in the city) with Granada Television, in particular, establishing a reputation for producing cutting edge, innovative shows thanks to the vision of people such as producer Johnnie Hamp and director Phil Casson.

Johnnie Hamp had moved north from London in 1956 at the behest of media baron Sidney Bernstein, chairman of the recently launched Granada Group and Manchester-based Granada Television. Hailing from a background in cinema management and concert promotion, Hamp was an ideas man with a thick contacts book which is why Bernstein wanted him in Manchester producing shows. In 1962, and again the following year, Hamp had been at the city's Free Trade Hall venue to witness package shows featuring well-known American blues musicians touring the UK. When details of another tour featuring, among others, Muddy Waters and Sister Rosetta Tharpe were unveiled in 1964, Hamp decided to book every act on the package to play a concert for Granada Television. Not just any old concert, but something unorthodox that would really stand out in the schedules. Which is where Phil Casson came in.

"Phil had really great modern ideas on how to stage a concert," says the Manchester-based author and broadcaster C P Lee. "Normally it would have been a case of tiers of seats and a stage. Phil built what were known as scaffolding sets and put the audience in different places. He also got them to dress casual, not formal. Phil said to Johnnie 'Let's not do it in a studio – let's do it somewhere different'. They knew about this semi-disused railway station in Chorlton (a suburb of Manchester) and things went from there. 'What if we could film it at the station? We could dress it up like an American station in the deep south. We could hire a train to bring the audience in, they can get off, and we'll do an outside broadcast of the concert'. And that's exactly what happened."

"The American Folk, Blues And Gospel Caravan", as the 1964 package tour was officially called, saw the acts – Muddy Waters, Sonny Terry, Brownie McGhee, Sister Rosetta Tharpe, Otis Spann, the Reverend Gary Davis and Cousin Joe Pleasant – scheduled to play 11 shows across England spanning the end of April and beginning of May. The night before the concert at Manchester's Free Trade Hall coincided with a rest day. Johnnie Hamp moved quickly to ensure that filming would take place on the evening of Thursday 7 May at Wilbraham Road station, closed to passengers in 1958 but still very much intact and witness to the occasional passing train. Tickets were distributed with the words "Casual gear essential – denims, sweaters" printed clearly across them. Many of those lucky enough to secure tickets took advantage of a special charter train laid on by Granada Television to convey people from Manchester's Central Station to Wilbraham Road, renamed "Chorltonville" for the occasion and festooned with bales of hay, chickens, a goat, fugitive "Wanted" posters and a four-wheeled surrey carriage drawn by a horse. Even the steam locomotive pulling the charter train (an Ivatt 2MT 2-6-0, just for the record) boasted an American-style cowcatcher on its front.

"It was a real novelty," says Brian Smith who was in the audience. "We'd been to the usual stage shows but it really was a stroke of genius by Johnnie Hamp and Phil Casson. The artists all performed on one platform, then across the railway lines on the opposite facing platform sat the audience. And, being Manchester, it rained. Sister Rosetta was probably going to do 'Didn't It Rain' anyway because it was one of her big songs but she came out, started singing that, and we all picked it up because we were sat there soaked to the skin. Muddy Waters was terrific because he was a colossus, a master of everything. Cousin Joe was one we really liked because he was so funny and witty. But Sister Rosetta was a revelation. To see this woman standing there in a fur coat with a Les Paul guitar strapped across her just mesmerised everyone. There were bits of Pete Townshend in there. He wasn't there but I believe he'd seen her in London, and she used to do the windmill arms and things like that. A phenomenal stage presence. At that time, girls just stood and sang love ballads so it was strange to see a woman playing guitar, lead guitar as well."

Three months later, in August 1964, Granada Television screened the show which appeared in the listings as the *Blues And Gospel Train*. The reaction among viewers was hugely positive. All that was missing from the transmission was the Reverend Gary Davis (a no-show on the night due, allegedly, to being worse for wear through drink) and the few minutes when filming came to a halt to allow a freight train to pass through the station.

"Can you imagine that happening now, the very thought of an outside broadcast taking place on a railway line that's still in use, albeit sparingly," says C P Lee. "When Muddy Waters did his turn he actually walked up the railway line before climbing some stairs onto the platform. I can see the headline now – 'Blues legend run over by freight train!' Health and safety just didn't come into it."

On Wednesday 7 May 2014, the Chorlton Arts Festival ran a special "Blues And Gospel Tram" to commemorate 50 years since Granada Television brought some of the most recognisable names in music to "Chorltonville". It ran from Manchester city centre to a tram stop near Wilbraham Road, the old station having long since succumbed to the town planners. "I expected a dozen or so souls to turn up," says C P Lee who acted as the on-board emcee accompanied by local musicians playing the blues. "Then the doors opened and about 200 people got on. It was absolutely rammed, testimony really to how this remarkable one-off 'concert' managed to influence a generation of music lovers growing up in the north west. And you know what? It poured with rain again!"

▬▬▬▬▬▬▬

A little over 12 years after Granada Television filmed the "Blues And Gospel Train", the Sex Pistols appeared at Manchester's Lesser Free Trade Hall, a large room upstairs from the more prestigious Free Trade Hall. The crowd was small, no more than 100 people, but it's said that almost everyone there (or who claims to have been there) was so inspired by the performance that they decided to do something creative with their lives, such as form a band. The "Blues And Gospel Train" TV show provoked a similar response among those who witnessed the recording or watched the transmission. Brian Smith, a self-confessed "fan with a camera," went on to photograph just about every major blues act to visit the UK during the 1960s as well as running the British arm of the Carl Perkins fan club. David Tomlinson, also present for the recording, became Dave Formula, playing keyboards in seminal post-punk band Magazine and new-romantic outfit Visage. "It did create a bit of a 'can-do' atmosphere," adds Brian. "It was like they were saying 'We're from the deep south of the USA, this is what we do, you too can be a part of this'. That meant a lot to us, the fact that they'd come and done it in Manchester and not London which was always seen as the epicentre of everything, even though it wasn't."

Staying put in north west England, however, wasn't an option for some of those swimming in Manchester's burgeoning musical talent pool. Young Graham Gouldman, just starting out as a musician and songwriter around the time the "Blues And Gospel Train" show was televised, knew full well that his dreams weren't going to be realised in Manchester. London was where the majority of the acts he aspired to write songs for were based and most of the deals done. By the summer of 1965, he was spending increasing amounts of time on trains shuffling between the Gouldman family home in Manchester and record company offices in the capital. Not that he minded. Riding trains gave him plenty of time to hone his craft.

"There is a romance about trains and a sort of escapism as well that really appealed to me," says the man who wrote a string of hit singles for bands such as The Hollies and The Yardbirds before co-forming 10cc in 1972. "Obviously now we've all got mobile phones but in those days once you got on a train until you reached your destination you were out of contact with the rest of the world. There was something rather nice about that. The train coaches still had separate compartments that you could sit in. If I was going down to London to do some work, then I'd take my guitar with me. Those compartments were an ideal place to get the guitar out and play for your own amusement or try and do a bit of writing. They were private. You were in your own little world. Sometimes there might be a few of you so you'd all pile in, get the guitars out, and that would be it for your entire journey."

It was while making one of those journeys, between Piccadilly station in Manchester and Euston station in London, that the song "Look Through Any Window" was born. "The actual title of the song came from somebody else. I was with a guy who was one of my co-managers at the time, Charlie Silverman, and he came up with it. We were looking out of the carriage window, trying to look into the windows of the houses alongside the track that were going by really quickly. He said the title and it stuck with me – '*Look through any window, yeah, what do you see?*' When I got home I mentioned it to my Dad who used to help me with lyrics. He wrote some lines, I wrote some lines. It happened that way, but it was conceived on the train."

Recorded by The Hollies, "Look Through Any Window" reached number four in the UK during the autumn of 1965, giving the band its very first top 40 hit in the USA early the following year. "Not bad for a couple of hours spent staring out of a train carriage window," says Gouldman with a smile.

The concept of north to south migration from Manchester to London, as experienced by Gouldman on those train trips, would be revisited in the 1980s by Morrissey and his songwriting partner in The Smiths, Johnny Marr. In their song "London" a man ventures forth for the English capital leaving his family and girlfriend behind, only to question his decision to bolt as the train hurtles south towards Euston station. The song itself is an echo of the 1963 John Schlesinger-directed film *Billy Liar* in which Tom Courtenay's character, a provincial dreamer and habitual fibber, finds himself unable to board a London-bound train which personifies reality. As with so many other songs, the train in "London" represents escape, except that this time the principal character is unsure whether escaping is really the solution.

▦▦▦▦▦▦▦▦▦

By the mid-1960s, Britain's skiffle kids were beginning to come of age. Many of those who had resisted getting a proper job were in bands starting to go places. They'd listened intently to rockabilly, blues, bluegrass and rock'n'roll records imported from America by merchant sailors and serving military personnel based in Europe after the Second World War. They watched spellbound as TV shows like the "Blues And Gospel Train" opened their eyes to a whole new way of making music. Now these influences were beginning to bear fruit. At the Railway Hotel in Harrow, adjacent to the Manchester to London railway line which was helping Graham Gouldman realise his songwriting dreams, The Who were playing their first gigs featuring a version of Howlin' Wolf's "Smokestack Lightning" that, as Pete Townshend's friend John Challis later told *Mojo* magazine, "felt like someone had driven an iron bar through my ears, had lifted me up, and I was hanging from it." On their debut tour of America, The Yardbirds managed to book some studio time with Sam Phillips in Memphis to record a version of "The Train Kept A-Rollin'", written by Tiny Bradshaw in 1951 and popularised five years later by Johnny Burnette, who reworked it as a rockabilly number. The song, an anthem to sexual prowess and staying power in which the "train" keeps a-rolling all night long (*"with a heave, and a ho, well I just couldn't let her go-oh-oh"*), would prove to have an enduring hold over the prime movers in Britain's sizeable rhythm and blues movement for years to come.

However, just because bands like The Who were singing about American steam locomotives in English pubs didn't mean the USA had mislaid its long tradition of writing songs about trains.

One afternoon during the summer of 1966, Bobby Hart was punching buttons on his car stereo while heading for home in Los Angeles. Pulling into the driveway he caught the fadeout to "Paperback Writer", the latest single from The Beatles. It was the first time Hart had heard the song.

40

Straining to make out the lyrics over the car's engine, he thought the words of the closing harmonies were "*take the last*" something.

"And I reckoned it had to be a train," recalls Hart. "The next day I heard it in full and realised it had nothing to do with trains or taking the last something to anywhere, but we were always looking for song titles. I told my [songwriting] partner Tommy Boyce that I'd misheard this thing but I liked the idea of taking the last train to somewhere. So we sat down to write it."

Whenever possible, Boyce and Hart would write together in the same room, conjuring lyrics, melodies and generally bouncing ideas off one another. At that time, the pair were writing and producing songs for what would be the first album by The Monkees, a four-piece band created specifically for a television show about a group desperate to emulate the success of The Beatles. The TV show was to be fun, jokey, light-hearted, but Hart liked the idea of including some kind of thinly-veiled protest song on the record. The American ground war in Vietnam had started the previous year and, despite initial public support for the deployment of soldiers, not everyone favoured military intervention in a foreign land on the opposite side of the world. Between them, Boyce and Hart decided this new protest song of theirs would have a Vietnam theme.

"We knew we couldn't be overt because this was The Monkees," says Hart. "We wouldn't get away with it and the powers that be wouldn't allow it. We started throwing names out and nothing sounded right. Finally Tommy said 'What about some of those little towns where you used to spend your summers in Arizona?' So I said to him 'Cottonwood, Clarkdale' and he said 'Clarkdale... what about Clarksville?' Then we started thinking about the guy who's leaving, not knowing if he's ever coming back because he's going to the war. He wants to spend one last night with a girlfriend. He's shipping out the next day by plane, but we brought her in by train – 'Last Train To Clarksville'. She was a little affluent, otherwise she'd have been on a Greyhound [bus]!"

From there, the lyrics quickly fell into place. Next came the music. "We always liked to get musicians in to get a few ideas together and rehearse," adds Hart. "I was playing with musicians in nightclubs at the time and rather than hire top studio musicians and an expensive studio I decided to bring the guys from the nightclub into a little 10 dollar an hour studio and work it out from there. So we went to this place, Rainbow Studios in LA, and we sang them the outline of the song and said that we needed an intro. It was [guitarist] Louis Shelton who said 'How about this?' And he

41

played dum-dum, dum-de-dum-de-dum, dum-dum. I don't know where it came from or whether he'd been rehearsing it but it was just there, kind of magical. That was the signature riff."

"Last Train To Clarksville" by The Monkees was released on 16 August 1966 in the USA and five months later in the UK, reaching number one and a relatively lowly 23 on either side of the Atlantic respectively (the song's appeal in the UK later grew as *The Monkees* television show soared in popularity). Its release stateside prompted speculation as to which Clarksville the song referred to. "I read one article which said there were 26 Clarksvilles in the United States and wondering which one it was," says Hart. "If anybody asked, we would say it was probably the one by Nashville because there was an air force base near there, although we didn't know that at the time we wrote it. Anyway, we got our protest song and nobody made a song or dance about it. Knock on wood it's still paying my rent, that and a few others. You don't get to write too many like that. People still seem to love it. Not so long ago I was doing a documentary on us, Boyce and Hart, in which [former Monkee] Mike Nesmith was involved. He was the one who did a lot of the singing and was probably the most serious out of them musically, and I couldn't believe how complimentary he was. He said all this bad stuff back then, like he didn't like the direction they were going in, but in this he said that he always loved 'Clarksville'. Maybe that's down to his country background because it does sound a little bit like that."

𝄞𝄞𝄞𝄞𝄞

The growing soul movement in the USA also moved fast to embrace trains, railroads and everything they embodied, hardly surprising really given that soul combined gospel, rhythm & blues and elements of jazz; all forms of music already littered with train songs. Traditional soul, the kind that originated in America during the 1950s before exploding during the 1960s, incorporated a litany of human emotions and experiences such as love, loss, pain, pleasure, heartbreak and sex which lent themselves easily to songs featuring trains (metaphorically, with regard to the latter). Some songwriters and artists wrote and performed original soul music featuring railways. Others adapted older pieces of train-related music to suit the genre. In the hands of James Brown the song "Night Train" – originally recorded in 1951 by Jimmy Forrest and integrated into the longer Duke Ellington composition known as "Happy-Go-Lucky Local" – became a roll call of cities on the eastern flank of America shouted by the singer in the style of a railroad porter barking destinations (the lyrics to most pre-Brown interpretations lean more towards a blues lament in which a man regrets treating his woman badly). Ultimately, trains became so closely associated with soul music that Chicago-based WCIU-TV chose the name *Soul Train* for its new television programme showcasing soul music performed by black artists. Launched in 1971, *Soul Train* went on to be syndicated throughout the USA, running to over 1,000 episodes spanning 35 years.

At around the same time as Tommy Boyce and Bobby Hart were conceiving "Last Train To Clarksville" another talented pair of songwriters were in the process of joining Motown, tasked with writing hits for the label's formidable roster of acts. Nickolas Ashford and Valerie Simpson had met in 1964 at the White Rock Baptist Church in Harlem, New York City, and soon became a couple romantically as well as professionally. Although they recorded together, it was as songwriters that Ashford and Simpson really made their names, crafting classic hits such as "Ain't No Mountain High Enough", "Reach Out And Touch (Somebody's Hand)" and "Ain't Nothing Like The Real Thing" for talents such as Diana Ross and the vocal duo of Marvin Gaye and Tammi Terrell.

One of the earliest groups to sign for Motown back in 1961 had been the five-piece all-girl outfit The Marvelettes, formed out of friendships forged while attending school in the Detroit suburb of Inkster. In truth, The Marvelettes never lived up to the high expectations that Motown had for them, enjoying a handful of hits (including a *Billboard* number one with "Please Mr. Postman") but suffering by comparison with their more successful label rivals The Supremes. Nevertheless, some of the singles that got away duly resurfaced long after The Marvelettes had split as lovers of soul probed the Motown back catalogue for hidden gems. "Destination Anywhere" by Ashford and Simpson proved to be just such a song.

"Destination Anywhere" is the story of a woman who has been hurt by love. Desperate to escape, she goes to the railroad station and demands a ticket just for one. The ticket man asks which destination and the woman replies that she doesn't care, she just wants to escape from her present predicament. She still pines for her ex but realises their relationship is doomed, and longs to get away to a place where nothing reminds her of him.

"What I remember most about 'Destination Anywhere' is that we tended to write very positive, uplifting songs but that was one of the few we wrote that definitely had a darkness to it," says Valerie Simpson. "I once called it the closest thing to a suicide song, you know, the idea that you don't care where you are going '*this old world ain't got no backdoor*'. It's certainly not a feel good things-are-going-well-in-my-life song. You're just going to get on a train and go anywhere. People have felt like that. We've all been hurt by love. It's a song that speaks to those people. It'll never go out of style because someone out there is always going to be hurt."

The lyrics to "Destination Anywhere" may have been borderline suicidal but the music that accompanied them had an undeniably positive groove. And there lay the secret behind the track's lingering appeal. In 1990, film director Alan Parker was searching for songs to feature in his screen adaptation of the Roddy Doyle novel *The Commitments*, about a group of working class Dubliners who form a soul band. "Destination Anywhere", with its world-weary lyrics offset against a catchy tune, fitted the bill exactly. When the film was released the following year, boasting an impressive soundtrack, the song stood out. On the back of the film's success in the UK, countless amateur soul bands were spawned playing many of the tracks featured in *The Commitments*. "Destination Anywhere" had finally found an audience 23 years after failing to dent the pop charts in Britain (even in the USA it only managed to reach a woeful number 63 in the *Billboard* chart).

"It got picked up for that film, *The Commitments*, and I think they play it a few times in it," says Simpson. "We'd written it for The Marvelettes and it had been a minor, minor hit. Suddenly, it was really picking up exposure after all this time. I still do it in my shows now. It's one of those that has just come back, which is always good. We wrote so many songs, and there are so many that I don't reach for anymore, but that is one that I do. Certain songs, you can see the picture as you write them, and 'Destination Anywhere' was definitely one of those. It kind of created what I call its own little play."

In Doyle's novel, the band play a version of "Night Train" at their gigs, lead singer Declan "Deco" Cuffe substituting James Brown's roll call of eastern American cities for stops on the Dublin Area Rapid Transit (DART) rail system: "Connolly, Killester, Harmonstown, Raheny, Kilbarrack, Howth Junction, Bayside, Sutton where the rich folks live", etc. However, it didn't work for the proposed film. So "Night Train" went out and "Destination Anywhere", which hadn't been in the novel, came in. Perhaps Deco's railway station ad-libs would have proved a little too parochial for US moviegoers. Miami, Florida, sounds exotic. Atlanta, Georgia, sounds exotic. Raheny? I don't think so.

Of course, Deco was being ironic, but back in the mid-1960s, embryonic bands like The Who and The Yardbirds were still transfixed by the sounds originating from America such as "Smokestack Lightning" and "The Train Kept A-Rollin'". Playing songs that felt British or referenced British (or Irish) place names, well, it just didn't seem right. It wasn't cool. But things were starting to change.

"When I worked on the railway, I was also in a band," says Dave Goulder who, prior to becoming a folk singer and songwriter, spent seven years cleaning and maintaining steam locomotives at the Kirkby in Ashfield depot in Nottinghamshire, England. "We wanted to do railway songs because we worked on the railway. It was all American stuff right out of the Lonnie Donegan song book and things like that. One night I was sitting in the mess room, practising my guitar. There was this other guy in there and he said 'I'm fed up of this American sound. When are you going to write something about the 6.15 to Wellingborough?' I went 'Don't be silly!' Then I went home and thought 'Yeah, he's got a point'."

"Singing about going from somewhere in Britain like Salisbury to Devizes can sound banal compared to, say, Memphis to Nashville or Tuscaloosa to Omaha," adds the singer and songwriter Robyn Hitchcock, raised within earshot of the railway line running south west from London's busy Waterloo station towards the English counties of Dorset, Hampshire and Wiltshire. "But... and here's the thing... a train is a train no matter where you are. Anything can happen on a train trip. It doesn't really matter where the train is coming from or going to."

In the spring of 1967, a song finally came along which demonstrated how railways in the UK could be just as alluring as any stretch of American railroad. It remains to this day about as quintessentially British, English, London-esque, as a pop song can possibly get. Widnes station might not have set Paul Simon's pulse racing, but the same certainly couldn't be said for Ray Davies when it came to Waterloo.

5

TIN LIZZY

By the mid-19th century, London had become the most powerful city in the world. The British Empire was in its pomp ruled largely by decisions made in the English capital a bastion of finance and international trade. As London's importance grew, so increasing numbers of people needed to go there on business. The railways helped them do that. Trains also enabled the masses to live on the fringes of the city where there was more room to move and fresh air to breathe, travelling in and out of London for work from their local station. Welcome to the wonderful world, or some might say necessary evil, of commuting.

One by one, a number of imposing railway termini rose up out of the ground across different parts of London, aligned towards the suburbs and far away towns they were created to serve. Heading west to Bristol? Then it's Paddington you need. Newcastle and the north east? That would be Kings Cross. Liverpool and the north west? Euston's your place. What about Brighton and the Sussex coast? Look no further than Victoria. Most stations were spectacular triumphs of Victorian engineering and sheer inventiveness, many of which survive in one form or another today. Waterloo, alas, was one of the exceptions.

Opened in July 1848 by the London & South Western Railway, Waterloo was initially named Waterloo Bridge station (although publisher George Bradshaw's popular 19th century rail guides also refers to it as Waterloo Road). Situated on the south bank of the River Thames in the borough of Lambeth, the station was never intended to be anything other than a temporary terminus. The L&SWR's plan had been to extend the railway north-eastwards from Waterloo right into the City of London. Because of that, little time or effort was spent on design and it grew to become a sprawling mess. At some point towards the end of the century, the L&SWR abandoned its idea of driving an overland railway into the City of London opting instead to rebuild the station at

Waterloo as a dedicated terminus. Work on this started in 1904 and was finally completed 18 years later.

There always was, and to an extent remains, something fascinating about the rebuilt Waterloo station. It's in the people you find there and the disparate nature of the communities to the south west of London that it serves – bankers from Surbiton and Guildford, secretaries from New Malden and Staines, Royal Navy personnel travelling to and from the docks at Portsmouth, racegoers making for Ascot, stockbrokers from well-heeled Esher and Richmond, passengers bound for ocean liners casting off from the port of Southampton, clergymen in London for the day from Winchester and Salisbury, families coming up from Weymouth on trains connecting with ships from the Channel Islands. All human life is present, which might explain why actor turned director John Schlesinger made a documentary film about the place in 1961 two years prior to helming work on *Billy Liar*.

Bereft of any commentary (and all the better, in this author's opinion, for it), *Terminus* charts a day in the life of Waterloo station. Rarely can so much have been crammed into 33 minutes of celluloid – commuters on their way to work, prisoners destined for a jail somewhere in south west England being escorted to a train, a distraught lost boy receiving a helping hand from a policeman, immigrants from the West Indies arriving on boat trains ready to begin new lives in England, the cat that lives in the signal box, a trainspotter receiving medical attention having received a smut in the eye from a steam engine, an elderly lady on a mission to track down a lost umbrella, tearful farewells as a boat train pulls out laden with people emigrating to far off lands. Some scenes were, in fact, staged using actors or, in the case of the lost boy, the 5-year-old son of an actress friend of Schlesinger's, but the majority of the footage was genuine fly-on-the-wall material. Even after all these years *Terminus* is captivating stuff, fully deserving of the BAFTA nomination it received (the film was also nominated for an Oscar before being disqualified after someone realised it had been released prior to the eligibility period).

Ray Davies had always felt drawn towards Waterloo station and the area surrounding it. Watching *Terminus* in his late teens, shortly after its release, only intensified his love of the place. "It's a wonderful documentary which John Schlesinger made when he was still quite young," says Davies. "I grew up in north London and had to catch the train to art school in south London which meant going through Waterloo. I was in hospital for a while by the station at St Thomas' [he had a tracheotomy at the age of 13] where the nurses used to wheel my bed to the window so I could look out over the river [Thames]. When I was older, I lived down in Surrey for a while and I used to get the train home from there most nights. You've got the river there, and when you cross the river [to Waterloo station] that means you're going on somewhere to the south by train. So it's always been a special place for me, an area that evokes certain memories and feelings. To me, *Terminus* really got the atmosphere around Waterloo at that time. I'd advise anyone to watch it, if they can find it, because it's a marvellous piece of film making. The attention to detail is staggering."

The Kinks, formed by Davies with his brother Dave, were already a hugely successful band by the time Ray came to write "Waterloo Sunset". They could be edgy ("You Really Got Me"), satirical ("Dedicated Follower Of Fashion"), world-weary ("Tired Of Waiting for You") or rueful ("Sunny Afternoon"). Observational would be one way of describing "Waterloo Sunset" which is to all intents and purposes *Terminus* dressed up as a pop song – the taxi lights shining bright, swathes of people milling around Waterloo's underground station, Terry and Julie, who meet every Friday at Waterloo station before crossing the River Thames to London's West End and whatever the night has in store for them. Who, in real life, were Terry and Julie? Davies has always maintained that they could in fact be anybody and most definitely were not actor Terence Stamp and actress Julie Christie who dated each other for a period during the 1960s. It's worth noting, however, that Christie played one of Tom Courtenay's love interests in *Billy Liar*, directed by Schlesinger, and is the girl Billy spinelessly abandons on the London-bound train at the film's climax. Maybe there was something about that scene deep in Davies' subconscious when he came to write "Waterloo Sunset" – railway stations, *Terminus*, Schlesinger, *Billy Liar*, Julie Christie? Just maybe.

"Waterloo Sunset" reached number two in the UK singles charts where it remained throughout late May and June of 1967, kept off the top spot by The Tremeloes' "Silence Is Golden". And silent, or at least a whole lot quieter, was what Waterloo station was about to become. For several years the powers that be who ran Britain's railways had been gradually phasing out steam engines, replacing them with new diesel and electric locomotives. That summer, Waterloo was the last of London's termini where you could still see steam engines in their glory. When it was announced that the second weekend of July would mark the very end of steam, not just at Waterloo but across the entire south of England, hordes of people – the curious, as well as Britain's army of trainspotters – drew up plans to witness the end of these elegant beasts for themselves. The soundtrack to this sad and somewhat historic event, inevitably, became "Waterloo Sunset" by The Kinks.

"Every time I hear those descending chords at the start of 'Waterloo Sunset' I'm right back at the top end of Waterloo's platform 11 watching steam trains coming and going," recalls Martin Lawrence who in 1967 was 15 years old and living with his parents in Kingston-upon-Thames on the outskirts of south west London. "I was there on that last weekend, on both the Saturday and Sunday, me and countless others, and it was like you were witnessing the end of an entire way of life, which I suppose we were. There weren't many steam engines left by that stage and those that were still running were in a rundown condition. Come Monday, they'd be off to the scrapyard so this was their last rites. I remember reading something in a newspaper at the time describing it as 'Waterloo's Waterloo' which I think summed it up perfectly. I went home that Sunday night, put my notepads away and never went trainspotting again. That was it for me, although I've always retained an interest in steam engines. But that was the end as far as trainspotting was concerned. Looking back, all these years later, I'm not afraid to say I get a bit sentimental thinking about it. 'Waterloo Sunset'... a beautiful song, but it doesn't half bring a lump to your throat. I saw him [Ray Davies] playing it a few years ago at the [London] Royal Festival Hall and I almost had to get up and walk out."

In 1967, Davies knew full well that the end of steam trains in Britain, not just at Waterloo, was imminent. Even so, the release of "Waterloo Sunset" and its presence in the pop charts that summer was purely coincidental. The following year Davies, who has often chronicled the march of so-called progress and its detrimental effect on picture-postcard England in his work, returned more specifically to the demise of steam in "Last Of The Steam-Powered Trains", a song that tipped its hat to Howlin' Wolf's "Smokestack Lighting" in terms of sound.

"There's a riff in it that alludes to it ['Smokestack Lightning'], a homage to it," says Davies. "The song itself ['Last Of The Steam-Powered Trains'] is very simple and was inspired by a train called the 'Tin Lizzy' – not the group! When I was small, I used to go hop picking in Kent with my family at a place called Rolvenden. There was this steam engine there that ran from one side of Kent to the other. That was 'Tin Lizzy'. You would see it in the mornings through the mist going about its business. It was very romantic and is an image that has stuck with me ever since. So much was changing at the time [when he wrote 'Last Of The Steam-Powered Trains'] and many of my contemporaries were changing, moving away from the things that had made them who they were, becoming more middle-class. I wrote it as a form of 'I'm the last person standing, I'm the last of the good old brigade', as someone who is determined to fight against progress, to retain individuality. I am 'Tin Lizzy'. I will stand alone. As long as I've got coal, I *will* keep going."

Davies would persist with railway references in other songs recorded by The Kinks such as "A Well Respected Man" (the metronomic life of a well-to-do commuter) and "Willesden Green" (personal reflection). But Waterloo has rarely strayed far from his side. In 1984, Davies wrote and directed a film called *Return To Waterloo* about a middle-aged man (known only as "The Traveller" played by actor Kenneth Colley) trapped in a monotonous daily commute from Guildford in Surrey to London.

"It was one of the first music films ever commissioned by [the UK's] Channel 4," says Davies. "He ['The Traveller'] was a real estate agent, his daughter had left home, and he sort of felt the world was passing him by, that he had been living a lie. When I wrote the script I took the train from Guildford through Cobham to Waterloo, and wrote the whole script in roughly about the same time as it took to make the journey. I used that train ride as a route map through the story. I'm in it as a busker. [Actor] Tim Roth is in there as well (appearing as a sneering 'punk' who boards the train carrying a firearm). I was the first person to teach Tim how to hold a gun... and he's been holding a gun ever since!"

Sadly both the film and its accompanying soundtrack (also performed by Davies) failed to capture the public's imagination, something which certainly couldn't be said for the song "Waterloo". No, not "Waterloo Sunset" but "Waterloo" as in Abba's 1974 Eurovision Song Contest winning entry. Written by Björn Ulvaeus and Benny Andersson, "Waterloo" referred to Napoleon Bonaparte's defeat by British and German forces near the Belgian town of the same name in June 1815 and had nothing to do with the London termini. However, after winning Eurovision in the English seaside resort of Brighton, the band's manager, Stig Anderson, hit on the idea of organising a photo opportunity at Waterloo station specifically for the London press. On the morning of 11 April, the four members of Abba played ball with photographers by adopting a variety of poses around the station (one picture of the group stood on a luggage trolley as two curious city gents wearing bowler hats pass by is pure comedy). This quirky publicity stunt partially backfired when elements of Abba's growing fan base, consisting largely of young people spread across many different countries speaking a variety of languages, came to the misguided if understandable conclusion that the song was actually about a London railway station.

But let's not get ahead of ourselves. Back to the 1960s.

ㅤㅤㅤㅤㅤㅤ

Like Ray Davies, fellow Londoner Rod Stewart was another teenager who found himself passing through Waterloo station on a regular basis during the first half of the decade (the pair had both attended William Grimshaw Secondary Modern School in Muswell Hill at around the same time, something they only came to realise years later). Stewart had discovered the flourishing south west London rhythm & blues meccas otherwise known as the Eel Pie Island Hotel and the Crawdaddy Club, which involved taking a train from Waterloo and alighting at either Twickenham or Richmond stations respectively. Late one evening, after attending an Eel Pie Island gig, Stewart began playing "Good Morning Little Schoolgirl" on his harmonica at Twickenham station while waiting for a train back to Waterloo. He was overheard by blues singer and musician John William "Long John" Baldry, destined to become Stewart's mentor, who happened to be standing on the same platform. The pair bonded immediately and, by the time the train pulled into Waterloo, Baldry had invited Stewart to join his band. The rest, as they say, is history.

"All true, except for the song," confirmed Stewart when I interviewed him in 1997 on behalf of the World Entertainment News Network wire agency. "It was 'Smokestack Lightning', or at least some kind of attempt at it because I think I'd had a couple [of drinks]. Talk about being in the right place at the right time. And he [Baldry] believed in me." So a song inspired by a train busked on a railway station platform got the young Rod Stewart the break he so desperately craved.

"Smokestack Lightning" and other American songs may have been *de rigueur* across the UK in early 1964, when Eel Pie Island and the Crawdaddy were *the* places to be, but within four years a sea-change would occur. "Waterloo Sunset" sent a message out to Britain's pop music production line that it was perfectly OK for them to mine their own country for material. American songs and influences would remain important, but they were no longer the be-all and end-all.

The Train Kept A-Rollin'

Having quit his job cleaning and maintaining steam locomotives in the English east Midlands to become a singer and songwriter, Dave Goulder – a highly respected figure in British folk circles whose work has been covered by such luminaries as Martin Carthy and June Tabor – was among the first to throw off the American shackles and embrace Britishness with creations such as "I'm The Man Who Put The Engine In The Chip Shop", a candidate if there ever was one for quirkiest song title of all time.

"That came from a press cutting someone sent me," says Goulder. "The chip shop in question was in Kirkby in Ashfield right at the bottom of the [railway] yard. There were what we used to call 'parking bays' for sticking steam engines while they were waiting for their crews to come and take them out. They were right at the end near a fence, then there was a road, and on the other side of the road was a chip shop. This young cleaner had climbed on an engine, literally fired up with excitement. He had this engine he could play with. So he started to muck about with it – put more coal on the fire, open up the dampers, put it in first gear, then put it in reverse. And then he left it. Unfortunately he left it in gear with the regulator, which is kind of a steam engine's accelerator, open a fraction. As the fire burnt up that was enough to create steam which moved through the glands into the cylinders which began to move the pistons. And the engine just gently rolled backwards through the fence and across the road. It didn't quite enter the chip shop, so there's a little licence there. But it came very, very close. I still get a lot of requests for that."

Travelling around Britain during the mid-to-late 1960s playing concerts on the folk circuit, Goulder got to spend a lot of time inside railway stations. They were places, so he found, that were unique. "There's just something about them," he says. "Arriving at stations, leaving from stations, watching people at stations. A railway station in a big city is a kind of oasis. I always think of Glasgow Central. Now Glasgow is not my favourite city but once I got inside Glasgow Central station then suddenly the city was outside. I could sit there on one of those nice wooden benches and look at these old Victorian buildings and frontages. It was peace. You don't get that at bus stations. It doesn't work with airports either."

At around the same time as Goulder started becoming acquainted with Glasgow Central station, approximately 45 miles to the east a young man by the name of Pete Brown was living the life of a "rather screwed up semi-alcoholic poet" in Edinburgh. He, too, was finding solace in railway stations, although the dire state of Brown's finances meant catching a train was rarely an option.

"Edinburgh had two stations at that time and sometimes, because I was stranded there in a kind of exile, I'd go down to one of them and watch the last trains going out late at night," recalls Brown. "I suppose it did something for me at the time because I was a kind of miserable sod. It was part of the general misery, trains leaving and you not being on them, thinking about somewhere better that you'd like to be."

That misery would, within a few years, pay off big time in the shape of a song written by Brown for a blues/rock supergroup drawing on his railway station experiences in Edinburgh.

Having gathered together enough pennies to return from Scotland to his native south east England, Brown settled in London and soon established quite a reputation as a performance poet, musician and songwriter. "I was around the jazz scene, doing my stuff, and I knew all the jazz musicians of the time," he says. "One of the guys in my band was living with Jack Bruce. So I met him and we had a residency at The Marquee with the jazz and poetry thing. That's how I also got to meet Ginger [Baker]. Jack and Ginger knew I was a writer and they got in touch when they formed Cream [with Eric Clapton]. And it went from there. At first, I probably did more with Ginger, but over time it became more with Jack. We had the chemistry."

Brown and Bruce continued working together long after Cream disbanded, right up until the latter's death in October 2014. It was a relationship that would generate a number of iconic songs including "I Feel Free" and "Sunshine Of Your Love", the latter with input from Clapton. While researching this book, Bruce confided that Brown "is completely obsessed with them," the "them" being trains. "I'm not a train freak, but they're always there," acknowledges Brown. In fact the pair's final collaboration, 2014's *Silver Rails*, used railway analogies to describe personal feelings both men had about the rapid encroachment of old age.

All of which leads us to "White Room", recorded in 1968 and quite possibly Cream's best known song both in the UK and America.

"'White Room' has got lots of trains and railway references in it," says Brown. "That's because I was living in Baker Street which is close to Euston, Marylebone and Kings Cross stations. Those are the stations that are alluded to. It's a watershed song, like a little movie. It's about being in and out of relationships at a critical time in my life when I had stopped taking drugs and was trying to make sense of my life. I was living in an actual white room in a very small place near the stations, so there's the opening line – '*In the white room with black curtains near the station*'. I'd been bumming round in people's places and finally started to earn a little bit of money from songwriting. I had lots of different girlfriends and there were lots of comings and goings. That's what it's about, the different relationships and how they fitted together, or rather didn't, seeing girlfriends off on trains from stations. There's an image in there about waiting '*in the queue when the trains come back*' and that came from living in Edinburgh and those night trips to the stations, waiting for people and watching other people waiting for people."

"White Room" doesn't namecheck any particular railway station or location, yet Brown's lyrics and Bruce's voice united with Cream's pulsating sound give it an undeniably British stamp. There's no mention of smokestacks, boxcars or hobos. This is a "*black roof country*" where people buy platform tickets and wait in queues. How much more British can you get? Even the old steam locomotives have gone, replaced by "*restless diesels*" bound for far off places (1968, the year "White Room" saw the light of day, also marked the official end of steam in the UK).

"Very often he [Bruce] would do the music first and then I'd do the lyrics, but in the case of 'White Room' the lyrics came first," adds Brown. "It's about my life at that time, but on reflection I think it could only be set some place here [in Britain] like London or Edinburgh. Maybe I'm saying that because those are two places I lived which influenced how the song came out; London especially because that's where I was when I wrote it. But the Americans liked it, so it crossed some boundaries there. It's a good song, and it still sounds good today. I'm proud to be associated with it."

"White Room" and its touching on casual relationships acknowledged what many male musicians and songwriters had grown to realise about trains – that there was a sexual element to them. Trains occupied a transient world where brief encounters could, and indeed often did, happen. In theory you could meet anyone on a train, or at a railway station, and if you liked the look of them and *vice versa* then anything was possible.

"I always found there was a slight eroticism about trains," says Graham Gouldman. "You could sit in an apartment on your own across from somebody and imagine all sorts going on. And sometimes it did, not that it ever involved me. Those compartments that I used to go in to write songs and play my guitar, well they also had blinds on the windows shielding the compartments from the corridor that ran down the side of the carriage. If you saw that the blinds were down, then you knew what might be going on inside and you knew not to enter."

"I remember hearing this thing about how the rhythm of a train was meant to get women aroused," adds Francis Rossi. "Whether that was just blokes and their wishful thinking, I don't know. But there was definitely something when you were in your early teens and you'd get on a train and think 'Ummmmm'. The vibe! Something was going on, but you didn't know what it was because you were too young to understand. Within a couple of years you get to realise that there's something about being on a train that can make you horny. Not romantic, but horny."

When it came to weaving railways and sex together in songs, the Americans still had one or two things they could teach their British cousins. In "Still A Fool", sometimes known as "Two Trains Running", Muddy Waters sings of a man juggling relationships with two women, one of them married to someone else. He knows he is a fool for doing it, but he just can't help himself. The two trains, needless to say, are the two women.

However, other songs like "The Train Kept A-Rollin'" were more sexually explicit.

▦▦▦▦▦▦▦▦

Metallica, Hanoi Rocks, The Yardbirds, Stray Cats, Screaming Lord Sutch, Twisted Sister, Imelda May, Shakin' Stevens, Skid Row, King Kurt, Aerosmith, The Tragically Hip, Bon Jovi, Motörhead. What have they got in common? All have at some point recorded "The Train Kept A-Rollin'". Johnny Burnette's 1956 rockabilly version is listed in the Rock & Roll Hall of Fame as one of the "500 Songs That Shaped Rock & Roll" but even that accolade doesn't really do it justice. From jazz to heavy metal, swing to rhythm & blues, boogie-woogie to rock, "The Train Kept A-Rollin'" has been moulded to suit just about every musical style going, although it tends to be regarded now as more of a classic guitar riff track thanks largely to The Yardbirds' 1965 interpretation featuring Jeff Beck's fuzzy power playing. Musicians return to the song because it's fun to play live and just downright sexy. The train, a sexual analogy, keeps rolling all night long with an awful lot of heaving, ho-ing and oh-oh-ing involving a *real gone dame* from New York City. It's about sexual prowess and many a lead singer and guitarist has taken the opportunity to emphasise theirs while performing the song, groin-led posturing and blue movie facial contortions to the fore.

"There is that *double entendre*, the spark plugs igniting as the pistons are pumping," says Brian Setzer who, despite covering "The Train Kept A-Rollin'" with his own band Stray Cats, still ranks Johnny Burnette's interpretation as the benchmark. "Oh God, I think that's the best one. Again, like 'Mystery Train', it's a gold standard song, the one that people tried to copy and get close to. But nobody can. There's been some good attempts, but that's right there at the top."

How ironic then that arguably the most influential, far-reaching recital of "The Train Kept A-Rollin'" occurred behind closed doors in a London backstreet with nobody other than the four musicians making the music present. In the late summer of 1968, Jimmy Page found himself at a loose end following the demise of The Yardbirds, the band he had joined two years previously playing dual lead guitar alongside Beck. Page wanted to form a new outfit from the ashes of his old group, one that melded blues influences with rock. Various personnel were considered – vocalists Steve Marriott and Steve Winwood, bassist John Entwistle, drummer Keith Moon and pianist Nicky Hopkins among them – but in the end a combination of circumstances and fate threw Page together with Robert Plant, frontman in a band called Hobbstweedle, drummer John Bonham of Birmingham group Band Of Joy, and session bass player John Paul Jones. Moon had been tempted but remained with The Who. He did, however, contribute a name for this collective which stuck in Page's mind – Led Zeppelin.

At the start of September Page, Plant, Bonham and Jones came together in a room below a record shop in Gerrard Street, London W1, to rehearse for a forthcoming tour of Scandinavia that The Yardbirds had been contracted to play (and which the four of them duly completed, billed as the "New Yardbirds"). Unsure what song to begin with but conscious that it had to be something they all knew, the quartet kicked around a few suggestions before settling on "The Train Kept A-Rollin'". We only have their words for it, but the chemistry was by all accounts instant. Speaking to Q magazine in 1990, Jones recalled the occasion as "quite a stunning experience, wonderful, very exhilarating." So blown away was Page that to this day he still can't remember what song they played next. When Led Zeppelin started officially touring as Led Zeppelin rather than the New Yardbirds during late 1968, "The Train Kept A-Rollin'" almost always opened each show (it returned to their set list for what proved to be the group's final tour in 1980 prior to Bonham's death that September). A sexy song for what many would agree were a sexual band.

Given their carnal connotations you can perhaps understand why so many virile male musicians enjoyed taking train rides during the mid-to-late 1960s, a period of radical change in attitudes towards sex. The vast distances between gigs in the USA gave aeroplanes or the all mod cons tour bus a clear advantage over the railroads when it came to touring. However, in Britain and mainland Europe it was a different story. Tight budgets meant buses or the ubiquitous transit van were the default choice when travelling from A to B, but given the opportunity the majority of bands or solo acts preferred to let the train take the strain.

"We went up to Leeds once on the train to do a show at Leeds University, and the whole thing was just 'Ahhhhhhh' compared to doing it by road," recalls Francis Rossi of Status Quo's early touring days. "You didn't have to worry about the driver falling asleep, or the smelly feet of the guy next to you in the back of the van, or getting a puncture and standing round wondering what you're gonna do and whether you're gonna make the show in time. You could just sit back, snooze, work on a new song, chat up a girl in the old restaurant car. Three or four hours from one end of the country to the other. Give me a bit of boom-chicka-boom-chicka-boom any day."

"We used to take the trains quite a bit," says Jeremy Spencer of Fleetwood Mac's nascent days on the road. "I for one always preferred it because you could do so much more like people watch, you know, looking around the carriage at everyone, thinking about their lives. Who they are? What are they up to? It would be 'Are we going by train? Ah, great!' It might take a bit longer than a plane but at least when you got there you weren't a nervous wreck."

Fleetwood Mac. The mere name, according to guitarist and group founder Peter Green, sounded like the sort of title that a "big American train" might carry. Trains lend themselves easily to the blues which is what Fleetwood Mac pre-Stevie Nicks and Lindsey Buckingham were all about. Listen to Spencer performing slide guitar while singing "Mean Old Fireman", a mournful song about *a mean old fireman and a cruel old engineer*" which is so far removed from "Don't Stop" or "Go Your Own Way" that it might as well be a different band.

Like just about every other British group of that era, the mark one version of Fleetwood Mac dreamed of touring America, in particular the west coast. California was where *it* was supposed to be at – San Francisco with its chilled vibe, the canyons and night life of Los Angeles, sun, sand, surf, the backdrop to Brian Wilson's world and the Beach Boys' masterpiece

Pet Sounds (an album that climaxed with the sound of a speeding train repeatedly blowing its horn as it approaches a road crossing, Wilson's dogs Banana and Louie providing some backing barking). Fleetwood Mac were there for the best of California circa 1968, and the very worst of it 12 months later. The whole contrasting experience would give them "Station Man", regarded by many as one of the most underrated songs to emerge from the band's earlier incarnation.

"We were sitting around and Danny [Kirwan] was a bit lost for words for this song that we had the music to," says Spencer. "So Christine [McVie], myself and him started thinking 'What about doing it about a train?' because there's something in the ba-du-du, ba-da ba-da ba-da ba-da movement at the beginning that reminded me of the shunting that happens when a train is just getting going, that clanking sound you get before it really takes off. We needed words and I said 'What about Station Man?' I was thinking back to the end of the hippy era which was something I'd become a bit disillusioned about.

"We'd been to San Francisco for the first time in 1968, right in the middle of it all with the Grateful Dead and all those guys, all these surf bands turned on with acid in their music, that kind of thing. Everyone was sunny and bright and 'Wow, love and peace, V-signs'. Then we went back in 1969 and it was just druggies on the street. The whole atmosphere had turned. There was a feeling of 'What was all this about anyway?' From my point of view that's what I was saying in the song – 'What's going on here?' The midnight train is leaving, you don't know what the future holds, you're looking for guidance. I guess you know a little about my history, but I kind of point a bit to God. You know, 'God, what's going on here? The whole love thing doesn't seem to be happening'. That's basically what it's about."

For those who don't know about Jeremy Spencer's history, here's the tip of the iceberg. On tour in America with Fleetwood Mac during February 1971, he quit the band just hours before a show at the Whiskey a Go Go venue in West Hollywood and subsequently joined a religious group called the Children Of God. The process leading up to that and what happened next is, safe to say, an entirely different book in itself.

Released in 1970 on Fleetwood Mac's fourth album, *Kiln House*, their last to feature Spencer's talents, "Station Man" continues to attract admiring glances from other artists, some of who weren't even born when the original was recorded. "I was out in the States in 2013 working with a young band, all of them about half my age apart from Evie Sands who was the lead singer," says Spencer. "And they were saying 'We want to work on your "Station Man" song'. They'd just clicked with it – at their age! We recorded a version and there were some things that I actually preferred about it. We took a bit of the clankiness out and made it more smooth which, as one of the girls said, made it kind of sexy. They were singing the 'Ah-has' which Danny had done. So sexy, yes, but the movement was still there, still quite sinewy."

❦

Just as Evie Sands and her young gunslingers felt the urge to put a different spin on a track recorded some 43 years previously, so The Rolling Stones finished the 1960s with a jaw-dropping cover version of a train song written by an idol of theirs before the Second World War. In fact, none of the Stones even knew what Robert Johnson looked like when they came to record "Love In Vain" for the 1969 album *Let It Bleed*, the three surviving authenticated photographs of the great Mississippi Delta bluesman only surfacing during the late 1980s. That was Johnson through and through, a blank canvas onto which all kind of myths and legends could be painted. And indeed were.

In his 27 years, Johnson recorded just 29 songs laid down over the course of five days (a three day session in San Antonio during November 1936 and a further two in Dallas seven months later). That much we know. Otherwise, well, why let the truth get in the way of a good story? It is said that as a teenager Johnson's guitar skills were nothing to write home about. Then he disappeared for a few months. On his return he had mastered the guitar like no other man alive. Finding himself one night at the crossroads where Highway 49 bisects Highway 61 in Clarksdale, Mississippi, Johnson sold his soul to the appearing Devil in exchange for the ability to play guitar in the finger-picking style that would, long after his death, make him famous. In 1938, Satan returned to Johnson, a notorious womaniser, and called in his debt. That's what happens if you dare make advances on a lady who isn't yours while playing a gig at a small juke joint venue – her man will serve up a bottle of whiskey laced with poison, and you will die.

Amid all the rumour and speculation, there was no denying his remarkable musical ability. Keith Richards, on first hearing a Johnson recording, was convinced it was two men playing guitar rather than one, asking "Who's the other cat?" His technique sounds simple, but is in fact remarkably sophisticated. Then there was the voice, a lonesome high-pitch cry unlike that of the stereotypical barrel-chested bluesman, conveying lyrics concerned with abandonment, rootlessness, the occult, alcohol abuse, sexual innuendo and, of course, the Devil himself.

It could be terrifying, piercing, edgy, sad or all of the above. And it never sounded sadder than on "Love In Vain", a song about a man in turmoil. The narrator carries his loved one's suitcase to the station, watches as the train pulls in, looks her in the eye amid the growing realisation that she really is serious about leaving, starts to cry, and is left alone as the train pulls out with its twin tail lights shining from the rear of the last carriage – a blue one for the narrator's mood, a red one for his fractured state of mind. Delivered in Johnson's inimitable style, the song was devastatingly effective and a must-hear track during the 1960s for the growing legions of British youths immersing themselves in the music of the Mississippi Delta.

"When I was a teenager I often hung out with guys who were a few years older than me, guys who were going to art college when I was still at school," says Graham Parker who moved with his family from London to Surrey, solid rhythm & blues territory during the sixties, at the age of four. "They were hip to a lot of old blues stuff and Robert Johnson was one of the artists they revered. Obviously his mysterious life and death got your attention as much as his music. I was struck then as I am now by the sparseness of 'Love In Vain' and how Johnson got huge dynamics out of his guitar which sounded like two guitarists playing but with very understated economy. The song itself puts you right there at the train station as his woman is leaving him. She's there one moment, then on a moving train the next. She ain't coming back by the sound of it and the narrator is left standing there like the loneliest man on Earth."

The Rolling Stones might not have known what Johnson looked like when the time came to record "Love In Vain" at Olympic Studios in London, but that didn't prevent them from capturing the essence of the late bluesman. The pain and desolation of Johnson's original song is still present both on *Let It Bleed* and the band's subsequent live album *Get Yer Ya-Ya's Out* which featured "Love In Vain" taken from a November 1969 concert in Baltimore (with Mick Taylor, another Johnson admirer, playing slide guitar on the latter).

"That's The Rolling Stones at their absolute best, around that time and playing those kind of songs, very bluesy and very emotional," says Tom Johnston of The Doobie Brothers. "You listen to 'Love In Vain' with that train taking off from the station and it's just sad, sad, sad. In fact it just breaks your heart. It's pulling out and there's nothing the guy can do about it. That's got to be right up there among the finest train songs of all time. It's certainly one of my own personal favourites."

The 1960s was the decade when every band or solo artist of British origin seemed to have a train song in their repertoire. Or two. Or three. To be honest, it reached cliché proportions. In the 1984 rock "mockumentary" *This Is Spinal Tap* friends since childhood David St. Hubbins and Nigel Tufnel (played by actors Michael McKean and Christopher Guest respectively) are filmed discussing the first song they ever wrote together. "All The Way Home" is probably the corniest train song you're ever likely to hear courtesy of the world's finest parody rock band. There's a boy, he's sitting by a railroad track, waiting for a girl to come back, if she's not on the 5.19 then he will cry all the way home. As with almost everything in *This Is Spinal Tap* the song is so purposefully trite that it borders on genius. Amplifiers go up to 11, drummers perish in odd circumstances, stage props malfunction in the middle of gigs, a train song must appear somewhere in a group's back catalogue.

The saving grace when it came to the majority of train songs performed by bands such as Cream, The Kinks, Led Zeppelin and Fleetwood Mac was that they were great tunes containing interesting, occasionally suggestive lyrics. The subject matter might have dipped into cliché territory but when done right nobody could deny its effectiveness. That in itself meant the music industry's love affair with the train song would show little sign of abating as the 1960s made way for a new decade.

6

PEOPLE GET READY

One evening in 1970 Jim Weatherly, then a 27-year-old songwriter struggling to make an impression in Los Angeles, picked up the phone and gave his actor friend Lee Majors a call. Majors, who would later star on television as *The Six Million Dollar Man*, wasn't in but his girlfriend, the model Farrah Fawcett, picked up and the two of them talked for what was probably only a couple of minutes.

"During the course of the conversation she said she was packing her clothes to go and visit her family in Texas," recalls Weatherly, a former quarterback at the University of Mississippi who chose songwriting as a career over playing football. "She said she was taking the midnight plane to Houston. After I got off the phone with her I sat down and wrote 'Midnight Plane To Houston' in about 30 to 45 minutes."

The story of how "Midnight Plane To Houston" became "Midnight Train To Georgia", as in the recording made famous by Gladys Knight And The Pips, is a convoluted one with a cast and plot worthy of a Broadway show. The song Weatherly wrote on his guitar that evening concerned a man who couldn't bear the prospect of being separated from a woman and revolved around the killer line "*I'd rather live in her world than live without her in mine*". Once finished, he filed the demo away before digging it out the following year on the insistence of recently hired manager/publisher Larry Gordon for inclusion on an album showcasing a batch of his songs, hoping they might attract the attention of some established artists. One track, "Neither One Of Us", was ironically picked up by Gladys Knight. "Midnight Plane To Houston" found a fan in the form of Atlanta-based producer Sonny Limbo who wanted it for another soul/gospel singer, Cissy Houston.

But there was a problem.

Cissy Houston loved "Midnight Plane To Houston" the moment she heard it, but felt the song needed a change of title. Her family were originally from Georgia and they didn't take planes anywhere. They caught trains. She wanted to record it as "Midnight Train To Georgia" which wasn't an issue for Weatherly. "I didn't mind the title change. I've always felt that if an artist wanted to cut one of my songs, changing certain parts of it was OK with me to make it fit the way they felt it." The plane became a train, Houston became Georgia, and Cissy Houston duly recorded the song in a country/gospel style.

Fast forward to 1973. Handed an exclusive contract by Buddah Records, producer Tony Camillo was waiting to see which artists the label had in store for him. Within days of signing on the dotted line, Camillo received a phone call from Buddah's boss, Neil Bogart. Would he like to produce "Midnight Train To Georgia" for Gladys Knight And The Pips who had just joined the label from Motown? Camillo said yes and immediately wrote two arrangements of the song having listened to Cissy Houston's recording which, it emerged, Larry Gordon had also sent to Gladys Knight. Deep down, Camillo wasn't completely satisfied with either arrangement, so he welcomed Knight's creative input. She wanted something sparky featuring horns and keyboards, the kind of record Al Green might make. Knight also asked to change a few words, for which Weatherly gave her his blessing.

Camillo then set about recording a new arrangement at his own studio in Hillsborough, New Jersey. In came Randy Brecker and Alan Rubin on trumpets, Michael Brecker and Lewis Del Gatto on saxophones, plus Meco Monardo and Dave Taylor on trombones. Jeff Mironov played guitar, Bob Babbit bass guitar and Andrew Smith drums. Having mixed their contributions together, Camillo took the tape to Detroit to capture the vocals. The Pips recorded their parts first (throwing in some train-like "Whoo whoo!" sound effects) followed by Knight. Take one went smoothly, but there was still something missing. It was Knight's brother and leader of the Pips, Merald "Bubba" Knight, who suggested the inclusion of ad-libs to keep the song moving along in places. Always more of a straight singer than an ad-libber, Knight was initially hesitant until her brother suggested that he feed her some lines through a headset: which is exactly what happened on take two. The song's crowning ad-lib lines such as "*My world, his world, our world*" and "*Gonna board, gotta board, the midnight train*" came courtesy of Merald, sung by Gladys. Some additional acoustic piano and Hammond organ was added later by Barry Miles and Camillo respectively, at which point the latest incarnation of Weatherly's *magnum opus* was ready to face the world.

"Midnight Train To Georgia" is a love song told through a narrator, by now a woman. Her boyfriend had dreams of becoming a superstar in Los Angeles but, alas, *"didn't get far"*. Crestfallen, he sells his car and buys a one-way ticket back to the security of his native Georgia, catching the midnight train. Despite being happy in LA, his girlfriend chooses to go with him (*"I'd rather live in his world than live without him in mine"*).

Released in 1973 in the USA and 1976 in the UK, "Midnight Train To Georgia" was a smash hit on both sides of the Atlantic and became Knight's signature song. At the time she recorded it her personal life was in turmoil. Immersed in recording and touring, Knight's marriage to saxophonist James Newman had reached breaking point. The more traditional relationship that he yearned for simply didn't correspond with her intense work schedule. The pair divorced shortly after "Midnight Train To Georgia" was released stateside. If Knight's vocals sound personal, then there's a clue why.

Written in less time than it takes to watch a football match, Jim Weatherly admits to being "amazed" at the way in which "Midnight Plane To Houston" evolved over a three year period, seemingly taking on a whole life of its own (albeit under a different title) on route to becoming a Grammy award winning US number one single. "When you write a song you never know the path it will take," he says. "Some songs never find that path. Some find a path that goes on forever. 'Midnight Train To Georgia' is one of those songs."

The early 1970s in America saw a number of songs featuring trains and railroads following the same exalted path taken by "Midnight Train To Georgia". From Sylvia leaving town on the nine o'clock train ("Sylvia's Mother", written by Shel Silverstein and recorded by Dr. Hook and the Medicine Show) to the Father, Son and the Holy Ghost catching the last train for the coast (Don McLean's "American Pie"), everyone seemed to be heading some place by rail. Raised on anthems conceived by the likes of Sam Phillips, Tommy Boyce, Johnny Cash and Howlin' Wolf, so the new breed of musicians and songwriters – Weatherly, Silverstein, Steve Goodman and The Doobie Brothers founder member Tom Johnston to name a few – began plumbing the older generation's influences for themselves. Just like their predecessors many of them had been raised within sight or sound of a railroad, often in small towns or cities built around stations or bustling freight yards. The hubbub of trains had been there 24 hours a day, seven days a week filtering into their homes, playgrounds, school classrooms and college lecture halls. Now it was time to take the source of that sound, and the emotions trains were capable of evoking, and use it to their advantage in songs.

Originally perceived as something of a tough biker band, by 1972 The Doobie Brothers had embraced a more melodic sound with songs such as "Listen To The Music" and "Jesus Is Just Alright" giving the group the breakthrough success it hankered after. Towards the end of the year the Doobies were ensconced at Warner Brothers Studios in North Hollywood cutting tracks for what would become their third album, *The Captain And Me*. Johnston, the band's founder and creative force, had for some time been playing an instrumental piece of music based on a train-like guitar riff. In order for it to make the album, this tune required lyrics. So far, try as he might, none had been forthcoming.

"The song was originally a jam," says Johnston of what would eventually become "Long Train Runnin'". "I'd been playing it all the time and it had this train quality, that chugga-chugga sound as it comes down the track. I'll be honest with you, the lyrics were the very last thing that happened on the song. One day I went to my favourite writing spot which was the bathroom [at the recording studio]. There was just something about that place. We even used to record vocals in there sometimes. It was somewhere you could get away. Nobody was walking around or talking or telling you what you've got to do. And it all just came together. I wrote it literally in about half an hour. I came up with this idea – '*Though I saw Miss Lucy, down along the track, she lost her home and her family, and she won't be coming back*'. It all seemed to go together, those words and the chugga-chugga rhythm of the guitar."

Visalia, Johnston's home city situated approximately mid-point between San Francisco and Los Angeles, certainly had form when it came to the railroads. Between 1889 and 1892, a group of bandits known as the Sontag-Evans Gang achieved widespread notoriety robbing trains travelling along the Southern Pacific Railroad. On 5 August 1892, the gang, led by brothers John and George Sontag together with farmer turned outlaw Chris Evans, were rumbled by police in Visalia. George Sontag was taken into custody and served 15 years inside Folsom State Prison, but John Sontag and Evans managed to escape, sparking what is still believed to be the largest manhunt in Californian history involving hundreds of lawmen, bounty hunters and armed civilians. Ten months later the pair were finally apprehended near Visalia following a shootout that became known as the Battle of Stone

Corral. John Sontag died later of his wounds whereas Evans survived, joining George Sontag inside Folsom's walls.

Much like Butch Cassidy and the Sundance Kid in Utah and Wyoming, the Sontag-Evans Gang elicited considerable public support in the area around Visalia, warped logic fostering a notion that the capitalist moneymen behind the railroads were in turn robbing the people. Besides the occasional earthquake, they remain the biggest thing ever to have hit the city. Johnston certainly tapped into the renegade psyche with "Long Train Runnin'". Miss Lucy might not necessarily have been running from the law, but she was itching to get away from something.

"Trains can mean all sorts of things in music – lonesome, exciting, happiness – but in the case of 'Long Train...' they symbolise escaping," says Johnston. "That's what she is doing. She's trying to get away from her situation. It doesn't get too specific about what has happened to her but she's lost her home, her family and she doesn't want to come back, so whatever's happened doesn't sound good. It's a powerful image. And yet despite the lyrics 'Long Train...' is generally associated with good times. That has always amused me. You've got this song about running away from a bad situation that people want to get up and dance to! I always loved 'Love In Vain' by The Rolling Stones which has that sad, mournful train taking off from the station. 'Long Train...' is a little like that when it comes to the lyrics but a 1,000 miles away in terms of sound. It doesn't sound sad. It sounds... exciting! It's become a party record but, hey, that's alright by me."

That party vibe and catchy guitar riff means "Long Train Runnin'" has rarely been short of an audience since the release of *The Captain And Me* album. It's been covered to the hilt by American university marching bands, dance acts, flamenco guitarists, amateur pub rock outfits and even the British girl group Bananarama. No air guitar contest is complete without someone launching into that distinctive chugga-chugga riff, or rather pretending to. As for the wailing harmonica solo that graces the original? Well that was the work of the late Phillip Jackson, for many years a member of the Steve Miller Band, who performed under the name Norton Buffalo. When it came to recording his part, Jackson had a particular sound that he wanted to evoke, that of a shrill steam locomotive whistle. Johnston pays tribute to his contribution with just one word – "Goosebumps."

While The Doobie Brothers powered from strength to strength during the early 1970s, young folk singer and songwriter Steve Goodman could only dream of emulating their success. Born into a middle class Chicago family in 1948, Goodman discovered shortly after turning 20 years old that he had leukaemia. Time on earth, he realised, would be short. Because of that Goodman decided to turn his back on further education and follow his dreams of making it in the music business.

As the sixties made way for the seventies, so Goodman's stockpile of songs grew ever larger. He played gigs to small but appreciative audiences in venues around Chicago, including a bar called the Quiet Knight. It was there one evening during the second half of 1971 that Goodman was finally discovered appearing as Kris Kristofferson's support act. Kristofferson introduced Goodman to Paul Anka which led to some demos being recorded and a deal being struck with Buddah Records. As far as Kristofferson was concerned one song in particular – "City Of New Orleans" – stood out and he sent a copy for his friend Johnny Cash to consider. Cash liked it but had trouble figuring out the chords, so he passed.

Big mistake.

Back at the Quiet Knight, one evening Goodman went to see Arlo Guthrie, son of Woody, who by then was making waves of his own as a singer and songwriter. Goodman asked if he could play a song for him. Guthrie agreed, on one condition – he had to buy him a beer first. Goodman went to the bar, purchased a beer, handed it to Guthrie and launched straight into 'City Of New Orleans'. Unlike Cash, Guthrie had no hang-ups about recording the song and it was his version that entered the public domain in 1972. The resulting royalties enabled Goodman to make a full-time career out of music.

The inspiration behind Goodman's best-known song was the news that broke in 1970 surrounding the daily "City Of New Orleans" train service that ran between Chicago and New Orleans. Ticket sales had plummeted to the point where the Illinois Central Railroad was considering axing it from the timetable altogether. America's love affair with train travel seemed to be on the wane and Goodman resolved to write a song about it. The result was a spellbinding piece of work that somehow manages to be uplifting and melancholic at the same time. It's all there – the passengers, the sacks of mail, the three conductors, the club car, the scenery rolling by the window, a majestic train capable of clocking up hundreds of miles in a day – and yet the scrapyard beckons. The chorus takes the form of a heartfelt plea from the train itself as it struggles to understand why

America, the land it helped to build, is allowing the railroads to die. As train songs go, "City Of New Orleans" takes some beating.

"An awful lot of train songs that I hear, I just find the lyrical content facile from a railway point of view," says Joseph Porter, founder member of the British indie rock band Blyth Power (a name itself taken from a railway locomotive). "But 'City Of New Orleans' isn't like that. It's a great tune, so upbeat, and it's more about the train and less about the people on it. It's not about the hobo riding somewhere or the prisoner on his way home. It's the train saying 'I'm a train! Look at me!' For me, it's got everything."

"It's not just one of the best train songs of all time, it's one of the best songs of all time," adds Soul Asylum frontman Dave Pirner. "It shows that side of America that has jack-shit to do with the busy freeways. It's got a life of its own, like a movie. You can picture it all as you listen to it, just like you're riding on the train watching the world go by. Man, what a song. What would you give to be able to write something like that?"

"City Of New Orleans" was never what you would call a big hit, Arlo Guthrie's recording reaching number 18 on the American *Billboard* Hot 100 chart (despite being released as a single in the UK it failed to make the charts at all). And yet its gravitas has increased over time. Goodman died in September 1984, aged 36. Five months later "City Of New Orleans" earned him a posthumous Grammy Award for Best Country Song in the wake of Willie Nelson's 1984 cover version. In time, Johnny Cash would see the error of his ways and figure out the chords for himself, performing the song at his own shows and as a member of country music super group The Highwaymen alongside Willie Nelson, Waylon Jennings and Kris Kristofferson. An American standard – that's what "City Of New Orleans" has become. Even *Good Morning America*, the country's long running TV news and talk show, took its name from the first three words of the song's chorus.

As for the "City Of New Orleans" train? Well, at the time of writing, it still runs between Chicago and New Orleans every day, taking approximately 19 hours to make the 934 mile journey. Whether the rise in passenger numbers that kept the train alive can be directly linked to the song's popularity is anyone's guess, but it can't have done its prospects any harm. If that is to be Steve Goodman's legacy, then it's a marvellously fitting one.

The idea of a train having a personality, as in "City Of New Orleans", was one that chimed with Ralph McTell. Goodman and McTell emerged on the US and UK folk scenes respectively at around the same time, kindred spirits separated by 3,000 miles of water, writing and performing songs formed around stories. McTell's paternal grandfather, Charlie May, had driven trains between London and the south coast of England during the 1940s and 1950s. On one occasion he had even taken his young grandson with him on the footplate of a steam locomotive bound for Brighton, an experience which left a huge impression on McTell.

"When I was a little boy, steam engines were these living, breathing beasts that actually had a heartbeat which went du-du-du-du, du-du-du-du," says McTell. "I just thought trains made that noise. It was only much later I realised that was the noise they made as they went over the joins in the track! I'd thought it was the train's heart that made that sound. I remember a mate of mine once calling them 'great singing kettles on wheels', which would be about right. There was something about the guys that drove them as well. There they were covered in crap and oil and dirt with this great big animal to look after, and loving every minute of it. As a songwriter you can take that and then add to it – the fact you are leaving somewhere, you are going somewhere, you are escaping from somewhere, you are beginning something. It's all that."

Inspired by the great singing kettles of his childhood and the fascinating world they inhabited, so the train songs began pouring out of McTell. There was "Last Train And Ride": "That's about relationships, a euphemism for I'm going to take the last possible train but I *am* going, as in getting out of this relationship. It wasn't autobiographical, no, but you always wonder if there's something in the back of your mind. I suppose I was borrowing from the blues tradition where the train was a means of escape."

...and "When I Was A Cowboy". "One of my biggest heroes was the singer songwriter Woody Guthrie who allegedly jumped freight trains and wrote lots of songs about it. I make a bit of a joke out of it in that song. There's a line which goes '*I travelled far from home, I even jumped freight trains, threw stones in the ocean, slept out in the cold rain*'. Well I didn't ever jump freight trains. If I'd jumped a freight train from my house (in Croydon) I'd have ended up a few miles away in Wimbledon where the train terminated, turned around, and came back again. I wouldn't have got very far. But the image, the representation of a free ride to somewhere new, is something that I love."

...and "Walk Into The Morning". "There's a line that goes '*I didn't need to hear a freight train to know Sonny Terry's harp was an aching cry for freedom whistling in my dark*'. Sonny Terry was one of the great harmonica players and a lot of the plaintive notes played on blues harmonicas are derived from the sound of the train. That eerie sound that starts on the left and moves to the right or vice versa as it travels through the night. It's a sound that also represents an escape from poverty, in particular freight trains which were a mode of free transport."

...and "Terminus". "That's a song where the story is being played out at a railway station. It's about saying goodbye to someone and the word 'terminus' meaning the end of something. It's the idea of these little dramas being acted out all day long every day by different people. There's all the paraphernalia as the train starts up, leaves the station and immediately you're left on your own. Then a bloke interrupts me and asks if I've got a light for a cigarette before noticing that I've been affected by something that has happened."

A train, as Robyn Hitchcock touched on in Chapter 4, is a train. Likewise a railway station is a railway station. The location is irrelevant; the stories and little dramas being played out around that train or station are nearly always the same. In other words, the ingredients for a good train song apply as much to the unfashionable English market town of Rugby as they do to jazzy New Orleans.

"In my early years as a musician I travelled everywhere by car, but after I had a near miss on the M1 [motorway] through tiredness and exhaustion I started taking the train everywhere to all my gigs, returning home the same night," says McTell, recalling how his song "Slow Burning Companion" came about. "For some reason the station at Rugby, which is a junction, was somewhere that I frequently found myself stuck at, ruminating on the meaning of life and so on. Now, a junction station is a very lonely place because it's not a terminus. It's not somewhere where people begin or end journeys. It's people crossing over, taking trains to other places. I used to smoke in those days and sitting there with a cigarette – my slow burning companion – started me thinking about people who were living in silence and alienated. There's nowhere lonelier than a railway station at midnight. The characters that you meet are very transitory, coming and going, on the edges of society. You can almost sense the ghosts all around. Then your train arrives and you get into your compartment and it's all warm and you rattle off to wherever you're going, which was usually London for me. But the experience that you've left behind while waiting there on that station stays with you."

Steve Goodman and Ralph McTell cemented their reputations as formidable singers and songwriters at a time of immense change in the music industry. Seven years spanning 1969 to 1976 – that's all it took to witness the emergence of glam rock, punk rock, prog rock, disco, funk, Krautrock and other early forms of electronic music, country rock, soft rock, reggae, blue-eyed white soul and heavy rock. All these genres would have their standout train song moments, some more so than others.

Heavy rock certainly didn't hold back when it came to trains. "Maybe it's the sound, the roar of a band playing at full pelt, which when you think about it sounds a lot like the noise you get when a train's going full speed down the track, rattling over the joins, all the trucks and coaches clattering together and the engine working hard," says Francis Rossi who as a member of Status Quo benefitted from the songwriting talents of Bob Young, often referred to during the 1970s as the group's unofficial fifth member. "Trains were about the blues, bringing countries together, building for the future, and Bob was very into that particularly when we were younger. We'd romanticise about being a couple of winos bumming rides on the old trains like obscure black blues musicians. Out of that came tracks like 'Railroad' [off the 1971 album *Dog Of Two Head*] and 'Slow Train' [from 1974's *Quo*]. '*Can't afford a ticket on a cattle trucking slow train*'. It was the cheapest ticket, a cattle train, cheaper even than the milk train. That was us playing the blues. Well, a rockier form of the blues."

Also playing a rockier form of the blues was a band hailing from the small towns dotted around Flint, Michigan, through which ran the Grand Trunk Western Railroad connecting Chicago with eastern Canada and parts of north east USA. In 1969 the three founder members of this band, heavily influenced by Cream's power-playing, had been looking for a name to call themselves, having decided to quit other groups and pool their talents. They didn't have to search far.

"I grew up in a little town just outside Flint called Swartz Creek," says drummer and singer Don Brewer, who had previously been in an outfit called Terry Knight And The Pack. "When I was a kid you would pull up to the railroad crossing as the barriers were coming down and you'd wait there for the train. Then it would come, and you would watch all these train cars going by with the words 'Grand Trunk Western Railroad, Grand Trunk Western Railroad, Grand Trunk Western Railroad' on them. It was the line that came down through Detroit into Michigan and it was a big part of our lives because it was always there right in your face. And that was it. Right about the same time a new term came along for music

– funk. And we all said, 'Yeah, Grand Funk Railroad instead of Grand Trunk Railroad'. It was very descriptive of where we came from and back then it was also a little risqué. People would say 'What's the name of your band?' and you'd say 'Grand Funk Railroad'. And of course they all thought we were saying 'Fuck'. It doesn't sound much now but back then it was like 'What did you say?' So it got a lot of attention. It sounded very big, and it sounded very romantic."

Just as Status Quo cracked Britain and Europe without ever really setting the USA alight, so Grand Funk Railroad became huge in America while failing to make an impression across the Atlantic. Loved by audiences and derided by the critics, in their own backyard they sold out stadiums and released singles and albums which shifted in eye-spinningly large quantities. Along the way there were several train songs (how could there not be with a name like that?) including "The Railroad" about the back-breaking life of a railroad yard worker featuring a drum impression of a steam locomotive played by Brewer which could easily pass as the real thing. And then there was the track that started off as a joke in the recording studio but went on to become a number one hit.

"We'd just had our biggest ever hit record with 'We're An American Band' and were in the studio doing the follow up album," says Brewer. "We'd recorded most of it including the song 'Shinin' On' which was to be the name of the album, but were really looking for a follow up hit to 'We're An American Band'. We needed something big. Mark Farner [GFR's guitarist] had gone home for dinner that day and the rest of us including [producer] Todd Rundgren were just screwin' around doing things when Mark walked back in nonchalantly singing '*Everybody's doing a brand new dance now*'. And we just fell over laughing. How stupid would that be for Grand Funk Railroad to do 'The Loco-Motion'? And we just went 'Yeah, let's do it'."

"The Loco-Motion" was a 1962 song that had topped the American charts for teenager Eva Boyd, performing under the stage name of Little Eva. Boyd worked as a babysitter for the prolific songwriting partners Gerry Goffin and Carole King, looking after the couple's daughter Louise while they were busy in the studio. Goffin and King knew Boyd could sing and were determined to deliver something that would suit her ebullient, poppy style. That something ended up being "The Loco-Motion" which, in turn, spawned a dance invented by Boyd herself. Swing your hips, jump up, jump back, move your arms in a chugga-chugga motion like a steam locomotive's pistons, form a chain just like an actual train. There, easier to learn than your ABC.

People Get Ready

A pop song, good for kid's parties, worthy of a Kylie Minogue cover version in her girl-next-door pre-sex kitten days. That's "The Loco-Motion". It certainly wasn't the kind of thing you would have expected coming from one of the loudest rock groups on the planet circa 1974. "It was a huge hit, and it still is wherever we play it," adds Brewer. "Every time it kicks in people are up on their feet doing line dances around the place and stuff. So, yeah, it started out as a joke, but it ended up being a pretty good one!"

When it came to dancing, there was hardly a club in the western world that didn't spin "Love Train" by The O'Jays during the golden age of disco. Despite being recorded as early as 1972, the song's driving rhythm slotted in seamlessly alongside any floor filler from Donna Summer or the Bee Gees. Written by songwriting partners Kenny Gamble and Leon Huff, "Love Train" echoed the 1920s and "This Train Is Bound For Glory", promoting the theme of unity at a time when disunity seemed to be dominating the world's news agenda. Lyrically it was much closer to "People Get Ready", Curtis Mayfield's call for greater social and political awareness written in 1965, yet as relevant as ever amid simmering Cold War tensions, violence on the streets of Northern Ireland and outright war in parts of the far east. "Love Train" and "People Get Ready" were clarion calls for people to stop persecuting one another and get on board the same train. You don't need a ticket or any baggage, just love for your fellow man and a little bit of faith.

"I love that idea of the train as a type of metaphor for people to get together and agree on a destination or goal, whether it's world peace or whatever," says Eric Bibb. "I tried it myself with a song called 'Get On Board'. That was inspired by songs like 'People Get Ready'. You know, 'What are we all waiting for? Just open the train door and get on board. Doesn't matter if you're rich or poor, weak or strong. All you need is some brotherly love. Trains really are like that. For however long you're riding on a train, you are surrounded by all kinds of people born into different situations and backgrounds. You are together like that for one, two, three hours or maybe more, breathing the same air, sharing the same space, co-existing in harmony. Why can't we live together like that always?"

Bob Marley was another who would urge people to board the train in "Zion Train", a reggae take on the "People Get Ready" theme of riding some kind of spiritual train bound for a better place. According to the

Rastafari movement to which Marley was committed, "Zion" represents a utopia of freedom, peace and unity, the polar opposite of "Babylon" where exploitation and oppression reins. Despite being the first country outside Europe or North America to benefit from a passenger carrying railway, trains played only a limited role in the social and economic development of Marley's Jamaica, hence what amounts to their walk-on part in the island's rich musical culture. "Remember, there was only one train for a time in Jamaica," says Ken Stewart, keyboard player and manager of enduring ska legends The Skatalites, by way of explanation [between 1992 and 2011 Jamaica didn't have a passenger service at all as a consequence of government cuts]. However, when they have appeared – as in "Zion Train" – the results have often been hugely effective. "Train To Skaville" by The Ethiopians not only sounds like a train but has lent its name over the years to numerous rocksteady/ska cover bands and club nights. But it was left to Marley's favourite singer of all, Dennis Brown, to fashion what has to rank as Jamaica's ultimate train song.

Dennis Brown was a prolific artist – and then some. Dubbed the Crown Prince of Reggae in deference to Marley's mantle as king, he released between 75 and 79 albums (the number fluctuates according to who you choose to believe) over the course of a 30-year career brought to a premature end in July 1999 by his death hastened by excessive drug use. Regarded as Jamaica's answer to Michael Jackson, in the wake of his first public appearance aged 12 sporting a mini-afro, Brown blossomed into one of the few reggae artists to achieve international success blending lovers' rock (a subgenre of reggae) with a hint of third world militancy. Many of his songs – "Some Like It Hot", "Cassandra", "Money In My Pocket", "How Could I Leave", "Ghetto Girl", "My Time" – are regarded as reggae classics. "Westbound Train" would be another.

Brown's lyrics to "Westbound Train", wrapped in a chugging, train-like groove, chronicle a man returning home to find a note from his woman. She has ended their relationship, taking the westbound train to a place where he will never see her again. Distraught, the man sets out to find her on board another train. At least that's how it appears on the surface. Dig a little deeper and the song is open to a darker interpretation. The woman is suicidal. The westbound train isn't taking her to a happier place in the physical sense. It has taken her to the afterlife in the most grisly of circumstances. Pining for his lost love, the man decides to end it all in a similar vein.

However you decode it, "Westbound Train" was a song that made waves way beyond the Jamaican shores on which it was recorded. With an opening guitar line pinched from the Al Green song "Love And Happiness", it proved that you didn't have to be born and bred in Visalia, California, or Manchester, England, to write a memorable train song. You could come from anywhere. Even Germany.

7

RIGHT DOWN THE LINE

On 28 January 1970, a package was delivered to the home of film director Mike Hodges containing a book accompanied by a brief note from the producer Michael Klinger. The note read as follows:

Dear Mike,
I did enjoy meeting you the other day.
I had a chat with Barry who felt you might be interested in reading a book with a view to directing and possibly writing the screenplay.

"Barry" referred to Barry Krost, Hodges' agent at the time. The book was *Jack's Return Home* by Ted Lewis, the story of a London mob enforcer called Jack Carter who travels to the north of England to investigate the mysterious death of his brother, sparking unease among other criminal gangs in the area worried that his snooping will interfere with their operations. Hodges read the book and was enthralled. Murder, revenge, corruption, sleaze and betrayal set against a gritty, industrial backdrop. Thirty two weeks was all it took to write the script, cast the actors, find a crew, choose the locations, film the scenes and edit the results into what is now widely regarded as the definitive British gangster movie. "Like a bottle of neat gin swallowed before breakfast," was how the musician and critic George Melly described *Get Carter*. Once seen, it's certainly not easily forgotten.

The city in which Hodges chose to set *Get Carter* was Newcastle, 285 miles north of London and completely unrecognisable from the trendy party mecca it has since become. To emphasise the cultural and geographical gap between London and Newcastle, Hodges filmed the opening title sequences from the front of a train as it sped through the changing landscape between the two cities, the same train conveying Jack Carter (played by Michael Caine) on his vengeful mission. To accompany this footage, Hodges wanted a piece of music with a sense of foreboding. Which is where the jazz pianist Roy Budd came in.

"I shot the title sequence on the way to shoot the film in Newcastle," recalls Hodges. "The idea was to put the titles as the [railway] tunnels blacked out the screen. This sequence fulfilled another function in that it showed Jack Carter on his way up north having been warned against doing so by his gangster employers (in London). When we showed this to Roy Budd he composed the very effective and exciting theme music to accompany the rhythm of the train. It subsequently became one of the United Kingdom's most played pieces of film music ever composed."

"Main Theme – Carter Takes a Train" had a sparse, menacing quality that stuck in the mind with all the subtlety of an ice pick. Electronic music was still wearing diapers in 1970 but, to some of those who would experiment with keyboards over the ensuing years, Budd's instrumental piece featuring a harpsichord, double bass and electric piano demonstrated how moods and atmosphere could be created through a less-is-more approach. Among those who sat up and took notice were Sheffield's The Human League who covered the track on their synth era-defining *Dare* album. At the time, many UK cities such as Newcastle and Sheffield, forged on heavy industry, were in a steep decline. The politicians and leaders at the wheel of a changing country were exterminating communities in the same way that Jack Carter had eliminated those who stood in his way. This air of decay helped shape the electronic music emerging from Britain, music that was also being influenced by what was coming out of West Germany where, by contrast, the situation was a whole lot brighter economically. Bright enough for a Trans-Europe Express to flourish.

⊪⊪⊪⊪⊪⊪⊪⊪⊪

Launched in 1957, the Trans-Europe Express (or Trans Europ Express as it sometimes appears) was an international rail service set up jointly between the companies responsible for operating trains in France, Italy, the Netherlands, Switzerland and West Germany. Aimed squarely at wealthy businessmen, it offered first-class travel only on routes between key European cities such as Paris, Frankfurt, Munich, Rome and Hamburg. Luxury, elegance and speed over national borders – that was the Trans-Europe Express which, by 1974, comprised of 45 separate trains sporting exotic names such as Adriatico, Bavaria, Erasmus and Rheingold. For a band such as Kraftwerk, whose music drew on the themes of travel, communication and mankind's relationship with nature and technology, the Trans-Europe Express was ripe for exploration.

Formed by Ralf Hütter and Florian Schneider in Düsseldorf during 1970, Kraftwerk raised eyebrows by producing minimalistic electronic music set to lyrics sung either through a vocoder or generated by early forms of computer-speech software. They first came to the attention of an international audience with the 1974 song "Autobahn" which described a journey along the A555 from Cologne to Bonn, the first German main road of its kind opened in 1932. In 1976, Kraftwerk turned their attention to another form of transport, retreating to the Kling Klang Studio in Düsseldorf to record the album *Trans-Europe Express*. It wouldn't be stretching things to say that the title track changed the face of music.

"Trans-Europe Express" is a song driven by the hypnotic rhythm of a train on a track, adapted slightly to make the beat danceable. The heavily vocodorised lyrics spoken by Hütter follow an imaginary journey on the *T.E.E.* through Europe taking in Paris, Vienna, Düsseldorf and a meeting with Iggy Pop and David Bowie (the latter, his head turned by "Autobahn", had met Hütter and Schneider in 1976 after relocating from Los Angeles to Berlin). Between the calling points, Hütter repeats the words Trans-Europe Express like a mantra. If, as has been suggested, Kraftwerk saw the album as a way of loosening their German moorings and being embraced as Europeans, then they succeeded. After its release in 1977, the continent took to them in droves, the album's two standout songs – "Trans-Europe Express" and "Europe Endless" – doing more for international relations than most politicians could ever dream of.

"I'd actually been to see them [Kraftwerk] in Liverpool in 1975 and I'm sure that they played an early version of what was going to become 'Trans-Europe Express' then," says Andy McCluskey of Orchestral Manoeuvres In The Dark. "They just absolutely blew me away, as in changed my entire life. 'Trans-Europe Express' has got that wonderful pulsing sound which is something of an anachronism because Europe's railways were all diesel and electric by then. They had been completely destroyed in the Second World War so they'd had to start all over again. It's strange that a band that is trying to sound like the future is actually generating their tone rhythms from the historic sound of a steam engine.

"'Europe Endless' doesn't mention rail travel. However, I see it as being an overview of travelling through Europe and I always assume, because it's on the *Trans-Europe Express* album, that it's more to do with travelling by train. There was me, a kid from the suburbs of Liverpool, being intellectually transported through a Europe that I hadn't personally experienced by these songs suggesting the elegance and the decadence of travelling through the capitals of Europe and the beautiful scenery. It's the opportunity afforded to a teenager's mind."

In 1977, pressing buttons while standing motionless behind a keyboard was the antithesis of music as far as large swathes of the record buying public were concerned. At the other end of the spectrum were those who saw "Trans-Europe Express" for what it was – the rejection of economic stagnation and any lingering Second World War sentiment in favour of a brave new world that sounded exciting. Within a remarkably short space of time many of the doubters would be swayed. Introduced to the song by lead singer Ian Curtis, by the end of the decade Joy Division were using "Trans-Europe Express" as their walk-on music at concerts. In America, it became pivotal in the birth of DJ culture, the only record Grandmaster Flash insisted on playing uninterrupted from start to finish. Afrika Bambaataa, whose electronic music influenced the development of hip hop culture, used the melody to underpin his trailblazing 1982 song "Planet Rock". If "Autobahn" offered a sneak preview of things to come, then it was "Trans-Europe Express" which barged down the doors and welcomed the new age in.

Given Kraftwerk's stamp of approval, train travel became something of a recurrent theme in the synth revolution that spanned 1977 to 1985. From "The Things That Dreams Are Made Of" by The Human League to OMD's "Locomotion", the message to young people living seemingly mundane lives in humdrum towns was clear – get out there, broaden your minds, take trains to interesting places, meet new people.

"Real life and picture postcard views are, in a broader context, the joys of travelling by train," adds Andy McCluskey. "You can completely disengage from the process of travelling in that you are not pushing the pedals, or walking, or driving a car. You get on, you sit down, you look out of the window, and you daydream. I think most people will tell you that their favourite thing to do on a train is gaze out of the window and let their minds wander. You're taken off into this fantasy world which is one of the things people find really positive about rail travel. It's not just the getting there. It's what can happen in between getting on and arriving."

The growth in air travel and improved domestic rail services meant the Trans-Europe Express had literally hit the buffers by the late 1980s. The last one ran in 1995, by which time the majority of routes had long since been withdrawn. While some of the coaches from the Trans-Europe

Express trains live on in museums, Kraftwerk's 1977 album of the same name still sounds ahead of its time. As indeed does *Station To Station*, David Bowie's long player from the previous year which also gets namechecked in the lyrics to "Trans-Europe Express". Bowie once stated that the title was in fact a religious reference to the Stations of the Cross rather than anything to do with railways, despite the album's entire opening minute being taken up by the sound of an approaching steam locomotive. The locomotive's strangely robotic, electronic tone has led some to believe that Bowie, like Andy McCluskey, may have witnessed Kraftwerk performing an early version of "Trans-Europe Express" on their 1975 tour and been suitably influenced. With Kraftwerk making no secret of their admiration for Bowie's cutting edge work, and vice versa, it's probably more a case of great minds thinking alike.

In terms of cachet and influence, "Trans-Europe Express" stands head and shoulders above all other train songs originating from Britain and mainland Europe during the 1970s. But that's not to say there weren't plenty of gems in the chasing pack. "Last Train To London" by the Electric Light Orchestra and Supertramp's "Rudy" (the latter sampling a train leaving London's Paddington station) trod the well-worn paths of love and regret respectively, while The Clash went for a combination of both on "Train In Vain" from their 1979 album *London Calling*. Why that particular title was chosen, given the words don't appear anywhere in the song, remains something of a mystery. Even Clash guitarist and co-lead singer Mick Jones, the man who wrote the lyrics, has gone on record as saying he can't remember. It is just possible that "Stand by me", the phrase repeated throughout the track, might have been deemed too risky in the face of potential interest from Ben E. King's lawyers regarding the soul singer's signature tune of the same name. The song did, however, have a tremendous train-like groove, and so "Train In Vain" it became.

█████████████

Killing time at a girlfriend's north London flat in the ebbing light of a grey 1977 day, Graham Parker set to work on a new song dissecting the "*dirty town*" outside which offered nothing to him except the midnight train bound for some place more inviting. "She was out and I was just staring out of the window, observing life going by with my guitar in hand, and out it came," says Parker of "Watch The Moon Come Down" from the *Stick To Me* album, recorded with his band The Rumour at a time when down-at-heel Britain, the so-called "sick man of Europe", seemed to be teetering on the edge of economic oblivion. "Like a lot of evocative imagery in songs, the train idea just came into it without any concrete reason. It can represent whatever you like, but basically from a songwriting perspective it is just very handy and it's hard to go wrong with the words 'train' and 'midnight'. In this case it fits perfectly with the melancholy of the song."

Across London in the leafy suburb of Richmond, the singer and songwriter Billy Nicholls also found solace during 1977 crafting a melancholic train song born out of his increasingly turbulent work/life balance. "I'd been out in LA recording an album with my two friends John Lind and Kenny Altman who were with me in a band called White Horse," recalls Nicholls. "I had a young family, I was living in Richmond, but the album was being done in Los Angeles and I found myself being away from home so much, up to 10 weeks at a time. When I'd come back home, my youngest daughter would hardly recognise me. I got really morose about it. A friend of mine called Bruce Rowland, a great drummer who played with Ronnie Lane and all sorts, was helping me do my demos in England. He came to my flat one day, I told him what I was doing, and he said 'Billy, you really should write a 3/4 song in waltz time. You've got to have at least one on the album'. So I went to my piano, started writing in 3/4, and that was it. 'I Can't Stop Lovin' You (Though I Try)' just poured out, a leaving song about a man and a woman and the woman is going to the station to catch the early train and the man doesn't know if she's ever coming back.

"It was an emotional song because I was in quite an emotional state. It wasn't trains I was leaving on all the time but aeroplanes, yet the principle was the same and, anyway, planes aren't nearly as romantic as trains. I'd also been listening to a band called Mother Earth at the time with this fantastic singer called Tracy Nelson, and she'd done a song about leaving on a train which had really affected me. So I got back to America, played the song to the band and it went straight on the album, it was so strong. Later a friend of mine in LA played it to Leo Sayer who was also doing an album out in Los Angeles and searching for songs. They didn't have a single, then they heard 'I Can't Stop Lovin' You' and realised 'Oh, *that's* a single!' It was a big hit for Leo which was great – it pays the rent – but it's still doing so because it has been recorded by all sorts of people since then including the Outlaws and even Phil Collins, who had a massive hit with it. It's one of those that still finds an audience."

And then there were the two wildly contrasting solo acts from the suburbs of Glasgow, Gerry Rafferty and Sheena Easton, whose train songs touched the masses and in the process changed their lives beyond all recognition.

Gerry Rafferty had emerged from the Glasgow folk music scene of the 1960s, joining forces with Billy Connolly in the Humblebums before enjoying greater success alongside old school friend Joe Egan as part of Stealers Wheel. By 1975, Rafferty was itching to go it alone, but couldn't. Stealers Wheel's management company had gone bankrupt leaving his business affairs in tatters and bank account shallow on funds. Over the next two years, Rafferty spent untold hours travelling on trains between his home in Glasgow and lawyers' offices in London while attempts were made to resolve the whole sorry mess so he could resume his recording career. It should have been purgatory. Instead it ended up being the most productive working period of Rafferty's life as he used what he later described as the "raw material" of those 800-mile round trips to write the songs that would eventually appear on his critically acclaimed and commercially successful albums *City To City* (1978), *Night Owl* (1979) and *Snakes And Ladders* (1980).

Some of those songs, for example "Baker Street", had nothing to do with trains but were nevertheless written or partly formed while travelling for hours by rail. Others had trains at their very core, among them "The Royal Mile" and "City To City" which disclosed the pain Rafferty felt at leaving loved ones behind to go to London and the pleasure of being reunited with them on returning to Scotland. Rafferty's musical stockpile also included a track that has to rank not only as one of the greatest train-related love songs of all time, but quite possibly one of the greatest love songs full stop.

"Right Down the Line" was written by Rafferty for his wife Carla, a song of heartfelt thanks and appreciation to her for standing by him through the thick and thin that comes with living alongside a moody, temperamental, albeit hugely gifted, musician. Rafferty's message was a simple one – my love for you, and only you, will go on forever like a railway line stretching away into the distance. One of 10 songs to make the cut on *City To City*, "Right Down The Line" was somewhat overshadowed at the time by the ubiquitous "Baker Street" which catapulted Rafferty into the big league on both sides of the Atlantic. It did, however, reach number 12 on *Billboard*'s hot 100 chart earning a citation for achieving one million radio plays in the USA (it also made number one on *Billboard*'s separate adult contemporary chart). While "Baker Street" unquestionably remains

Rafferty's calling card, "Right Down The Line" is the song of his most likely to wash up on people's lists of desert island discs.

"It would be my funeral song, it would be my wedding song, it would be the song I would want playing at any important moment in my life," says the English singer and songwriter Elly Jackson, more commonly known under her performing name La Roux. "What a metaphor – my love for you will go on for as long as a train track, which is basically the longest of lines. How much more powerful a statement can you get than that? I remember when I first heard it in the car with my mum [the British actress Trudie Goodwin]. She had an old Citroen 2CV which was purple and black with these grey quilted seats. Anytime you went anywhere in that car was amazing because there was no seatbelts, the door handles were a weird kind of shape, and it had a little tape cassette deck. We only had a couple of tapes in the car and one of them was *City To City*. My mum and I would drive for fairly long periods when I went with her to the TV studios and that's what we always played. It had to be Gerry Rafferty every single time we were in the car. 'Baker Street' I was never really bothered about. It was all the other ones on there that got to me.

"There's no other song that does what 'Right Down The Line' does to me, and I think that says something. A really special song has that kind of effect. It's so true, so honest, a simple love song with this beautiful melody, the texture of his voice, and his delivery. What makes it sadder for me is the fact that he's almost forgotten about now which gives it this melancholy feel. It can still make me cry now and I must have listened to it a million times."

The kind of fame that "Baker Street" and the *City To City* album generated didn't sit easily on Rafferty's shoulders. He wanted the music, not himself, to take centre stage. Thrust into the limelight by the recording industry's relentless publicity machine, his diffidence was never more evident than when asked to mime the track "City To City" on the Dutch television show *TopPop* in 1978. In a scene that wouldn't have looked out of place in *This Is Spinal Tap*, Rafferty was forced to share the stage with a model steam locomotive performing loops of a small track intended to emphasise the song's central train theme. The whole embarrassing experience only succeeded in underpinning Rafferty's aversion to making such appearances. Unwilling to promote his work and with a reputation in some circles for being difficult and aloof, Rafferty's career suffered as his consumption of alcohol spiralled. In 1990, he and Carla divorced after 20 years of marriage. While "Baker Street" remained tethered to radio station playlists, Rafferty withdrew from public life and resisted all attempts to make him go sober until it was too late. He died in January 2011, aged 63.

"It ['Right Down The Line'] is a beautiful, beautiful piece of work and I hope, wherever he is now, that he knows that," adds Jackson. "Those people who love it do so to insane levels. [Singer] Lily Allen feels exactly the same way about it as I do. I remember when I first met her and I said that one of my favourite tracks was 'Right Down The Line'. She was like 'What? That's one of my favourite songs!' It's either got in there or it hasn't. For those people who've got it, then they've *really* got it."

*

At around the same time as Gerry Rafferty was starting to battle his demons, not to mention miniature train props in Holland, so producers at the BBC in London were busy working on ideas for the next series of *The Big Time*, a popular British television show that took members of the public with specific talents and placed them in the limelight to see how they fared. One of the ideas put into production involved following an unknown singer as he or she attempted to conquer the pop charts. Auditions were held and a young Scottish woman barely out of her teens was chosen to be the subject of the programme. That was Sheena Easton.

Born Sheena Orr in April 1959, Easton grew up in Bellshill some 20 miles from Rafferty's home town of Paisley. Her father, a steel mill worker, had died when she was aged just 10 leaving mum Annie Orr to support a family of six children, Sheena being the youngest. In 1975, she earned a scholarship to attend the Royal Scottish Academy of Music and Drama in Glasgow where she studied by day to become a speech and drama teacher, singing at night around local clubs in a band called Something Else. In reality, she never wanted to be a teacher, enrolling on the course as a way of improving her singing, hoping some kind of big break would come her way. In an era well before reality TV shows parading unknown singers became omnipresent, *The Big Time* with its audience of millions represented a once in a lifetime opportunity.

Easton was pretty and could more than hold a tune, yet recording *The Big Time* during 1979 proved to be anything other than a cakewalk. She sang for Dusty Springfield and Lulu who both offered encouragement, but that didn't prevent the latter's manager Marion Massey from saying she was unlikely to make the grade. Nevertheless, EMI signed Easton and had her record a single, "Modern Girl", the story of a fiercely independent

The Singing Brakeman.

Above: Jimmie Rodgers, the Singing Brakeman. *(Michael Ochs Archive)*

Right: The boxcar; not so much a way out of poverty as a means of survival. One hobo helps another aboard a freight train as it pulls out of Bakersfield, California, 1940. *(Rondal Partridge)*

Top: Jimmy "Duck" Holmes outside the Blue Front Café in Bentonia, Mississippi. When a train comes thundering past, you hear it. *(Mick Gold/Redferns)*

Above: A promotional sketch of the Orange Blossom Special luxury passenger train, which inspired the song of the same name. *(Tichnor Brothers. Boston)*

Right: "High balling your way". An advert from the American entertainment trade magazine *Variety* promoting "Freight Train" by the Chas McDevitt Skiffle Group featuring Nancy Whiskey. *(Courtesy Chas McDevitt)*

On the ED SULLIVAN Show

CHARLES
McDEVITT
SKIFFLE
GROUP

featuring
NANCY
WHISKEY

SUNDAY
MAY 12
CBS-TV

HEAR THIS GREAT HIT PERFORMED BY THE
U.S. NAVY'S RANDY SPARKS (U.S.S. PRINCETON)
CVS-37

the **ORIGINAL**
HIGH BALLING
YOUR WAY...
CHIC RECORDS

FREIGHT TRAIN

Chic
THOMASVILLE, GEORGIA

CHIC#1008

P. O. BOX 732   CAñcl 6-1423
'VILLE, GEORGIA

In England It's OMOLY RECORDS
In Canada It's SPARTAN RECORDS

VARIETY   Wednesday   VARIETY

Above: Lonnie Donegan takes the *"mighty good road"*
to Liverpool's Empire Theatre, 1956. *(Courtesy Brian Smith)*

Top and above left: "I followed on from all the other kids with trainspotting."
The spotting mecca that was York station, England, during the summer of 1981.
(Trevor Ermel)

Above right: The end of the line. Steam engines breathe their last inside
Stockport Edgeley shed, northern England, 1968. *(Trevor Ermel)*

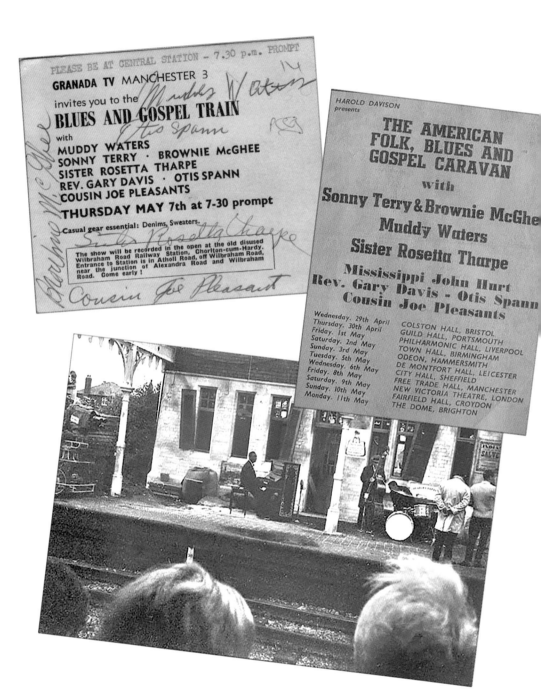

Top left and right: A ticket for the recording of Granada Television's *Blues And Gospel Train* at Wilbraham Road station, Manchester, England, signed by the majority of the acts who appeared, plus a poster for the tour. *(Courtesy Peter Goldsmith)*

Above: Otis Spann takes to the stage, or rather the platform, on 7 May 1964 to record his slot at Granada Television's *Blues And Gospel Train. (Brian Smith)*

Top left: Widnes station, where Paul Simon is supposed to have written "Homeward Bound" in 1965. *(Spencer Vignes)*

Top right: "That isn't going anywhere." The latest of several plaques to appear at Widnes station commemorating Paul Simon's composing of "Homeward Bound". *(Spencer Vignes)*

Above: 123 Coroners Lane, Widnes, former home of the Speed family and the more likely setting for the genesis of what became "Homeward Bound". *(Spencer Vignes)*

The plaque in the image reads:

At Widnes Station
in 1965
Paul Simon
wrote the song
Homeward Bound

Top: A Britannia class steam locomotive, a favourite with Chas Hodges, climbs Shap Fell in Cumbria, England, during July 1967. *(Trevor Ermel)*

Middle: Waterloo sunset. Padstow, a West Country class locomotive, caught on camera one evening at the London terminus during the dying days of steam in southern England. *(Trevor Ermel)*

Above: "The Paul McCartney of trains." The Flying Scotsman, her fan club out in force, storms through north London in 1969. *(Trevor Ermel)*

woman with a casual boyfriend and a job in a London office which she commutes to by train. Despite some heavy promotion, it stalled in the UK charts at number 56. Not to be undone, Easton recorded a second single, "9 To 5", the tale of a not-so-independent woman whose man takes the morning train to work, then catches another one home again in the evenings to find her waiting for him. By the time "9 To 5" was released Easton's episode of *The Big Time* had been screened on national television. That kind of massive exposure propelled "9 To 5" to number three during the summer of 1980 and encouraged EMI to re-release "Modern Girl" which promptly followed it up the charts to number eight. By the end of the year, Easton had appeared in the annual Royal Variety Performance at the London Palladium in front of Her Majesty Queen Elizabeth The Queen Mother, all on the strength of two massively popular train songs featuring young women as their central characters.

The best part of four decades on, Easton is quick to attribute credit for her early success to the man responsible for crafting those singles. "They were literally the first two songs I ever recorded, back when I was still a student," she says. "I was young and very green about the whole process. As I gained a little more experience I chose my own material, but the credit for those two songs and any meaning or inspiration behind their subject matter goes exclusively to Chris Neil who was my record producer and, of course, the writer of the songs. I did not choose them because of any metaphor or deep meaning. At that time they were simply fun, catchy pop songs that were a blast to sing. I would be a total fake and poser if I claimed to attach any cultural significance to my reasons for singing them."

Unlike Rafferty, Easton embraced the glitzy side of the music business. She was confident, refined and media savvy, qualities that went down well in America where Easton ventured in 1981 to promote "9 to 5", released in the USA as "Morning Train (Nine to Five)" to avoid confusion with Dolly Parton's song "9 To 5" from the film of the same name. America duly embraced her and the single went to number one for two weeks, selling over one million copies in the process. Her career there never looked back and in 1992 she became a US citizen.

By contrast, Rafferty failed to play so much as a single live gig in the land of the free, torpedoing his career stateside in the process. Not that it appeared to bother him. Whereas Grammy nominations (at the time of writing she's had six, winning two), a James Bond theme ("For Your Eyes Only") and Las Vegas (where she has performed regularly) befitted Easton, Rafferty always seemed more at home riding the London to Glasgow night trains celebrated in his song "City To City". Which, listening back to all the great music conceived on those railway journeys of the mid-1970s, is something we should perhaps be thankful for.

8

THE PULL OF THE RAILROADS – A SONGWRITER'S TALE

You've probably never heard of Jack Wesley Routh. Unless, that is, you are a country music aficionado, or a country music artist who recognises a top notch songwriter.

Routh – whose songs have been recorded by an A to Z of country luminaries including Johnny Cash, Emmylou Harris, Waylon Jennings and Linda Ronstadt – was born in Kingman, Kansas, in 1950. The railroads provided the backdrop to his formative years. Placing a shiny new penny on the tracks to have it flattened by a passing train was a rite of passage. During the days, Routh and his friends would jump from the railroad bridges that spanned the local river into the deep channels below, returning in the evenings to fish from the same locations. Lying in bed at night, the last thing he heard before drifting off to sleep was usually the lonesome sound of a train whistle. The railroads, he remembers, always had a sense of freedom about them.

"My childhood was spent in the farm and ranch land of Kingman County, south central Kansas, where my family homestead was built in the 1800s," says Routh. "Most of my family still lives within 50 miles of there to this day. It is rural farm and ranch country where the farmers raise such crops as wheat, barley and corn and the ranchers raise cattle. A lot of folks do both just to survive, or at least better their odds at survival. The trains were a means of transporting the crops and cattle to the cities such as Wichita, Kansas City and onward. Nowadays, tractor-trailers are another means of transportation. As a teenager I worked on the farms and ranches and also loaded the boxcars with various grains and cattle. Some of those trains would stretch more than a mile long and if you didn't get to the other side of a railroad crossing when one was coming you often could be in for a long wait. Sometimes you would just turn your truck or car off to save fuel, or to keep it from overheating until the train had passed. I knew a guy that got his girlfriend pregnant while waiting for a train to clear the track!"

Having turned 17 in 1967 Routh, together with one of his best friends, caught the Santa Fe Chief from Wichita to Los Angeles to spend the summer of love in California, "getting an experience that will never, ever pass through this universe again." Over the years that followed he rode many more trains across North America and Europe. They were a fun way of seeing the countryside and cities. Routh also loved watching people arriving and departing from railway stations, or "depots" as they're known stateside. By that time he had been playing guitar for several years, cutting his first record at the age of 15 with the band Robin's Hoods. In March 1973 he moved to Nashville to work with Johnny Cash. The "Man In Black" knew nothing about this arrangement, but the rookie was determined to engineer some kind of meeting and have Cash listen to his songs. After several failed attempts at catching the legend at his office and studio in Hendersonville, Tennessee, Routh's dollars were rapidly disappearing. In one final shot at glory he decided to drive by Cash's mansion overlooking Old Hickory Lake on the off chance that something life-changing might happen. And, lo and behold, it did.

"To the right of the house I saw Johnny Cash dressed in black on a hillside operating a rototiller ploughing his garden. I couldn't believe my eyes and thought for sure I was seeing things. It's not unusual for tour buses and fans to be lined up outside the fence taking photos with hopes of catching a glimpse of him and June. An older man came through a gate and went up to talk to John so he turned the tiller off. I later learned it was John's dad, and when he left I yelled out to John and asked if I could talk to him. To my surprise he came over to me and I introduced myself and said I had some songs I'd like for him to listen to. He told me that he was doing something that was very important to him [his garden], and for me to leave a tape with his sister at the office. I told him that what I was doing was the most important thing in my life, and that I'd rather just play them to him. He said OK, and that he would meet me at his office in 30 minutes. I walked in his office with him, and his sister [Joanne] was shocked that I had connected. I played him some songs that I had written and ended up leaving that first meeting with an exclusive songwriter contract and a cheque. I was in hog heaven!"

Routh not only wrote songs for Cash but opened for the great man live, played guitar with him in the studio, produced some of his songs, briefly dated his eldest daughter Rosanne, and later married June Carter Cash's eldest daughter Carlene (Johnny already had four daughters when he met June, a mother herself of two daughters, and the pair went on to have a son of their own, John Carter Cash). In essence, John "took me in and nurtured me and let me develop as a songwriter, musician and producer." The two men shared many of the same passions, including railroads, so it was inevitable that some of the songs resulting from their union would feature trains. And of them all, probably the choicest cut – certainly in this author's opinion – was "Crystal Chandeliers And Burgundy" from Cash's 1974 album *The Junkie And The Juicehead Minus Me*.

A hobo jumps a freight train in San Antonio, Texas. However, in climbing aboard he injures an ankle which "*shoots pain that feeds*" his dreams of living a more comfortable lifestyle surrounded by some of life's luxuries. Unlike Bill in Waldo O'Neal's "Hobo Bill's Last Ride" he is not at death's door, but the situation in that boxcar is grim. As a hobo he is free to go wherever he wants to go, but it's the kind of freedom that comes at a price. Our man is born to drift, and he knows it. Crystal chandeliers and fine wine? No chance.

"'Crystal Chandeliers And Burgundy' is one of the first songs I wrote after John signed me as a songwriter," says Routh. "John's studio was previously an old dinner theatre and very elegant with plush blue carpet and crystal chandeliers hanging, and I had also been over to the house for dinner and drank his vintage wines. So, looking back on it, I guess some of the furthest things from riding in a boxcar are crystal chandeliers and burgundy. The song has a pretty and lonely melody and the line about my mother's heartbeat from the tracks has to do with the pulse of the clickety-clack and the knowing of never turning back to where you came from. The pain of leaving home."

Another track that the pair collaborated on was "When The Trains Come Back Again", destined not to be heard in public until well after Cash's death in 2003. "John and I both loved the old west, trains and women, and this song is about a guy dealing with a woman or two in his own way in another place and time. Shortly after John signed me, Rosanne – John's oldest – who'd recently moved to Tennessee from California, invited me over for dinner and we dated for a few months. Then John offered me a place to live in one side of a duplex on the property near his studio. Carlene – June's oldest – lived in the other side of the duplex. Before long, we became involved and turned the duplex into one house, married, and had a son. One evening John and June came over for dinner and while

June and Carlene were in the kitchen, John and I were in another room passing a guitar back and forth writing a song. He'd be writing down the lyrics while I was playing the guitar, and then I'd be writing down the lyrics while he was playing. We finished the tune before dinner was ready. That was "When The Trains Come Back Again". We talked about the song afterwards but never recorded it and somehow it was forgotten.

"A few years ago, I was going through some letters and papers inside an antique 1864 Colt 45 gun box that John had given me for a birthday present one year, and there was the folded yellow legal pad paper that John and I had written the lyrics to this song on. Half of the lyrics were in his handwriting and the other half in mine. Unfortunately John had already died, but I remembered how the song went and recorded it on an acoustic album I did in 2009 (called *Another Season*). It was a perfect John song and I really wish he could have laid it down on record before he was gone."

Songwriters are always on the lookout for stories, real or otherwise. For as long as Jack Wesley Routh can remember, railroads have had all the ingredients necessary to make great stories. They're not the only thing he writes about, far from it, but trains and the world they inhabit are a seam that he – in common with so many other songwriters throughout the generations – has found himself returning to time and time again for inspiration and material. Occasionally, as Routh himself has discovered, life does indeed end up imitating art, so embedded are the railroads in the social and cultural fabric of North America in particular.

"When I was married to Carlene, one night we had a fight and she went over to John and June's house about a mile from our house," Routh recalls. "I had been drinking and I called over to the house and John answered the phone. I told him to tell Carlene if she didn't come on back home, I was going to go out back and hop on the train and get the hell out of there – we had a railroad track that ran behind our property that the Amtrak and a few freighters mostly used. John started laughing and said 'OK Jack, I'll give her the message, but I just want you to know that the train is usually going about 40 miles per hour when it passes by your house, so it's going to be a little tough hopping on, my friend'. That was kind of sobering. I loved John. He always had a way of looking out for me.

"Trains cover a lot of ground, not just physically but metaphorically too. Besides being a major means of travel and transportation for many years, it's very inspirational and romantic. You can have the romance of two lovers kissing goodbye beneath a lamp post and the clouds of steam rolling off the waiting train in the darkness of the night. And you have the romantic life of a down-on-his-luck hobo climbing aboard a boxcar on a slow moving train that's pulling out of some big city rail yard. He cares not where it's going or how long it will take as long as he's gone from the situation he's been in and maybe, just maybe, he might have a shot of luck and change somewhere faraway down the line."

9

BLUE TRAINS

Romance, escape, hope, adventure, sex, the kind of freedom that comes with sitting in the open doorway of a boxcar bumming a westbound ride across the wide open plains of Nebraska. That's the sunny side of the train song where life's glass is, by and large, somewhere between the brim and half full (providing an ankle wasn't injured while climbing aboard).

Then there's the darker side where the glass isn't so much empty as non-existent.

A man enters a London Underground station at night. He's heading home to his wife with a takeaway curry. A gang of thugs corner the man, beat him up, take his money and house keys. Lying wounded, the victim of "Down In The Tube Station At Midnight" by The Jam realises his unsuspecting wife is also now in danger. He slips either into unconsciousness or the afterlife.

A woman watches as a man, possibly her boyfriend, injects himself with hard drugs. He is a habitual user. His skin is riddled with lines which remind the woman of railway tracks. Her inability to do anything to save this man from himself equates to a train ride of utter despair, a journey she will never recover from. He dies and the narrator of "Been On A Train" by the late Laura Nyro is left grieving for someone who was hell bent on letting the needle do its damage.

Ever since steel driver John Henry dropped dead of exhaustion, hammer in his hands, singers and songwriters have found themselves drawn towards crafting and performing train songs laden with doom and foreboding. Forget about the suicidal undercurrent of Dennis Brown's "Westbound Train". These are songs where the sinister subject matter jumps right out of the speakers and punches you between the eyes – hard. Infidelity. Mortality. The exploitation of poor migrant workers. Bereavement. Our inability to protect those closest to us. Second World War Nazi death camps. Nuclear catastrophe. It's all there in an inventory of misery including, in the shape of Jethro Tull's majestic "Locomotive Breath", a song that examines mankind's very own self-destruct gene.

Written by Ian Anderson in 1969 and recorded late the following year, "Locomotive Breath" (a nod towards the exhaust emitted by the same steam engines which terrified Anderson as a child in Dunfermline) chronicles the train wreck that one man, and in essence all of us, is making of his life. "It uses the notion of a runaway steam train which is a metaphor for our species on its lemming-like rush toward oblivion," says Anderson. "It's a song that was born out of the earliest awareness that I had about issues like population expansion, greed, people being determined to fight their way up the ladder at the expense of their fellow man. It's a rather ugly song, driven more than anything else by the idea that we are out of control and we can't get off this crazy train."

Issues that, as Anderson acknowledges, apply just as much today as they did back in 1969, if not more so. "It's impossible to take a step back now that we've got used to all these economic benefits in modern life. Throw the wife's iPad away and she will kill you. So, yes, it's a song with lasting value. For me as a performer it is much easier to sing a song that I find has an impact on me today, one I can sing with authority and fervent declaration. Where are we going as a human race? Do we ever stop to think about that? Not nearly as much as we should. We're all on board a train that won't slow down. In fact, it only seems to be picking up speed."

Twelve years after "Locomotive Breath" appeared on Jethro Tull's multi-million selling *Aqualung* album, Anderson turned to one of the most graphic examples of mankind's increasingly lemming-like existence in "Trains" from his 1983 solo effort *Walk Into Light*. "That's a song driven by the whole commuter experience," he explains. "It has always struck me as poignant, but quite horrific, that people will live in one place and spend perhaps three or four hours each day commuting in what generally are not very pleasant circumstances. The song is about the unpleasantness of travel that you have to do, or have chosen to do, in order to spend the evenings and weekends in a leafy glade somewhere in Berkshire or Wiltshire. The awful penalty is that you have these wasted hours of your life commuting, wasted perhaps less so today because now we have our laptops, iPhones and iPads which you can catch up on work with. Nowadays, people use that travel experience to stay connected. I know I try and make travelling by train a productive part of my life. An office desk with an ever-changing picture window – that's how I try and look at it."

Even allowing for modern electronic gizmos, the whole concept of commuting amounts to a parody of travel. For millions of people worldwide it is a chore which jars with the sort of freedom that trains are supposed to represent. Or maybe we have all, quite literally, been taken for a ride.

"The 20th century American songwriters created a cliché with their idea of the train being a journey to freedom, a journey of expression, a metaphor for life's journey with the ability to go where you want – but it's actually a lie," suggests Andy McCluskey. "They presented this freedom of choice, expression and destiny, whereas in reality a railway journey is almost always by definition predetermined. There is a set place of departure and there is a definite terminus and the stops along the way are preordained. So in actual fact it's much more of a metaphor for the strictures of life. Railways were built and controlled by rich entrepreneurs. They were constructed by workers who were exploited and often died, and they were operated by underpaid staff. In actual fact, that is a metaphor for modern industrialised life, and particularly modern life that's in the grip of international corporate control. This concept of trains being a personal journey to freedom, determining your own fate, is in some ways complete bullshit. Perhaps the 'King Of The Road' boxcar hobos felt they were usurping the system by freeloading rides, but were they really making any difference to the world? Perhaps they, and the songwriters who glorified them, were happy to delude themselves that they had the freedom of the road, but you could argue they were marginalised parasites on a system that could tolerate people taking a free ride."

Occasionally, those predetermined destinations have been about as far removed from briefcases and boardrooms as you can get. In times of war, trains have been used not only to transport troops to and from the front line but also to convey civilians displaced by the fighting and political upheaval. Al Stewart's 1993 song "Trains" recounts how the railways of mainland Europe were clogged with soldiers during both the First and Second World Wars. It then takes an altogether darker direction by reminding us of the role trains played transporting people on what was often a one-way journey to the Nazi concentration camps. Looking on as young and old are escorted aboard a train by disdainful guards, the driver of a steam locomotive makes a chilling cut-throat gesture with his hand. His "passengers" may be oblivious to their destination but he, having made this trip many times before, knows exactly where they are bound. Stewart recalls the brightly coloured trains with names which lit up his own childhood and contrasts them with these cold accessories to murder. Alarmed by a combination of indifference towards the Holocaust and the lingering presence of anti-Semitism in northern Europe during the early nineties, the late Israeli singer Ofra Haza also recalled this heinous abuse of the railway system during the Second World War in the song "Trains Of No Return" from her 1992 album *Kirya*. Urging modern Europe to guard against complacency and learn from the mistakes of the past, Haza's message is clear and passionate – *"Don't let them roll again"*.

Despite masquerading as a means of employment, the conditions for migrant workers in and around the mines of South Africa during the apartheid years also plumbed the depths of man's inhumanity to man. Raised in the coal mining town of Witbank, around 100 miles north east of Johannesburg, musician and singer Hugh Masekela witnessed first-hand the plight of labourers who came from as far afield as Angola and Tanzania, not to mention other parts of South Africa, to work underground. Masekela's grandmother, Johanna Mthise, brewed beer made from sorghum plants which the miners drank while gathered at her house. As the drink flowed so the heartbreaking stories of their struggle for survival would pour out. Masekela never forgot those tales of woe and in 1972, while holidaying in upstate New York, he composed "Stimela (Coal Train)", a song about men forced to work 16-hour days for virtually no pay, who curse the trains responsible for bringing them to the grim South African mining communities from other parts of the continent.

"The train in 'Stimela (Coal Train)' is emblematic of the cruel, destructive, deceitful power of that period," says the English singer and songwriter Sarah Jane Morris who covered the song on her 2013 album *Bloody Rain*. "It [the train] seems to promise work but it delivers enslavement. It seems to promise survival but it delivers dislocation. Instead of hope, it delivers despair. I'd always loved Hugh Masekela and had been doing some research when I found a clip of him performing it. I thought 'Wow, this speaks to me'. It's a song that comes right at you and hits you round the head."

Masekela's emotionally charged performances of "Stimela (Coal Train)" have long been regarded as a highlight of his live shows. The lyrics are mainly spoken rather than sung, accompanied by panting, screaming and screeching that veer between the sound of a steam train and the anguished cries of a physically and mentally exploited miner. Small wonder Morris was affected. As a major player in the anti-apartheid movement in Britain, Morris was someone with a pretty good understanding of events in South Africa between 1948 and 1994. During the 1980s she played host to many displaced South African musicians at her flat in Brixton. Dali Tambo, founder of the Artists Against Apartheid organisation and son of former African National Congress president Oliver Tambo, was a former boyfriend. When not writing or performing she could often be found protesting outside South Africa House in London's Trafalgar Square, megaphone in hand. Morris had also once supported Hugh Masekela at the 100 Club in Oxford Street and, in a bizarre twist of fate, first met Jimmy Somerville with whom she would perform in The Communards at a benefit concert for striking British miners. If anyone was destined to cover "Stimela (Coal Train)", then it was probably her.

"He [Masekela] is a pretty hard act to follow but I felt it was the kind of song that I could do something with," she says. "When I perform it, I do the sound of the steam train at the start – choo, choo, choo, choo – and then the other performers join in and we get this wonderful percussive steam train going. That's when I do my gut wrenching scream which is the train shooting through. I wanted it to represent a scream of violence, the scream of being wrenched from the womb of your country. It's utter despair. I did it [the scream] at the Union Chapel in London when we launched the album and I held onto it for a long, long time. Somehow it managed to be dark and moving and terrifying all at the same time. I'd always wanted to work with the Soweto Gospel Choir and that was the perfect track to get them involved with. I had hoped to involve Hugh as well but it was around the time of his 75th birthday and he couldn't fit it in. But he gave us his blessing."

Over time, Masekela has expanded the meaning of "Stimela (Coal Train)" to encompass economically exploited workers worldwide, not just in South Africa. Morris, a perennial champion of minority rights and the oppressed, does likewise whenever she performs the song live. "It's about getting the message out there," she says. "This kind of stuff still carries on. People are being exploited today perhaps more than ever. You've got to try and stand up against it."

"The coal train is a motherfucker." So Hugh Masekela once said while addressing the subject of African migration. But it doesn't just stop with coal trains. Any old train, given the right (or rather the wrong) set of circumstances, has the potential to represent fear, heartbreak, pain or misery, something Dennis Locorriere came to realise when, having quit as lead singer of Dr. Hook, he started attending songwriting nights while living in Nashville.

"You'd go along with your friends and sit around and every-fucking body had a train song," he recalls. "And they're all written in the same way, about how trains make you feel romantic and blah blah blah. Maybe I was just feeling rebellious, but I thought I'd try a different slant. Maybe I should write that whenever I hear a train I don't get melancholy in a good kind of way; it tears my heart out. It's that train in the distance thing. I hear that train and at the other end of wherever it's going *you* might be there, and that thought kills me. I kind of liked that angle. This is the sound of a train that makes you want to put a pillow over your head so you can't hear it." The song born out of those Nashville nights, "The Sound Of A Train", ended up on Locorriere's 2010 album *Post Cool*.

Locorriere's angle was certainly something that Nick Cave, a songwriter renowned for exploring life's darker tracts, could identify with. "There are certain songwriters, I guess, who love the symbol of the train because it is a powerful, masculine, journeying machine that literally eats space and time, flying along on its own narrative drive, big, black and ferocious," he says. "But it is not just that. If you have ever sat alone in a hotel room in a small American town and heard its ghastly, lonely whistle, it is literally the saddest sound in the world. It is the sound of the terror-riven soul in flight, full of ghosts and regret."

Cave's second album with his band The Bad Seeds, 1985's *The Firstborn Is Dead*, had included "Train Long-Suffering" written as "a kind of homage to those sorts of rattling train songs" recorded during the fifties and sixties by the likes of Elvis Presley and Johnny Cash. Nineteen years later, Cave did away with the rattling and slowed the train down to walking pace with "O Children" from the double album *Abattoir Blues/ The Lyre Of Orpheus*. Little did he realise at the time that the track would arguably do more for his public profile than anything he had previously recorded in a career already into its fourth decade.

"'O Children' was a song I wrote about our inability to protect our children and the ones we love," adds Cave. "It's got a slow beat, full of suspended dread. The train is used as a symbol of deliverance. It comes and takes the children away. There is a false sense of hope, a bit of gospel singing, and the train rolls off to 'The Kingdom', whatever that may be."

One of those who sat up and took notice of "O Children" on the album's release was Matt Biffa, an English-based music supervisor responsible for finding songs to accompany movie footage. Biffa stored the song away in his memory banks and had almost forgotten about it completely when the call came to work on the 2010 film *Harry Potter And The Deathly Hallows: Part 1*. At the time, Biffa was in the process of separating from his wife and the uncertainty over how the split might affect the couple's two young sons terrified him. Tasked by the film's director David Yates with finding a song for a scene in which Harry and his friend Hermione Granger share a dance while struggling in their quest to overcome the dark wizard Lord Voldemort, "O Children" immediately sprang to mind.

"I went for a meeting at Leavesden Studios where they made the Harry Potter films and they said, 'There's this dance that Harry does which is not in the original book. We've written it in. Go away, read it and let's have a chat'," recalls Biffa. "So I read it and it just leapt off the page. There was always something about 'O Children' that I knew would be absolutely incredible for the right scene. Over the years all sorts of scenes came up that it would have been really good for, but I deliberately held it back. At that time, the lyrics were incredibly relevant to me because of what was going on in my personal life and how I was feeling about my children who were three and one years old. It was horribly on the nose. I kind of sensed straight away that this was the scene I'd been waiting for."

Even so, Biffa prepared three CDs full of potential songs to present to Yates, together with the film's producers David Barron and David Heyman. Between them the four men agreed that the track they were looking for needed to be a piece of relatively unknown music so as not to overshadow the gravitas of the scene. Various soul songs were considered but rejected because "we found they were far too much of this world and not enough of theirs." Biffa had included "O Children" on the first CD and, sure enough, Yates also fell under its spell. "He liked it because it was melancholic yet uplifting, bittersweet and haunted, and he loved the tempo and the meter," says Biffa. "He also liked the fact that it wasn't too pointedly romantic. Then he said to me 'So what I want to know now is, is there anything better than 'O Children'? Over the next month or so I sent him another six CDs during which I was definitely scraping the bottom of the barrel. To cut a long story short, there wasn't."

Getting permission to use the song from Cave proved to be a painless process. "I think he was pleased that we weren't using something like 'Red Right Hand' or one of his better known songs," adds Biffa. "After that there was a debate about whether the scene would even make it into the film. I think it went in, went out, then went in again. I was thrilled it was used because it was the closest I could ever get to writing a song for my children. I'm not a songwriter. It was a little love letter from me to them, sort of telling them that I was terribly worried about what we [Biffa and his wife] were potentially doing to them. I knew it was the right piece of music but you live very much on your nerves in this business. When it comes to shooting a scene you have no plan B – you're committed to it. Dan [Radcliffe] and Emma [Watson] might not have done as good a job as they did and it could have been awful. But when I turned up Dan rushed over, gave me a big hug and said 'You've made Harry Potter cool!' I said 'Listen Dan, I think you're doing a good job of that all by yourself! He's very enthusiastic about his music and he was thrilled that it was Nick Cave. When they were filming it I was looking round and the make-up girls were crying and people were visibly moved, so my nerves sort of dissipated. I thought 'Yeah, we've got this right'."

Cave's career was doing very nicely long before *Harry Potter And The Deathly Hallows: Part 1* was released. Aimed squarely at older children and the young adult market, it's unlikely many of those who went to see the film had even heard the name Nick Cave before. Given his traditional source material – lechery, sin, redemption, death – that's arguably no bad thing. However, something changed once the Potter hordes stormed cinemas worldwide. Biffa estimates that prior to the film's release "O Children" had approximately 20,000 hits on YouTube. That soon became one million, then two, then three, until all the various uploads featuring the song and/or the scene had by 2016 clocked up in excess of nine million views. The comments accompanying the pages were, in the main, left by young people drawn to "O Children" through the film. This particular author's daughter has now discovered Nick Cave. Much as I admire his music, I have to confess that was Harry Potter's doing, not mine.

"I don't really know what the song is about, even to this day," confesses Biffa. "But then a lot of Nick's music is like that. You can almost read into his lyrics what you want. I used to think that it was the train taking people to heaven like in the old spiritual gospel songs. Now I think it's actually more about the train taking our children away into their lives. But I love that train metaphor, whatever it is. In *Harry Potter And The Deathly Hallows: Part 2* there's the scene where Harry Potter dies and he's with Dumbledore in this big, white, bright sort of railway station between life and the afterlife which Harry identifies as Kings Cross station. Harry says, 'I have to go back, haven't I?' Dumbledore replies 'You could board a train'. Harry says 'Where would it take me?' And Dumbledore just says 'On!' That was very serendipitous and I wish I could tell you I was such a genius for putting two and two together, but it was just a happy accident that the train metaphor happened to carry over from 'O Children' and *Part 1*."

"Our inability to protect our children and the ones we love," to echo Cave's words, has to rank as any caring parent's worst nightmare. In July 1977, while in the middle of an American tour, Led Zeppelin vocalist Robert Plant heard the news that his 5-year-old son Karac had died suddenly of a stomach virus. Grief stricken, he immediately returned home to Britain and put the band on hold. Twenty one years later, Plant offered up a glimpse into his world of pain in "Blue Train", a poignant hymn to Karac from the album *Walking Into Clarksdale* recorded with his former Led Zeppelin cohort Jimmy Page. And yet how can we be expected to protect our children and loved ones if sometimes we can't even protect ourselves?

In 1999, the year he turned 50, Dire Straits co-founder member, bass player and backing vocalist John Illsley decided to go for a mid-life health check. The results made pretty good reading – low cholesterol, low pulse rate, the blood pressure of a man half his age – but there was one area that concerned his doctor. Illsley's white blood cell count was high. He had further tests involving a bone marrow biopsy with a small amount of fluid being collected from the bone using a syringe. The results from that revealed Illsley was suffering from a condition called chronic lymphocytic leukaemia where a person's bone marrow generates too many white blood cells which don't work properly, reducing the number of normal blood cells that a body produces, causing no end of problems. In short, he had cancer and 10 years at best left to live.

On the advice of a consultant, Illsley played the waiting game to see how his symptoms developed. That kept the wolf from the door until 2002, when his blood count started to go awry. Illsley had chemotherapy every month for three months which bought him time until 2008 when he began to feel increasingly weak. Another round of chemotherapy followed after which only one further option, a stem cell transplant, remained. That involved using drugs to kill off his own bone marrow and replacing it with stem cells taken from a donor's blood and marrow. Which is where Illsley's older sister, Pat, stepped in.

"She didn't even know I'd been ill, so I had a bit of explaining to do both to her and the rest of my family," says Illsley. "I hadn't wanted to worry them so I'd kept everything low key, but obviously I'd got to a position where I couldn't do that anymore. Pat ended up being a perfect match and so she came to London where I was being treated, and her cells were taken out and frozen for when they would be needed."

Which proved to be January 2011. "I knew when I was admitted to hospital that I was going to be in there for a minimum for four weeks because that's how long the transplant is supposed to take. I asked the doctors 'When you say I'll be in isolation, what does that mean? Can I take things in with me?' They said 'Of course you can'. So I said 'Can I take my guitar with me?' and they said 'Yeah'. They just didn't want anyone coming in with colds or bugs because they were taking me down to zero and I was going to be susceptible to all sorts of stuff. So I got myself prepared with my gear in a fourth floor room of this clinic in London with a view down Marylebone Road, so I still felt connected to the outside world even though I couldn't go out. And I wrote some things around when the doctors and medical people were doing things and coming in to see me."

If that makes having cancer seem like a breeze, don't be fooled. Illsley, an optimist by nature, needed something to sustain him throughout the physical pain and associated side-effects such as hair loss. Lying there in hospital, a striking analogy of his 12-year journey from diagnosis to stem cell transplant came to mind:

> *"Life doesn't run on railway tracks*
> *It twists and turns*
> *It's not white or black"*

Slowly but surely, a song emerged which Illsley called "Railway Tracks". "I tried to get down on paper the feeling of what it was like being in that situation," he recalls. "There's the first verse – you're in a white room, you can't wait to get out and have the glass of beer or wine that you're not allowed – through to the last verse when you bounce back, the blood flows strong. It struck me that I wasn't the only one going through all of this. All the other rooms were full of people undergoing the same thing. I tried to describe the journey through the illness that I, we, were all going through, using the idea of the train taking us on that journey. '*Life doesn't run on railway tracks*' – sometimes the train derails and you have to deal with the wreckage. The song itself was quite simple but the journey element to it was probably the strongest part because it was relevant to what was going on at the time."

The stem cell transplant worked and Illsley was given the all-clear in 2012. "Railway Tracks" subsequently found its way onto his 2014 album *Testing The Water* and has since proved inspirational to other people undergoing transplants and/or treatment for cancer. Illsley is far from the first musician to have compared life's journey to a train ride. He knows that. However, there can't be many who have done it under such testing personal circumstances.

By contrast, the personal hell Matt Johnson experienced which formed the backbone of his song "Slow Train To Dawn" was more of a self-inflicted nature. The prime mover in, and founder member of, the influential British group The The, Johnson has trains in what he describes as "my ancestral DNA", his great-grandfather Edward Johnson's name appearing on the memorial plaque at London's Liverpool Street station to the Great Eastern Railway employees who lost their lives during the First World War. Writing The The's critically acclaimed 1986 album *Infected*, Johnson had the building blocks of a song that was perfect for another painful train analogy.

"The 'Slow Train To Dawn' is simply a metaphor for a long, sleepless night," says Johnson. "We've all had them, where time slows down and we slip into that strange space between day and night, tossing, turning, wrestling between sleeping and waking." As for what was causing his state of sleeplessness? "It's about infidelity and lies," he adds. "In the case of this song, it's about male infidelity. The protagonist is conflicted as he still has feelings for his partner, feelings of companionship, friendship, security, yet he just cannot resist straying – '*I'm just another western guy with desires that I can't satisfy*'. Due to the feelings of guilt and inner conflict though he twists things against her as he attempts to justify his unjustifiable behaviour – '*making it easy upon myself by making it hard on you*'."

Johnson wrote the song for himself to sing as a duet with a female singer, the lyrics taking the form of dialogue between a couple sparring over the man's betrayal. The subject matter required a woman who came across as hurt and confused yet feisty. Neneh Cherry, then a relatively unknown Swedish-born singer and rapper, got the job after an alcohol-fuelled meeting between the pair at Johnson's home.

"I had enjoyed her work on [the band] Float Up CP and arranged to meet her," he recalls. "She visited my flat, we got on very well, in fact we got roaring drunk together on vodka and upon leaving my place I think she fell halfway down the stairs, all the while laughing. She was a pleasure to work with, a lovely person full of enthusiasm and talent."

Cherry's voice helped make "Slow Train To Dawn" work as a song while her enthusiasm extended to a memorable performance in the accompanying video while tied to a real-life railway line, something we will return to in the next chapter. The chemistry between the pair and the somewhat steamy video led some to assume, given the song's subject matter, that Cherry could well be the real life source of Johnson's infidelity. The assumption was wrong – the song came before they had even met – but Johnson admits "Slow Train To Dawn" was inspired by "personal experience."

"Slow Train To Dawn" was something of a rarity when it came to *Infected*, a song about sexual tensions and desires from an album dominated by the politics of the 1980s. Released at the apex of Conservative Prime Minister Margaret Thatcher's free-market years, *Infected* questioned the direction in which Britain was being taken and its all-too cosy relationship with Ronald Reagan's America. Johnson genuinely believed, and he was far from alone, that the UK was in danger of becoming the 51st state of the USA, an opinion formed by questionable decisions such as allowing American nuclear weapons to be based on British soil at RAF Greenham Common in Berkshire (even as the album was being recorded, Reagan gave the go-ahead for an air-strike on Libya with some planes taking off from bases in the UK). The word "nuclear" didn't actually feature in the album's lyrics, yet in songs such as "Sweet Bird Of Truth", sung from the perspective of a dying US airman flying his bomber back from a Middle Eastern raid, it hung over it in much the same way as radioactive particles from the defective Chernobyl nuclear power plant (which had exploded in April 1986) permeated the air above Europe.

Ever since 1956, Britain had been developing its own nuclear energy, building a number of power stations at locations such as Dungeness on the Kent coast and Trawsfynydd in North Wales. During the early 1960s, containers known as flasks were introduced to transport nuclear material by rail from these power stations to the British Nuclear Fuels reprocessing plant near the town of Sellafield in Cumbria. For years, the British public seemed to quietly tolerate the nuclear freights which ran along the same tracks as passenger trains, often through built-up areas. Every so often people would ask questions and a Member of Parliament, just to show

how safe the flasks were, would set up a photo opportunity of him or her kicking one. But that was about as combative as things got.

In the 1980s, with Britain at odds with itself over everything from the future of the mining industry to events at Greenham Common, that changed. Well-organised local pressure groups, in tandem with organisations such as Greenpeace, started asking serious questions about the safety of these trains and whether they should be running past the end of people's gardens. In July 1984, the powers that be, keen to allay concerns, staged a deliberate accident by smashing a driverless train travelling at 90 miles an hour into a flask filled with water placed across a railway line in Leicestershire. The flask withstood the hit but a sceptical public remained unconvinced. The horror that was Chernobyl and the subsequent soul-searching over the safety of the entire nuclear industry meant they had every right to continue asking questions.

"I used to live in Finsbury Park in north London and I got to hear about this nuclear train that went all the way from Cumbria down to Kent pretty much past my house, and it did so in the middle of the night," says Paul Simmonds of The Men They Couldn't Hang. "There was this graffiti on a wall in a cutting nearby which read 'Death train comes at midnight'. CND [the Campaign For Nuclear Disarmament] were very prominent at that time so I did a bit of research and saw that the route of this train took it through so many built up areas. And it did it in the dark, out of sight and out of mind with no fanfare. I found that rather scary."

On the other side of London, Tim Smith – better known as TV Smith, one-time lead singer with punk band The Adverts who had since embarked on a solo career – heard about another nuclear train which ran close to his home in Shepherd's Bush. "There had been a lot of talk about these trains taking nuclear fuel rods through populated areas," he says. "The big fear was 'What happens if there's an accident?' but of course the propaganda was "They're safe, they can't have accidents'. I thought 'How can you be so sure about that?' You've got terrorists, human error, any number of things that can happen. Are you absolutely sure that nothing can go wrong? I for one wasn't convinced."

Simmonds channelled his fear and outrage into the song "Midnight Train" charting the passage of one of these nuclear freights from the English Lake District through Lancashire, Nottinghamshire and London to the Kent coast, "*seven boxcars full of trouble*" heading for "*the end of the line*". Smith, however, decided to put a different spin on the subject in "Runaway Train Driver".

"I was driving along one day, next to this huge embankment which the railway runs along carrying these massive, huge, heavy and sometimes quite lethal trains," he says. "Right at the bottom of this embankment was a petrol station. I thought 'OK, even allowing for the fact that there might be a derailment or some kind of accident. What happens if the train driver, because he's pissed off at the world, just decides to wreck his train or deliberately make an error?' You can make these trains as safe as you like, but you can't legislate for something like that. I wanted to raise awareness into this. Songs about trains are always great, but I wanted to make people aware that there are some trains out there that aren't necessarily great. Far from it. This was a plausible scenario. It could happen."

It could but, at the time of writing, it hasn't. The trains continue to run, yet over the intervening years the issue has, to a degree, slipped off the radar. Pressure groups still exist, among them the Nuclear Trains Action Group run from an office only a short walk from Simmonds' old home in Finsbury Park, but the safety records of such trains and the precautions taken surrounding them have been robust.

"Runaway Train Driver" retains its power to move people, albeit not always in the way that TV Smith originally intended. His concerts have been known to feature congas of people who form their very own trains as the song strikes up. "When you're in an environment where there is this regular beat going on it can become very infectious," says Smith by way of absolution. "I think maybe that's where the conga comes from. But underneath the message remains the same. Unfortunately, we live in a dangerous world. If you were a terrorist, wouldn't you think one of those trains was an easy target? God forbid it ever happens, but it's more than just a possibility."

10

RAIN, STEAM AND SPEED

Dawn breaks over the small Swedish town of Tumba. At the local railway station a beautiful blonde haired woman waits for the train that will take her to work in nearby Stockholm. She catches the eye of a fellow commuter, a male. The pair make sure they board the same carriage where some increasingly seductive smiles are traded as the train makes its way through the early morning light over the majestic spans of the city's Årstabron Bridge. The pair embark on an intense relationship which transforms the woman's previously mundane existence into something meaningful where she doesn't have to rely on watching episodes of the television show *Dallas* for entertainment. No matter where this relationship is heading, she knows her life will never be the same again.

Long before moody Scandinavian noir became cool there was the video to "The Day Before You Came", the last song ever recorded by Abba back in August 1982. Now regarded as something of a mislaid classic, the single bombed in the UK and many other countries where audiences had abandoned the group and moved on to the likes of Duran Duran, Spandau Ballet and Culture Club. The woman in the video was Agnetha Fältskog, the reluctant star whose voice – and looks – played such a prominent part in Abba's success story, the role of her love interest going to the suave Swedish actor Jonas Bergström. The problem was that in 1982 the record buying masses didn't want videos of atmospheric Scandinavian dawns promoting sensual songs from a band that represented the 1970s, no matter how attractive the leads. They wanted Simon Le Bon on a yacht, Spandau bassist Martin Kemp in soft focus and Boy George pouting down the camera lens. Ultravox, who were at least current, had already bagged the moody step with their atmospheric video for "Vienna". Abba simply didn't fit in anymore. At least not at that moment in time.

106

When the first rays of the Abba renaissance began to shine down on the world during the early nineties, the very same record buying public that had turned its back on the four Swedes seemed to realise *en masse* what they'd missed out on during the dying embers of the group's active career. These were people who since 1982 had left school, got jobs, had serious relationships, married, become parents and, in some cases, divorced. Songs such as "When All Is Said And Done" and "The Day Before You Came" now had relevance. Through the repackaging of the group's singles and videos, the latter song in particular started getting the sort of attention it had perhaps deserved all those years previously. More than a few commuters found themselves daydreaming of train carriages shared with an Agnetha Fältskog or a Jonas Bergström. Almost overnight, the song started topping people's lists of favourite Abba tracks. Those who had loved "The Day Before You Came" from the start mocked Johnny-come-lately fans in the same way that long suffering fans of a football club resent those who gravitate to the cause once success has been achieved. It was all slightly bizarre and yet, as far as the four members of Abba were concerned, sort of reassuring. Their recording career *had* finished on a high note after all.

Although "The Day Before You Came" failed to set the charts alight, the song's accompanying video didn't go unnoticed within the world of moving pictures. Videos, or promotional clips as they were widely known during the 1970s, had (with one or two glorious exceptions) tended to be tame affairs showing bands performing or miming along to songs. Then the MTV music channel came along. Suddenly videos became an increasingly important marketing tool meaning a different approach was required. Made by director Kjell Sundvall and cinematographer Kjell-Åke Andersson, the video to "The Day Before You Came" demonstrated what could be achieved on film inside a few minutes with a decent storyboard. Abba's star might have been on the wane but trains and railways, coupled to a happening band, were a director's wet dream when it came to eye-catching props and locations.

Musicians had been exploiting railway art and imagery to enhance both their credibility and creative output long before the arrival of promotional clips and the video age. Besides death, escape, hope, love, loss, mystery, romance, sex and all manner of human experiences and emotions, the railways also stood for integrity and the kind of working class/blue collar fibre that couldn't be bought. Woody Guthrie, Jimmie Rodgers and Johnny Cash were all keen to rubber stamp their humble beginnings and gritty credentials with publicity pictures of themselves sitting atop boxcars, strumming guitars on station platforms or standing beside the colossal wheels of steam locomotives. Recognising a good thing when they saw it, future generations simply fell in line.

One of the more iconic album covers of 1982, the same year as "The Day Before You Came", showed all four members of The Clash hunched beside a railway track in Thailand where the band were touring. The picture, taken by the English rock photographer Pennie Smith and used on the front of *Combat Rock*, has a lawless air about it almost as if they intend to rob the next train that comes their way. Singer Joe Strummer is positioned behind the other three with his right hand covering the right side of his face, something conspiracy theorists inevitably probed for hidden significance. Strummer later told writer Chris Salewicz that he'd simply been trying to focus his short-sighted eyes, but the suspicion remains that the shot held clues about the mindset of the group at that time (The Clash would never surpass the commercial high water mark of *Combat Rock*, the sacking of drummer Nicky "Topper" Headon in the midst of his heroin addiction just days after the album's release precipitating their demise).

As The Clash, like Abba before them, began to implode so a band arrived on the British pop scene who were as political and outspoken in their own way as the former had been under Strummer's vocal tutelage. Bronski Beat were an openly gay three-piece synth group. Their songs, with lyrics delivered in the unmistakable falsetto of lead singer Jimmy Somerville, reflected this, commenting on issues that until 1984 had rarely, if ever, been addressed so openly in mainstream music. Signed by London Records having performed only a handful of live gigs, the band's debut album *The Age Of Consent* listed on the record's inner sleeve the varying ages for consensual gay sex in different countries around the world (the age of consent for sexual acts in Britain at the time was 21, compared to 16 for heterosexual acts, many countries having far more liberal laws on gay sex than the UK). It sold well on the back of a breakthrough single which, in the same vein as "Wuthering Heights" by Kate Bush or Kraftwerk's "Autobahn", sounded unlike anything that had gone before it.

"Smalltown Boy" tells the story of a young gay man who deserts his family and home town. The physical and verbal abuse that comes with his sexual persuasion has reached a tipping point, so he leaves one morning with all his possessions crammed inside a small black case. His mode of escape? The tried and tested train. For the video, London Records brought in Bernard Rose who had an impressive track record directing mini-films to accompany singles by UB40 and, most notably, Frankie Goes To Hollywood, arguably the hottest group in Britain during 1984. Rose created a visual subplot to complement the lyrics in which the young man, played by Somerville, tries befriending a male diver at a swimming pool. The move backfires when the diver and his homophobic friends beat him up. He is returned to his family home by a policeman, but enough is enough. The teenager makes for the railway station and buys a train ticket from the small town to the big city where his sexuality won't be such an issue.

"I was approached because I had just made a Frankie Goes To Hollywood video for their song 'Relax', and so I was the king of gay videos at that moment in history," laughs Rose, now a successful film director. "It was the record company rather than the band who wanted me because they thought it would be more commercial if I did it. That was my understanding anyway. They were interested style-wise in the work I'd done with UB40 which was more social-realist videos like little movies. The song, I guess, was semi-autobiographical about Jimmy Somerville. He was from Glasgow and had come to London, although in the video he takes this little suburban train which is unlike anything that would take you from Glasgow to London! A lot of what was done with the video was under the aegis of a man who was running London Records at the time called Colin Bell. Colin was very supportive of doing something that was (a) openly gay, and (b) politicised, because that was their [the record company's] thing. So that was very much the brief. The song is almost like a country and western song, even though it's a disco song. It has a Woody Guthrie thing going on. It has a very clear narrative and a very clear message, so in that sense it was a question of trying to put it across without being too illustrative. If the song and the pictures are too closely illustrative it becomes horrifically banal. There has to be a kind of counterpoint. So it was just a question of making what is really a very simple story about him being alienated in the vaguely northern or provincial surroundings that he's in and leaving and going to London."

Rose shot the video around London with the swimming pool scenes filmed in the eastern suburb of Hackney and the train parts at various locations on the railways running into the termini stations of Paddington and Marylebone. When screened during the summer of

1984 the finished article, in tandem with the song, was compelling. Young people, gay and heterosexual, had been running away to London for years and for all sorts of reasons, with trains often providing their escape route. Those who had made the journey found the video brought back memories, often extremely painful ones. For those that hadn't, but were considering bolting from their own small towns, it showed they were not alone.

"I think 'Smalltown Boy' is quite unusual for a music video," adds Rose. "At the time I was getting slightly bored with making music videos. I just wanted to make films. 'Smalltown Boy' really does function like a silent movie in that there are no shots of anybody performing the song at all. I used the band, and in particular Jimmy Somerville, but the rest of the cast are actors with the exception of the policeman who was actually played by Colin Bell himself. It's not really a video in the normal sense of the word. It's cut to the music, but not slavishly cut to it. It's not obsessively kind of bang on every beat. It was something you really had to watch from the beginning to the end, not just a piece of it. To understand it you had to see it all."

Rose was far from alone in wanting to make videos of real substance that amounted to mini-films. For several years, the musician and songwriter Robyn Hitchcock had been experiencing a recurring dream based around a railway journey through southern England. "It takes place somewhere between Winchester, Oxford, Reading and Basingstoke on the labyrinth of lines and capillaries and veins that used to go everywhere in the pre-Doctor Beeching days," says Hitchcock. "It's set on a Sunday in a 1930s style railway carriage which has a bar in it and old fashioned looking beer glasses. I'm not drinking, but I can see them. We go on this route between two very kind of medium places like Basingstoke and Reading. The summer is turning to winter, and it's all very vivid. Every year there's usually at least one afternoon where the weather is exactly like in my dream. It would be around the last week of October. It still looks like summer but the leaves are starting to go. It's the kind of atmosphere you might get in a classical painting where you have nymphs and satyrs and swains wandering around some ruined columns. If you put some 1930s railway carriages in there, then they would blend perfectly. It's a sort of idyllic world that doesn't really exist."

During either 1982 or 1983, he can't recall which, Hitchcock decided to turn his night time excursions of the mind into a song. Released in 1984 as the title track of his third solo album, "I Often Dream Of Trains" came with a video made in black and white of Hitchcock surrounded by trains on two very different railway lines, one fortunate enough to have escaped the sweeping cuts to Britain's railway network made during the 1960s and early 1970s, the other not so fortunate.

"We started off at Waterloo and filmed going down the main line to the south west of England through Weybridge and Woking to Basingstoke," Hitchcock recalls. "It's quite ironic in a way because it now looks so old fashioned. When I'm in the buffet car you can see a luncheon vouchers sticker. I've got a roll-up [cigarette]. There are windows you can open. If you look at the indicators at Waterloo station, they're the old fashioned ones that used to spin round. I also took a phone receiver with me. I thought 'This will be a fun prop. Imagine a phone on a train. That'll be a novel idea'. So I pull it out and you see me talking into the phone. What no one knew was that 20 years later everyone was going to be doing that on trains with mobile phones. It was an unwitting echo of what was to come."

From Basingstoke, Hitchcock and his lone cameraman boarded a bus in order to reach the Watercress Line in Hampshire, a heritage railway reopened in stages between 1977 and 1985, having initially been shut by British Rail in 1973. "There were loads of these old steam engines and carriages there dating back to the twenties and thirties waiting to be restored, so we filmed stuff of me walking among and through them," he recalls. "They were beautiful things which were old then, so must be positively ancient now, but are probably still running."

The final edit proved to be everything that Hitchcock hoped it would be – dreamy, comic, slightly surreal, the antithesis of all things new romantic. Today it also serves as a portal into a world that has long since disappeared. "It's interesting how lower key everything seemed to be back in the seventies and early eighties," adds Hitchcock. "Everything nowadays seems like it's had more salt and pepper put on it. Everything's full of additives to make it zing. The eighties is now seen as a time when a lot of that happened. Suddenly you had shoulder pads, digital reverb and fairy dust on everything. We were trying to make the opposite of whatever Spandau Ballet or Duran Duran were making in their videos. They were shoulder pads to the max. And I think we achieved that. I'm really glad we got to do it."

Hitchcock continues to perform "I Often Dream Of Trains" at the majority of his live shows despite having a vast back catalogue of other tracks to draw on. "That song has stuck there for ages," he admits. "It's part of my repertoire because I'm pleased with it and it's quite respected. People pick up on it for a variety of reasons." So does he still have the dream? "Oh yes. It's a fixed scenario that never changes, chugging round the Home Counties on a Sunday. That in itself is untrue to life because the weekends now mean engineering works. The chances are you'd get to Basingstoke and have to get a coach to Reading. There's nothing romantic about that at all."

Unlike, that is, the atmosphere preservationists strive to recreate on the dozens of heritage railways like the Watercress Line scattered throughout Britain. One of the longest and most popular of all is the Severn Valley Railway, a 16-mile stretch of line straddling the counties of Shropshire and Worcestershire which was originally closed to passenger and freight traffic in 1963. It was here that Matt Johnson came in 1986 to make the video for The The's single "Slow Train To Dawn". Directed by Tim Pope, the shoot resulted in probably the most visually stunning (not to mention daring) piece of railway video art ever made, starring Johnson alongside his co-lead singer Neneh Cherry and a 68-tonne steam locomotive celebrating its resurrection from the dead.

Let loose from British Rail's workshops at Swindon in 1955, 75069 – it only carried a number, never a name – was among the last steam locomotives ever built in the UK. One of 80 of its type (a BR Standard Class 4MT 4-6-0), it hauled passenger and freight trains mainly around southern England until September 1966 when it was withdrawn and carted off to a scrapyard in Barry, South Wales. There, 75069 sat gathering rust for six years before being saved and taken to the Severn Valley Railway to be restored, a job that due to its dilapidated state seemed to take forever. In 1985, it emerged reborn from the Railway's works at Bridgnorth. When Johnson and Pope arrived a few months later looking for a steam engine to appear in their video, the locomotive's size and excellent condition meant it passed the audition with flying colours.

The storyboard for the "Slow Train To Dawn" video goes something like this. Johnson is a railwayman in charge of a steam train barrelling down the line towards Neneh Cherry, sporting the smallest of dresses, who has her hands and legs tied to the track like some damsel in distress from a 1920s silent movie. Cherry manages to look vulnerable yet sultry while Johnson's face and clothes are covered in sweat and dirt (remember

– this is a song about male infidelity and lies). At one point, the action cuts to beneath the track where the couple face each other crouched inside an inspection pit used to maintain the underside of locomotives. As they trade lyrics, so the immense frame of 75069 rolls slowly over their heads, venting steam and dripping boiling water. It's intense, gripping and borderline dangerous especially with Cherry's braided hair literally in the firing line.

"Neneh was a real sport throughout, especially when allowing herself to be tied to the railway tracks," says Johnson who, by making the video, got to follow in the footsteps of his great-grandfather Edward Johnson, late of the Great Eastern Railway. "It was pretty damn cold as I remember and she only had a tiny dress on, but she didn't complain once. That was quite an experience being allowed to drive one of those trains. An abiding memory is just how filthy it was as my face soon became blackened by coal smoke, heat and steam. The noise too – the hissing, steaming, chugging, puffing. It was thrilling stuff."

"End Of The Line" by the Traveling Wilburys; "Back In The High Life Again" by Steve Winwood; "Pink Houses" by John Mellencamp; "Live Together" by Lisa Stansfield; "Breakthru" by Queen; "Fields Of Fire" by Big Country: all those songs plus many, many more came post-1982 accompanied by videos loaded with railway imagery. For sheer spectacle, Queen certainly deserve a big hand, all four members miming along to their 1989 single while being towed at speed through the English countryside on a wagon converted into a stage behind an ex-Great Western Railway steam locomotive sporting "MIRACLE EXPRESS" on its sides (*The Miracle* being the group's album of the moment). The video allegedly cost £300,000 to make, with the group insured for £2 million in the event of an accident. It's good, in an over-the-top Queen sort of way, but "Slow Train To Dawn" remains the train video to beat all train videos; brilliantly shot and oozing raw sexual and mechanical power. Watch it. You won't be disappointed.

Alas, in the music business trends have a habit of changing almost overnight. At some point around 1991 the kind of videos that directors such as Bernard Rose and Tim Pope liked to make were deemed obsolete. "What killed it dead was that somebody in marketing at these record companies decided that if you didn't see a band performing with their instruments, then people wouldn't believe they were a real band," says Rose. "This was the era, don't forget, of Milli Vanilli [whose two lead singers, Fab Morvan and Rob Pilatus, were memorably exposed as not having sung on the group's records]. The producer ruled supreme. And there were a lot of these bands who couldn't play their instruments. Back in 1984 it could have been an issue with Bronski Beat as they were not widely known at all. What were their instruments anyway? Of course they played on their songs, but now you had to prove that bands could actually play. Suddenly everything changed. You had to see them, their faces, and some instruments. There was no room for anything else."

The golden age of the video was over, and with it went the sort of storyboards where trains and their surroundings took centre stage. But the desire to use railway imagery for other promotional purposes continued. When Bob Seger was mulling over potential album covers for his 1994 *Greatest Hits*, he went for a shot of himself standing alone astride a railway track, guitar slung across his waist, the line bending away into the distance behind him towards who knows where. Post-drug addiction and a spell in prison, the American singer and songwriter Steve Earle posed for pictures of himself leaning against old passenger carriages and freight wagons in a yard in Nashville, the subliminal message from artist to fan being "I'm back on track". Journalists receiving review copies of Metallica's 1996 album *Load* found it came with promotional stills of the band standing in an empty, decaying railroad yard. The train tracks might have seen better days but, judging by the look of them, here was a group that could be relied on to do the business in an uncertain world.

Rather than putting themselves on the cover of their single "Rain, Steam & Speed", The Men They Couldn't Hang chose a painting of a British Coronation class steam locomotive hauling a passenger train past a group of men busy maintaining the tracks. The song itself had been inspired by another piece of railway-related art. In 1844, *Rain, Steam And Speed – The Great Western Railway* by J. M. W. Turner went on display for the first time at the Royal Academy in London. Long regarded as an iconic piece of work by an artistic genius, the oil painting shows a steam train speeding out of the gloom across what is widely believed to be Maidenhead Railway Bridge on the Great Western Railway. "The world has never seen anything like this picture," remarked the contemporary critic William Thackeray at the time, and you can see why he said it. The painting manages to unite water, land and sky while encapsulating much of what was new about Britain in 1844 – a steam locomotive, travelling on a railway linking two of England's most important cities – London and Bristol – crossing a formidable piece of modern architecture. Is it nature and technology in harmony or, as some have suggested, technology challenging nature? Nobody really knows, an imponderable that only adds to the painting's allure.

Inspired by the painting and the historical period that it represents, Paul Simmonds of The Men They Couldn't Hang set to work on a song that became "Rain, Steam & Speed" from the band's 1989 album *Silver Town*. "It's about the explosion of railway building in this country and the people who came from Ireland and all over to do the work," he says. "I know it mentions [Isambard Kingdom] Brunel who built the Great Western Railway and the bridge over which the train is travelling in the picture, but it's not just about him. These guys worked in the most dangerous of conditions using stuff like dynamite and so many of them died and were just buried alongside where they'd been working. If they were lucky they ended up in a graveyard but many of them had to make do with unmarked graves. It was brutal but what they achieved was staggering. At the time I wrote the song they were busy building the Channel Tunnel, so that was also going on in the back of my mind. It's my, our, tribute to those men who built the railways and specifically those men who gave their lives doing so."

Despite boasting a large and loyal following, The Men They Couldn't Hang never achieved anything like the commercial success of, say, their British contemporaries Blur. There is every chance, however, that someone at Blur's record company remembered the cover of "Rain, Steam & Speed" when the time came to choose the artwork for the band's second long player. After all, what better way of accentuating the *Modern Life Is Rubbish* slogan than having a picture of Mallard, the fastest steam engine in the world and a symbol of great British design and engineering, on the front of your album?

In 1984, the artist Paul Gribble (then living in Bristol) was asked by his licensing agent, Michael Woodward, if he would be interested in producing a picture of the legendary Mallard for a greetings card. It was, in all honesty, a no-brainer. Gribble, a lover of trains, had worked on many commissions depicting railway scenes from around the world and was also close friends with Oswald Stevens Nock, better known as O. S. Nock, one of Britain's foremost rail historians. Gribble delivered a striking oil painting of the big blue locomotive in full flight, a throwback to 3 July 1938 when Mallard set a world speed record for steam engines of

125.88 miles per hour on the East Coast Main Line south of the English market town of Grantham. The company behind the commission, Royal Publishing, were more than happy with Gribble's work and paid to reproduce the painting on a greetings card which sold well for several years. "It always seemed to be very popular, but especially during the early nineties," recalls Jenny Gribble, Paul's wife.

In early 1993, Woodward took a call from someone at either Food Records or Parlophone (Blur were signed to Food which had close associations with the latter; exactly who the caller was nobody seems able to remember). Gribble's painting of Mallard (called simply *Mallard*) was wanted for the front cover of Blur's forthcoming album *Modern Life Is Rubbish*. Gribble gave his consent, a fee was agreed, and the artist thought little more about it... until later in the year that is, when word filtered through to Paul and his wife about the hugely positive response to the album and its cover. At the time, Blur were searching for a career reboot having slipped from view in the wake of their moderately successful debut album *Leisure*. Released in May 1993, *Modern Life Is Rubbish* was an unmissable presence in UK record shops and many people (this particular author included) bought it on the strength of the cover combined with the album's strong opening single "For Tomorrow". Great song, great cover design, great train – how could you not be seduced?

Jenny Gribble cites two incidents soon after the album's release which underlined the new-found fame that *Mallard*, and by association her husband, was enjoying. Strolling through Bristol city centre, the couple came across the local branch of the HMV record chain. There, in the window, was a floor to ceiling display plugging *Modern Life Is Rubbish* complete with a colossal cut-out of Paul's picture standing just inside the door. "It was like walking into his own painting," says Jenny of the memory. A few weeks later, Paul dropped by the school where his son taught to give him a lift from work. Walking from the car towards the reception area, he was suddenly besieged by dozens of children all wanting to know about *Mallard* and what it was like being a "famous" painter. "Street cred at last!" Paul remembers thinking.

Blur's career never looked back after *Modern Life Is Rubbish* and a new generation went away to discover Mallard for themselves. Now living with Jenny in Somerset, Paul Gribble continues to be fascinated by trains and music, albeit jazz rather than Britpop. A one-time trumpeter in various jazz groups around Bristol, he is someone who appreciates the important role that railways have played in that musical genre, taking the time to list several tracks – "Take The A Train", "Happy-Go-Lucky Local" and "Night Train" among them – which have become standard numbers. He remains "delighted" that Blur used "Mallard" for the cover of *Modern Life Is Rubbish* as "railways from an early age was, and still is, a passion of mine."

▓▓▓▓▓▓▓▓▓▓▓

The release of *Modern Life Is Rubbish* came, aptly, at a time when modern life was on the cusp of massive changes that would affect the way mankind communicates and shares information. Between 1993 and 2000, millions of us would buy a mobile phone for the first time, get an e-mail address for the first time, visit a website for the first time and, as a result, start changing our behaviour patterns. Thanks to the internet, substantial amounts of railway-related art commissioned by the music business – from promotional photographs of Woody Guthrie bumming a ride, to Bernard Rose's video for "Smalltown Boy" – became readily available at the touch of a button. Just about every band or solo act of any substance, not to mention plenty of songwriters, now have a website through which to channel information and assert their image by way of quality controlled still photography or moving pictures. Musicians are no longer at the mercy of journalists, staff-photographers or mean sub-editors. If they want the world to see a picture of them looking pensive while stood beside a railway track, then all they have to do is stick it on their website for everyone to see.

"When we were working on our latest website we went on the internet looking for pictures of railroad tracks, and man we just found these beautiful, gorgeous photographs of railroad tracks with sunsets and mountains and valleys and streams and rivers in them," says Don Brewer of Grand Funk Railroad. "They all had this romantic feel to them which was just what we wanted. You look at them and you get that feeling of getting on a train and disappearing, or getting on a train and looking for adventure and just going and going and going. It's like sitting on a beach that goes on forever. It makes your mind wander. That's what you do when you look down a desolate stretch of railroad track. You wonder what could be up ahead. Hopefully anyone who looks at our website will also think like that. You wonder what's up ahead for the band, and maybe you might start to thinking what's up ahead for yourself."

In recent years the music industry has also witnessed something of a revival when it comes to videos or mini-films featuring trains. Today musicians make more money out of touring than selling their music. That means more time and effort goes into making the live experience something to remember for the fan – hordes of dancers, dazzling pyrotechnics, lorry loads of merchandise; you get the picture. The gradual ramping up of the visuals has resulted in musicians utilising back projections of films which play throughout concerts. Just as Johnny Cash often performed in front of screens depicting trains at his shows, so the 21st century's live acts have taken to screening the kind of videos/films that Bernard Rose once made while playing their setlists. Trains and railways, they have come to realise, make for good visuals.

But there's a catch – good visuals can overshadow what a band does onstage. When The Who played London's Roundhouse in 2006 (itself a former railway locomotive shed) they performed the song "Who Are You" in front of three large screens each relaying the famous black-and-white film, taken from the front cab and speeded up, of a train travelling the 50 or so miles from London's Victoria station to Brighton in just four minutes. Despite Pete Townshend giving it everything with his trademark windmill guitar action, there were considerably more heads watching the screens than the band. Contrast that with the Pet Shop Boys who, for several years, have used footage shot at London's King's Cross station during 1987 by the late Derek Jarman to accompany live performances of their song "King's Cross". The track itself was written by singer Neil Tennant as a metaphor for Britain in the late 1980s, a time when King's Cross was a depressed, crime-ridden area, and the UK was increasingly polarised under Margaret Thatcher's leadership. Jarman's grainy black and white images of trains delivering optimistic people into a landscape where there is little optimism fits perfectly with Tennant's delivery of a haunting, thought-provoking song.

Haunting, thought-provoking; words that could equally apply to one video from 1993 which did manage to buck the Milli Vanilli "must-show-bands-playing-their-instruments" production trend. In fact, it bucked virtually every trend going in the most startling of ways. When spliced with the toxic subject matter of the single it was made to promote, you could argue that "Runaway Train" by Soul Asylum is the most powerful train song of all time.

11

RUNAWAY TRAIN

Ask someone to name a train song off the top of their head and they will probably come back at you with "Mystery Train", "Last Train To Clarksville", "Midnight Train To Georgia" or one of around 20 truly iconic tracks that have entered the collective trans-Atlantic post-war consciousness. The answer is unlikely to be "Runaway Train" by Soul Asylum, unless the person happened to be in their teens or twenties during the mid-1990s with a taste for American alternative rock. In which case, they just might tell you there's no train song out there capable of holding a candle to "Runaway Train".

Soul Asylum were a band formed in Minneapolis during 1981. Originally known by the name Loud Fast Rules, they toured hard for years building up a loyal following in and around their native city. Despite recording five albums during the eighties (including two while on A&M Records) and supporting such illustrious names as Hüsker Dü, that was about as good as it got. By 1990 Soul Asylum were broke, low on morale and close to disbanding with their main creative force, lead vocalist and songwriter Dave Pirner, suffering from hearing problems. Ironically it would be the band's softer approach, adopted as a coping mechanism in light of Pirner's health issues, that would give them the big break – and the big fat hit single – they so craved.

"I'd had this tune in my head for a while, but it was going nowhere lyrically," says Pirner. "At the time I'd gone through a real personal transformation. I was having, more or less, a nervous breakdown because I thought I was losing my hearing. I'd be calling my friend in New York, who was part of my music life, at three or four in the morning and was just totally hysterical because I thought 'That's it man, I'm going deaf'. It was during that time that I switched to the acoustic guitar and, at some point within that period of soul searching, the lyrics [to 'Runaway Train'] came to me in an evening.

"I had this body of around 25 songs that I had made in retreat from the loud electric scenario that we'd been practising. I'd been discovering Woody Guthrie and Johnny Cash – but specifically Woody Guthrie – and one night I went to my local punk club in Minneapolis and taught these guys in a local punk band a couple of Woody Guthrie songs. We played them on stage and it was really, really different to anything that was happening in the club at that time. Everyone was sort of shocked that they could play the songs. And I had a kind of revelation – we're *all* playing folk music! It's all the same. The music is similar. We're playing the same chord progressions and singing about a lot of the same things. That picked up a thread that had been going through my entire life, right back to watching *Casey Jones* on television as a kid. I had loved that show. It had a big effect on me, the kind of things that he [Casey] got up to, this train engineer who was like a hero. I got thinking about that and the model train that I'd had as a kid passed down from my father, and from my grandpa to him sort of thing. It's still around, this old Lionel train. All of that came together – my hearing, Woody Guthrie, *Casey Jones*, that model train. And at last I had the words to go with this tune I'd been carrying."

Soul Asylum's new semi-acoustic approach saw them picked up by Columbia Records and the band set to work recording some of the songs that Pirner had assembled during his retreat from the electric guitar. In October 1992, the album *Grave Dancers Union* went on sale. By the start of 1993, Soul Asylum's public profile was such that they were called upon to perform at the first inauguration of US President Bill Clinton. However, it wasn't until June that "Runaway Train" was released. The lyrics reflected the extent of Pirner's inner torment over his hearing problems. Sung from the heart, it's the story of a man in turmoil riding a runaway train of the mind. The tale was Pirner's but, and here lay the song's universal appeal, it could easily have applied to anyone who has ever felt like running away from a challenging situation. Which is where the video came into its own.

"The director of the video was a British guy called Tony Kaye who went on to make movies like *American History X* with Edward Norton in it," says Pirner. "He was just brilliant. He said to me 'Milk cartons'. I went 'What?' And he goes 'Milk cartons – we'll put kids in the video, like you get pictures of missing kids on milk cartons'. He was making a word association with the word runaway. He wanted to put pictures of missing kids in the video. I thought 'That's pretty interesting. Yeah, let's really try and find them, let's fucking do it!' That was Tony's idea. From that point on, the song sort of took a new angle. When the video was added to it, well, it just blew me away. And everybody else from what I can gather."

Rather than just one video, Kaye made several versions to be screened in different countries. All featured the band playing the song interwoven with a series of harrowing film exerts; a child witnessing his grandfather assaulting his grandmother, a girl being dragged into a van by a gang where she's raped and beaten, a distraught mother chasing after an older woman who has snatched her baby from a stroller. These were interspersed with still photographs of real life missing children and young people, followed by their full names in capital letters and the year of their disappearance. Three different versions were made: for the USA: one for the UK; one for Australia and so on, each containing people reported missing in that particular country. They made for uncomfortable viewing, a little too uncomfortable for some. 'If you have seen one of these kids, or you are one of them, please call this number' Pirner told viewers at the end of each video prior to a telephone number (which changed from country to country) appearing on screen. Except that MTV, worried viewers might confuse the video with a public service announcement, took the decision to cut this out. Other channels were, however, brave enough to show the videos in their entirety.

"Runaway Train" was always likely to be a hit record. With the video in its corner, the song became something else entirely. Released inside a sleeve showing a distorted picture of an electric train on the cover, the single sold in huge quantities around the world and won Best Rock Song at the 1994 Grammy Awards (where, ironically, the video lost out to Peter Gabriel's "Steam" in which the singer's face is superimposed onto the front of a steam locomotive). Pirner had, at the time he wrote the song, been in mourning for his own lost innocence – being a kid, playing with a toy train, watching episodes of *Casey Jones*, all the happy things that came prior to adulthood and the anguish caused by his hearing problems. The video served as a reminder that there were, and indeed still are, plenty of children and young people out there dealing with infinitely worse situations.

Sadly, and perhaps inevitably, several of the individual stories behind the people featured in the videos to "Runaway Train" had unhappy endings. Kaye has claimed that 26 of the missing children were subsequently found alive. Vicky Hamilton and Dinah McNicol, who both appeared in the UK version of the video, weren't so fortunate. Vicky, 15, was last seen in

February 1991 as she waited to catch a bus in Bathgate, Scotland. Dinah, an 18-year-old student from Essex, hitch-hiked with a male friend from a music festival in Hampshire during August 1991. The male friend was dropped off at Junction 8 of the M25 motorway near the town of Reigate, while Dinah remained in the car with the driver. She was never seen again. In 2007, the remains of both girls were discovered buried in the back garden of a house in Margate, Kent. Peter Tobin, a former resident who had previously served 10 years in prison for a double rape committed in 1993, was subsequently convicted of their murders together with the rape and murder of Angelika Kluk, a 23-year-old student from Poland visiting Glasgow. The Australian video included a number of foreign backpackers reported missing. Some turned out to have been victims of Ivan Milat, dubbed the "Backpacker Murderer", who was given seven life sentences for murder at his trial in 1996. As Soul Asylum guitarist Dan Murphy has since admitted, "Some weren't the best scenarios."

Nevertheless, Pirner has no regrets over the band's decision to go along with Kaye's flash of inspiration for the video. "We challenged what can be done with a music video in ways that were great," he says. "I think we broke a boundary. I have a kid. You imagine someone taking them. It's one of the most fucked up things ever. It [the video] is still with me. It continues to have a profound effect on me because I've done research into missing kids now I'm a dad, and it's so disturbing. Some, of course, don't want to be found. They've run away from a bad situation and are trying to put things right elsewhere. But some are also taken against their will. It's the kind of subject that if you think about too much, it will completely fuck your mind up."

On the plus side, Pirner's hearing has steadily improved. At the time of writing, Soul Asylum remain a going concern, "Runaway Train" being what might be described as Pirner's pension plan. His interest in railroads also continues, especially since re-locating to New Orleans just as the nineties gave way to the noughties.

"I really look forward to the day when we can have more passenger trains in America," he says. "I just think it's inevitable, you know, a more eco-friendly way of moving people around. Since I've come down here [New Orleans], you get wrapped up in the majesty of the Mississippi River and of jazz music – and how jazz helped transform rock music – and you realise how much the trains had to do with that movement of people getting around America when all this music was born. When I first started coming to New Orleans seriously, like when I wasn't just coming through with the band, I'd take that train down from Minneapolis and it's the same train that Arlo Guthrie sings about [in 'City Of New Orleans']. It's so romantic, the kind of real fun experience that everyone should have at least once. It's movement; it's expansion; it's happy – but there's also something sad about it too, all the people coming and going, saying goodbye to each other, this big huge thing that maybe we've taken for granted too long. It's part of America. It's our soul. We gotta keep it that way."

12

THAT'S WHAT
I LIKE

Cast your mind back to Chapter 2. Ian Naisbitt, in the days before he became a sought after session drummer, is busy driving lorries for Edwin Shirley Trucking, the first dedicated rock 'n' roll haulage firm in Europe. It's 1975 and Johnny Cash is on tour. During their down time, the man in black and Naisbitt have been discussing trains. Naisbitt tells Cash all about growing up in Stockton, north east England, within earshot of the steam locomotive engine sheds, and how his father would take him to watch trains at the nearby North Shore signal box – the very same signal box that Naisbitt, on leaving school aged 15 with zero qualifications, would get his first proper job working as a cabin boy. "I'd have done it for nothing," he says. Cash smiles and nods in agreement. Naisbitt talks about his favourite British trains and Cash comes back at him with the best America has to offer. He knows a lot about railroads, and then some. In fact, it strikes Naisbitt that Cash could almost be British, such is the wealth of his knowledge. Naisbitt doesn't say this but, on reflection, he wishes he had as it was intended as a compliment. Because nobody does trains quite like the British.

That is in no way intended as a slight to America where railroads are in the DNA; the way they opened up the entire country back in the 19th century, the vast number of families whose livelihoods have depended on them, the important role played by railroads in the emancipation of the people. But when it comes to the actual trains themselves – where they were built, what names and numbers they carry, how many miles a particular engine has travelled (and at what speed), when they were withdrawn – then Britain is in a league of its own. Americans appreciate trains and what they stand for. In Britain, it's a passion bordering on the obsessive. People write down the numbers of trains, take their pictures, spend large amounts of money travelling behind specific locomotives. Or at least they used to. American kids have never stood on bridges armed with pens and notebooks waiting to write down the number of the engine pulling the Empire Builder from Chicago to Portland and Seattle. That, as any one of the many railway enthusiasts and ex-trainspotters ensconced within the UK music industry will tell you, is something the British have a virtual monopoly on.

Within months of finishing work on Johnny Cash's tour, Naisbitt had quit his truck driving job and started session drumming for a living. By 1978 he was part of Chris Rea's regular band playing live and in the studio. One day between takes, he and Rea fell into conversation about trains, or rather one particular type of train – Deltics. Designed during the late 1950s and introduced onto British Railways during 1961 and 1962, the Deltics were the fastest diesel locomotives in the world at the time, built for hauling express passenger trains along the East Coast Main Line between London, Leeds, Newcastle and Edinburgh. Aesthetically stunning, they also sounded terrific. Imagine an E-Type Jaguar crossed with a Lancaster bomber; enough, in other words, to make the hairs on the back of your neck stand tall.

"I was telling him about Deltics and in particular how powerful they were," Naisbitt told me during the early stages of my research for this book. "He was a good listener, Chris, and I'm always full of talking. I told him 'You need to hear them'. Chris was well into his Ferraris and that, but I said 'No, you need to hear a Deltic start up mate. That'll blow a Ferrari away'. They had the noise, the power, the speed, everything. They were just marvellous, unlike anything that had gone before or indeed since, and exactly the kind of reason why people fall in love with trains. That was the beginning of how 'Deltics' came about."

"Deltics" was a song from Rea's second album, overseen by Elton John's producer Gus Dudgeon, which also ended up being called *Deltics*. The track is a rousing salute, featuring Rea's gravelly voice and distinctive guitar sound, to iconic trains that travelled fast – the stainless steel American Burlington Zephyr streamliners built in the 1930s, the A3 and A4 steam engines that predated the Deltics on Britain's East Coast Main Line, and of course the Deltics themselves.

"We got it in one take," recalled Naisbitt who, instead of using a click track to keep time, always drummed to the rhythms secreted inside his head by years of listening to and watching trains. "I remember that we were going to have a picture of a Deltic on the cover of the album as well. We'd been to the Science Museum where the prototype Deltic was and taken a load of great pictures of it, but the record company didn't like them. They didn't want a picture of a diesel locomotive on the front, so it ended up being one of Chris walking on the beach at Saltburn. It's a nice shot and one that a lot of people are familiar with now, so I suppose it served a purpose in that it helped raise Chris' profile. But I still think a Deltic would have been better!"

For three decades the prototype Deltic, withdrawn from service in 1961 after six years of trials, was one of the main attractions inside London's Science Museum (in 1993 it became the property of the National Railway Museum at York). Its immense frame and sky blue livery meant you simply couldn't miss the thing. "The first time I ever went to the Science Museum was as a 10-year-old," recalls Andy McCluskey of OMD. "I saw the blue Deltic diesel... and that was it. A personal love affair of mine started at that moment. It was blue but it also had these cream flashing chevrons on the front. It looked staggering, very American with all the curves, but engineered in Britain. I've always had a soft spot for machinery but in particular for that Deltic diesel."

In 2013, OMD's twelfth studio album, *English Electric*, was released. The title was a nod in two different directions – not only are OMD regarded as being an integral part of the synth sound from the early 1980s, but English Electric was also the name of the company that built the Deltics. "We're English, and we were an electric band – still are," says McCluskey. "That's the analogy. But it's actually more about that love affair of mine with the big blue Deltic which has been there ever since I was 10. I don't think that will ever go away."

The success of the prototype Deltic saw English Electric commissioned to build 22 production models which were called after famous racehorses or army regiments based in England and Scotland – Ballymoss, The Green Howards, Pinza, Gordon Highlander, St Paddy, The Royal Northumberland Fusiliers, Crepello – names that embodied speed and a sense of history. There are those who will tell you that Britain's love affair with the railways, and in particular trainspotting as a hobby, began to wane with the final withdrawal of steam locomotives in 1968. Others point to the beginning of 1982 when the Deltics bit the dust. On 2 January that year, Tulyar hauled a special farewell train from London's Kings Cross station to Edinburgh, with Royal Scots Grey returning the 700 people lucky enough to get tickets back to the English capital the same evening. Thousands upon thousands of people lined the route to watch the train go by, while ITV's national news covered both its departure and return, presenter Jon Snow giving a wry smile at the sight of grown men in tears pressing their hands (and in one extreme case lips) against the side of the locomotive.

"The day the music died," is how Naisbitt described 2 January 1982. Well not quite. Six of the 22 production Deltics were later saved from the cutter's torch by groups of rail enthusiasts such as the Deltic Preservation Society, of which Ian Naisbitt was a proud member right up until his death in February 2014 following a long illness. And so the music does live on, albeit on a more intermittent basis and usually in the retirement home setting of a volunteer-run heritage railway.

▬▬▬▬▬▬▬

While the demise of steam and the Deltics certainly hammered plenty of nails into the trainspotting coffin, a sizeable army from across the UK continued with the pastime throughout the eighties and into the 1990s. Among the foot soldiers was Joseph Porter, driving force behind the rock band Blyth Power, whose incessant touring made them the darlings of the *New Musical Express* weekly gig guide for many years.

"For me, the railways came before the music," says Porter. "I started going spotting with my brother in Somerset. That was during the seventies, although I probably did most of my 'hard core' following during the eighties and nineties. You'd go away to all the roughest places in these towns to see trains with all your expensive photographic equipment, places like Teesside and Immingham. We must have been absolutely mad. Just sitting targets. Then you would go home and write your notes up, and that's where the music started coming in. You'd get back, put the radio on, write up your notes, and listen to music. Every time I hear 'Sugar Baby Love' I think of Crewe station in the dark with the floodlights shining down on the depot. That for me is the link, the childhood association between trains and music."

That childhood association spawned many a Blyth Power song loaded with railway imagery and references. "There's one called 'Signalman White' which is essentially a love song about a girl not phoning you back. It's based on Charles Dickens' *The Signal-Man* and is about this guy working in a signal box who keeps on getting this phone call coming through. That's one I'm really pleased with because it's got specific technical railway references in it. It's not just 'Oh, it's a train and the whistle goes whoo-whoo'. Most train songs that I hear, the people behind them are writing about an emotion, the romance, not the actual railway. They don't use terminology. A lot of people when they think about trains might think of the 'Flying Scotsman'. For me, the 'Flying Scotsman' is the Paul McCartney of trains; this old thing that's a national treasure but now passed its sell-by date. When I'm writing about railways, I'm writing about something that I know, that I love, and that I've experienced. All those locomotives that I grew up with are, in a way, individual characters. You're not just seeing a train. You're seeing 47097. It's a series of memories that you associate with it – where you saw it, what livery it was in, the people you used to hang around with at the time. It all comes together. Some people are hooked on ships. Some have a thing about planes. For me, it's very much the railways."

Even the name Blyth Power had its roots in the railways. "One of the engines that used to pull coal trains into power stations in the north of England was called 'Blyth Power'. It was a name that seemed to mean something on a number of levels. I wanted a name for the band that had some kind of sense, not 'It's going to be the first thing I see when I look over this hedge'. Blyth Power had this feeling of benign strength like a locomotive, which of course it was. A class 56 for anyone out there who cares about these things, 56076 to start with before the nameplates got transferred to 56134. But it was the name that really did it for me rather than the locomotive. 'Blyth Power' – it's strong without being evil, if you know what I mean."

Folk singer Dave Goulder was another musician who, like Porter, always made sure he used the correct terminology when it came to writing songs about railways, drawing heavily on his own previous existence cleaning and maintaining steam engines for a living. "Ewan MacColl managed to collect one or two cracking train songs of which 'Song Of The Iron Road' is probably my favourite," says Goulder. "It's about the men who kept Britain's railways running and how hard their jobs were. That [song] is what really kick-started me into seeing if I could also write my own songs. With MacColl all the right terms were there, but not necessarily in the right order or the way you would use them. That's where I started to score with my own songs because they were from the inside. I spoke the same language as those men because I'd been one of them."

Another for whom the railways came before the music was Nigel Fletcher, drummer with the group Lieutenant Pigeon famous for their 1972 UK number one hit "Mouldy Old Dough". "At about the age of six or seven I just became fascinated by things that ran on rails," he recalls. "I had a father who wanted me to follow in his footsteps and play rugby, football, tennis and cricket. I had that rammed down my throat and I think I rebelled a bit and disappointed him. He played in a cricket team and wherever they went I was supposed to sit in the stands spectating or scoring. Instead, I used to slip away to the nearest railway line and sit there watching the trains go by. Oddly enough, that was one of the main reasons why I got into partnership with Rob Woodward (Lieutenant Pigeon's keyboard player and guitarist). We were interested in music but he was also mad keen on railways. We often used to go out and sit and write songs by the railway line. You couldn't get a better working environment – if you could call it working."

Between them, Fletcher and Woodward concocted several train songs (some featuring vocals, others purely instrumentals) which they recorded with Lieutenant Pigeon and the band's forerunner Stavely Makepeace, including "Meet Me Off The Royal Scot" and "Steam Train Stag". The pair even carved out a healthy sideline making actual live recordings of British diesel locomotives, such as the Deltics, released through the Argo Records label. However, when the royalties and acclaim started drying up Fletcher found himself at a crossroads familiar to many pop stars on the downward trajectory, the one where all the signposts read "What do I do next?" Fortunately he didn't have to think too hard.

"Back in 1963 after I left school, they were taking on cleaners at the railway sheds in Basingstoke," recalls Fletcher. "It was either that or join the Merchant Navy for a living. I ended up joining the Merchant Navy and went away to sea for three or four years before coming back and getting into music. We [Lieutenant Pigeon] wrapped up our last LP in 1978 and after that I gigged around for a bit, but you have to do something to put food on the table. In 1983 I had a complete change of lifestyle and applied to work with British Railways as a signalman. I was accepted and went to work in a [signal] box on the Coventry to Nuneaton line. We had five boxes on that line when I started, which gradually shrank to three, then two. Now they're all gone, victims of modern technology. I worked there for five years and then moved over to another box on the Great Western [Railway]. I was 37 when I started and it was like a new lease of life doing something I loved and that I'd missed out on in 1963. Wonderful days."

Fletcher's love of the railways continues, even though most of his beloved steam engines and vintage diesel locomotives have long since been consigned to the history books. It was Fletcher who Pete Waterman, the record producer and keen rail enthusiast, sought for advice when he wanted to buy a train (the pair went to Derby in 1985 and checked out a class 25 diesel which Waterman purchased, the first of several locomotives he has owned). When Michael Palin of Monty Python fame was researching for an episode of the BBC television series *Great Railway Journeys Of The World* he wrote to Fletcher asking for his input (Palin's letter remains a treasured possession). Noddy Holder, ex-frontman of the band Slade, still greets Fletcher with the words "Hello Nigel, how's the trains?" We are, after all, talking about a man who during Lieutenant Pigeon's heyday still found time to venture abroad and catch the dying embers of steam in West Germany. "Basically I'm a trainspotter who got lucky in the recording industry," is Fletcher's own honest assessment.

▓▓▓▓▓▓▓▓▓▓▓

As indeed is Chas Hodges, although hard work and sheer talent have also been to the fore in a musical career that began during the 1960s with session work for such trailblazers as Gene Vincent and Jerry Lee Lewis. "I grew up listening to Lonnie [Donegan] and Chuck Berry so the trains, as well as the trainspotting, were always there," says Hodges. "Songs like 'Rock Island Line', 'Wabash Cannonball' and Chuck's 'Rockin' On The Railroad' which we [Chas & Dave] do quite a bit. We do songs about all sorts of things, but the trains creep in every now and then. You've got 'Clive Of India' after one of the old Britannia class of steam engines, which we did for Derek Lawrence of Retreat Records who put it out in a box set. There's 'That's What I Like' where we both sat down and wrote lists of things that we liked off the top of our head and put a chorus in the middle, so the trains had to go in there. And of course there's that train sound all the time. You'll have a song that's not about trains, but the sound – that rockin' rhythm – is the sound of the old trains going down the track with their pistons turning, that beat you used to get with steam trains. You know, back in the days when it was all silver service in the buffet car, not hamburgers in a box."

"He's right," says poet, songwriter and train admirer Pete Brown, endorsing Hodges' line of thought. "Train rhythms are terribly important when it comes to music. Lots of structures and grooves come from the railways. Trains have been making groove sounds for longer than any of us have been around. Jimmy Forrest, James Brown, Duke Ellington, Muddy Waters, Howlin' Wolf... they all knew that. You listen to the music they made and you know where the groove is coming from. It's a train. That boogie-woogie style of piano playing they [Chas & Dave] and so many others do is very train-like. It's not such a big thing now. The steam trains have gone and taken their beats with them. The tracks don't make that clickety-clack sound as you go over them anymore because it's all one long continuous welded rail. But it was a big thing and it helped shape the music we all listened to."

In 2012, the East Midlands Trains company, operator of services out of London's St Pancras station to cities such as Derby, Nottingham and Sheffield, approached Chas & Dave about using one of the duo's songs in a marketing campaign. "Gertcha" was the track in question, "Gertcha self down to London by train" being the strapline of the proposed campaign (Chas & Dave's influences and music hall style have always given them an undeniably London flavour). The pair said yes and East Midlands Trains plastered their stations with posters showing Chas & Dave superimposed in front of the Palace of Westminster and the London Eye. "They contacted us and came up with a figure and we enjoyed doing it," says Hodges. "I think all that's left for us now is to get our name on the side of a train like the ones I used to spot as a kid. I would love that, but I can't see it happening. 'Chas & Dave'... it's nice, but it's not exactly 'Hereward The Wake', is it?"

The British obsession with trains – the kind that made Ian Naisbitt, Joseph Porter, Nigel Fletcher and Chas Hodges want to spot as many different locomotives as possible – is, it has to be said, almost entirely a male thing. In fact, the vast majority of train songs, regardless of their country of origin, have been written by men. There are of course exceptions; "Destination Anywhere" by Valerie Simpson, Elizabeth Cotten's "Freight Train", Carole King's 50/50 share of "The Loco-Motion" with Gerry Goffin. But in the main, railways and the songs they inspire are very much a masculine preserve. Quite why is anyone's guess. Is it really a case of machines being able to press the kind of emotional buttons that exist largely within the male psyche?

Peggy Seeger has her own theory, and it's a good one. "I think it has to be something to do with the fact that men are hunters. Hunters follow a straight line, they don't look to right or left, and that's what the railways did. They went relentlessly through communities in as straight a line as possible, certainly in America. Women like to live in 360 degrees. They like to be settled, to look all around them. The railways brought a lot of things that women wanted, but the actual act of riding on a train is a hunting one. It's goal-orientated, not looking to the right or the left, you just want to get there. That fundamental difference between men and women is certainly something that comes across in songs that have been written about trains."

Francis Rossi, however, has another suggestion. "I was watching [British TV programme] *Tomorrow's World* a long, long time ago and they were talking about how the Scottish used to be sent into battle with this marching music playing which was written just a few beats above the heart level which, of course, rouses you. It gave them this thing, this spirit, to go in and fight. It riled them up. That whole thing with the music, the beats per minute, is like a train. If you get the rhythm right – boom-chicka-boom-chicka-boom – then subliminally you've got this movement going. You can't help but move your body. Much of my childhood was spent on trains. We went everywhere on them. I even went to school by train and there was something about that boom-chicka-boom. I think that applies to men probably more than it does to women. It stirs that little Scottish soldier inside of you."

The male fascination with trains within the music industry also extends to the model ones than run around floors, on tables or, in Rod Stewart's case, the attic of his house in Los Angeles. Musicians on both sides of the Atlantic have been tinkering with model trains for decades, losing themselves in miniature landscapes instead of worrying about the day job or the hazards of straying beyond their front door into the real world. Frank Sinatra dedicated an entire section of his ranch in California to model trains, an area he called "The Train Building". Roger Daltrey of The Who has made no secret of the fact that he enjoys chilling out with friends around his train set, while Johnny Cash not only had an extensive Lionel layout but also endorsed the company's products in a series of TV adverts. To relieve the boredom between shows while on tour with Genesis, Phil Collins would even bring along a portable train set for entertainment (the larger version remained safely at home in his basement).

In America, Neil Young took his involvement with model trains to another level by developing pioneering remote control and sound systems for Lionel products, something he had initially concocted at home for his son Ben to use. Discussing his passion for trains of the smaller variety with David Letterman in 2012, Young told the TV talk show host "I was out Christmas shopping back in 1977, or '78, maybe '76, when I was just

Top: "As long as I've got coal, I will keep going." Ray Davies (far right) with The Kinks in 1967. *(Pictorial Press Ltd/Alamy Stock Photo)*

Middle: Gladys Knight And The Pips enjoyed a smash hit on both sides of the Atlantic with a song which began life as "Midnight Plane To Houston". *(Pictorial Press Ltd/Alamy Stock Photo)*

Above: Abba play up for the photographers at Waterloo station after winning the 1974 Eurovision Song Contest with "Waterloo". *(John Downing/Stringer)*

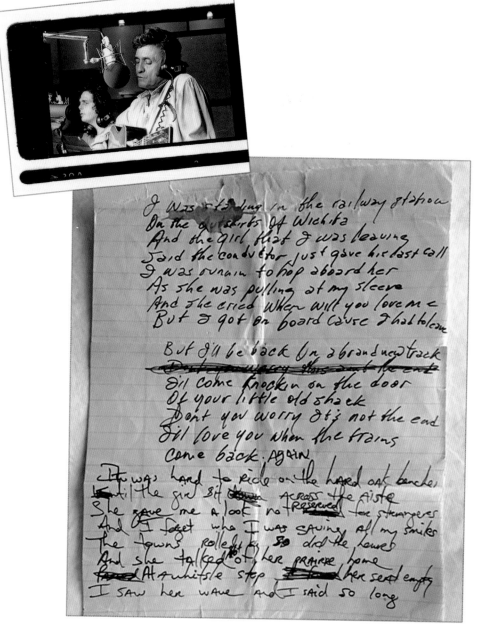

Top: Johnny Cash and Jack Wesley Routh, two lovers of "the old west, trains and women" together in the recording studio. (©Al Clayton, used with permission of Al Clayton Photography, LLC)

Above: The handwritten lyrics to "When The Trains Come Back" with Johnny Cash's contribution at the top of the page and Jack Wesley Routh's towards the bottom. (*Courtesy Jack Wesley Routh*)

Opposite: From station to station. David Bowie lets the train take the strain while travelling through mainland Europe. (©LFI/Photoshot)

Top Left: Luxury, elegance and speed over national borders.
A Trans-Europe Express train, as immortalised by Kraftwerk. *(Shipley43)*

Top right: "*Seven boxcars full of trouble.*" A freight train designed for carrying nuclear waste makes its way along the English Cumbrian coast. *(©Construction Photography/Photoshot)*

Above: "I saw the big blue Deltic diesel… and that was it." The object of Andy McCluskey's affection, and the inspiration behind the title of Orchestral Manoeuvres In The Dark's album *English Electric. (Bethany Marsh)*

Top left: "The culture of 1,000 years is shattered with the clanging of the cell door behind you." Johnny Cash stares down from the cover of *At Folsom Prison*. *(CBW Alamy Stock Photo)*

Middle right: A sign of the impending apocalypse or a symbol of deliverance? The cover to Bob Dylan's 1979 album *Slow Train Coming*. *(CBW Alamy Stock Photo)*

Middle left: The UK version of the cover to Madonna's single "Holiday" portraying the "Golden Arrow" luxury Pullman car service, the very same train that had entranced a young Graham Parker. *(razorpix / Alamy Stock Photo)*

Above: The cover of Blur's 1993 album *Modern Life Is Rubbish* depicting Mallard, taken from Paul Gribble's oil painting of the fastest steam train in the world.

Top: Brian Setzer in Johnny B. Goode pose, strumming his guitar beside the railroad tracks. *(Russ Harrington)*

Above: "Give me a bit of boom-chicka-boom-chicka-boom any day." Status Quo prepare to ride the rails in style aboard the Orient Express. *(©LFI/Photoshot)*

Top: "Oh that's a title, that's a great title." Metro-Land, as the Metropolitan Line wanted potential passengers to see it. *(Lordprice Collection / Alamy Stock Photo)*

Above: Tea break on board one of Britain's night mail trains, the inspiration behind a film, W. H. Auden's "rap before rap" poem, and Public Service Broadcasting's song. *(UPPA/Photoshot)*

Top: Squeeze at the Kent and East Sussex Railway,
Tenterden, England. *(Rob O'Connor)*

Above: Public Service Broadcasting on location at the video shoot
for "Night Mail". *(Dan Kendall)*

getting together with my wife. I was shopping for presents and I found this huge Lionel thing. It was like many thousands of dollars. I'm going 'My goodness, this is very expensive'. And being a rich hippy I bought it immediately! Then I took it home, and I opened the box, and I found all this stuff in it, I mean that was extra that I didn't know I had. So I got into it."

Inspired by the view over Highgate's railway marshalling yards from his family's terraced house in Archway Road, north London, Rod Stewart was bought his first train set at the age of seven and never looked back. By 13, it had expanded onto a six foot by four foot board. As his career took off – and the houses got bigger – so the layouts grew steadily in size. After moving to Beverly Park, LA, in 1993 Stewart set about constructing the mother of all train sets based on a fictional American city just after the Second World War and featuring models of both steam and diesel locomotives (not to mention entire streets, factories, an oil refinery, a port, skyscrapers and a replica of the Brooklyn Bridge). In 2007, *Model Railroader*, the world's largest selling magazine on model trains, featured Stewart and his layout as its cover story (something the magazine repeated during 2010 and again in 2014). It was, he admitted, the ultimate accolade, better even than landing the front of *Rolling Stone* magazine. And he wasn't joking. As far as Stewart is concerned, the layout, which occupies a room 50 feet long and 21 feet wide, is a serious business. Just don't call it a "train set". It's a "model railroad".

In his 2012 autobiography Stewart recalls his father saying that every man needs three things in life to be contented – a job, a sport, and a hobby. Stewart's job has more than paid the bills over the years. Football became his sport of choice. As for the hobby? That would be model railroading. It might just be that Mr Stewart's philosophy comes as close as any to explaining the male infatuation with trains.

"Is it just us who are like this, the British I mean? Are there any trainspotters in Sicily? Do Belgians go misty-eyed at the thought of seeing the 12.16 to Antwerp? Do Swedes save up all year for a Hasselblad to photograph a Stockholm to Gothenburg coal train breasting a 1 in 57 gradient?" Those were the rhetorical questions asked by Michael Palin while presenting his *Great Railway Journeys Of The World* episode first broadcast in 1980, the one he approached Nigel Fletcher for input prior to filming. While railways occupy a hefty chapter in American history and remain the social and economic backbone of India, Britain still rules in terms of the whole A to Z train smorgasbord. Although, admittedly, the love affair has become somewhat strained over recent years with exorbitant fares, underinvestment in the infrastructure and overcrowding on services testing people's patience and bank accounts to the limit. Trains are something everyone in Britain seems to have an opinion on, for better or for worse. Trading e-mails with Matt Johnson of The The while researching this book, the often controversial subject of rail privatisation came up. "It has never made any economic sense apart from to the vulture capitalists who always attend the flog-off of our public assets," Johnson wrote of the decision to privatise Britain's railways made during the 1990s. "Call me an idealist but our railways should be non-profit and run by people who love them and also understand the public's love affair with this most civilised mode of transport."

"We do have this sort of love/hate relationship now with trains which, and I might be wildly wide of the mark about this because I wasn't around in the 1930s, there didn't seem to be a few decades back," says John Illsley. "We hate them when they're late, but we still seem to love being on them. I use the train to travel from Hampshire [where Illsley lives] to London because I find it incredibly relaxing. In the car, I'm being talked at by the radio, or the phone is ringing. The phone doesn't work properly on the train. You've got this hour, or two, or three, of tranquillity where you can read, or write, do the crossword, or just stare out of the window. Personally, I love them. But, and here's my gripe, don't get me started on the food. I remember taking trains up to the north [of Britain] and going into the restaurant car and they'd have those white tablecloths and stainless steel knives and forks, and a perfectly dressed guy would come out and serve you. Now it's just a trolley full of crap. And they call that progress?"

Regardless of political leanings, or opinions about privatisation, there's no denying the British care about their railways and how they are run. Maybe John Illsley, Chas Hodges, Rod Stewart, Nigel Fletcher, Joseph Porter and Matt Johnson should be approached about taking control of the UK's rail infrastructure. Vintage steam engines and diesel locomotives on the front of every train, china cups and silver service for all in the buffet car, the reintroduction of old-style signal boxes with polished levers and ringing bells. The vulture capitalists might despair, but it wouldn't half be fun.

13

UP THE JUNCTION

It's now 1989. Rod Stewart has taken a punt and covered "Downtown Train", written by Tom Waits. The gamble will pay off big time as the single puts him back on the map in both Britain and America after several years in the wilderness. The Pogues, purveyors of Celtic folk punk, release *Peace And Love* brandishing two rollicking railway numbers in "Boat Train" and "Night Train To Lorca" (the former documenting a booze-soaked trip from the Welsh ferry port of Holyhead to London, the latter a song Johnny Cash might have written had his heart resided somewhere between Galway and Granada). Guns N' Roses are on the "Nightrain" although singer Axl Rose is playing on words, Night Train Express being a cheap brand of Californian wine popular with the band rather than a method of transport. And Lenny Kravitz, together with the Mexican/ American poet Ingrid Chavez, are collaborating on "Justify My Love" for Madonna in which the singer will breathily declare her intention to make love on a train travelling cross-country. One hundred and sixty one years since Arthur Clifton wrote "The Carrollton March" to mark the start of construction work on the Baltimore & Ohio Railway, it seems there's still a place for the train song in popular culture.

But music, once again, is changing.

In Europe, the acid house and rave scene is in full swing. Gone are the new romantics and so much of what constituted the pop charts during the first half of the 1980s, washed away by a tsunami of frenzied beats championed by the next generation. It's the same story in North America, where rap and hip hop have challenged the older orders. DJ culture is becoming ever more conspicuous. The catalysts behind this brave new world aren't old enough to remember the sounds and smells generated by steam trains, or the *Six-Five Special* TV show, or the kind of carriage compartments Graham Gouldman used to frequent writing songs on his guitar. Do trains and railways have a future in this evolving musical landscape? In the short term, yes. British acid house band The KLF will soon enjoy a huge hit with "Last Train To Trancentral", Trancentral being the name of the group's recording studio in the basement of an old Victorian terraced house in Stockwell, south London (and, in the context of the song, a journey of spiritual adventure). A sudden unscheduled halt in the music set played by a DJ will, in club parlance, become known as a "train wreck". But long-term? Only time will tell.

The early 1990s saw a cluster of older, established acts adding their names to the extensive roll call of train song performers. With words written by Phil Collins, "Driving The Last Spike" by Genesis followed in the footsteps of "Rain, Steam & Speed" from The Men They Couldn't Hang, acknowledging the huge sacrifices made by those who built Britain's railways during the 19th century (the term "last spike" was often used to mark the end of construction work on a railway line). Berlin's Zoologischer Garten railway station, a renowned hangout during the 1970s and 1980s for junkies and prostitutes, became the inspiration for U2's "Zoo Station" from the *Achtung Baby* album. Elton John enlisted his old friend Eric Clapton to sing and play guitar on "Runaway Train", a song where the protagonist is out of control but determined to get his life back on track (a feeling both men knew only too well given their respective battles with drink, drugs and, in John's case, bulimia). And Squeeze, their creative juices flowing after a spell in rehab by the band's lyrical font Chris Difford, earned widespread critical praise for the albums *Some Fantastic Place* and *Ridiculous* both of which featured train songs showcasing the darker and lighter corners of the human condition respectively.

For the best part of two decades, Difford had enjoyed a drink virtually every day. However, by 1992 he'd become a full-blown alcoholic on the verge of a nervous breakdown. That summer, Difford checked into a clinic in Kent where he underwent 12 weeks of intensive therapy. The experience completely transformed his life and he emerged a much happier, healthier person clutching a bundle of lyrics charting the ups and downs of the previous few years. Among them were the words to "Third Rail" which would become Squeeze's first single from 1993's *Some Fantastic Place*.

"The third rail is the source of power that drives a lot of the trains around where I grew up in south London," says Difford. "All the Underground trains have it and quite a few of the ones that run on the surface. It's lethal really – touch it and you're probably going to die, which is why all the schools used to show these little awareness films about the importance of not playing on railway lines. 'Third Rail' [the song] is talking about a relationship that has lost its power. There was a lot of that going on in my life at the time, or there had been, so that's what it's about. Without a third rail, you're not going to go anywhere. Alcohol had also been my third rail, and I was questioning that. It's me looking back with the benefit of hindsight having been given this new lease of life."

Determined to make the most of his personal and creative rebirth, Difford started attending songwriting weekends working with other singers and musicians from outside Squeeze, something he had never done before. It was during one of these getaways that the words to "Electric Trains" fell into place. Difford knew straight away that these were some of the finest lyrics he had ever penned. Nevertheless, he initially gave the song to Francis Dunnery, former vocalist with the band It Bites, rather than keeping it for Squeeze to record. When Glenn Tilbrook, Difford's songwriting partner in Squeeze, realised this he was less than amused. To cut a long story short, Difford went back to Dunnery, explained his predicament, and Dunnery graciously agreed to step aside. It was an awkward experience for all concerned, but Difford and Tilbrook had been around the block long enough to let bygones be bygones and immediately set to work on Squeeze's next long player, *Ridiculous*, with "Electric Trains" taking pride of place as the album's opening track.

"Electric Trains" harks back to Difford's childhood at Combe Avenue, Greenwich. It's about growing up, coming of age, and all the stops along the way – listening to Julie Andrews and Jerry Garcia on the radio, collecting records, playing with a model electric train set (which Difford, like many boys, kept beneath his bed), masturbation, counting your first pubic hairs, chasing girls and eventually forming a band. Despite being lyrically and musically upbeat, "Electric Trains" is a song that resonates so strongly with some men, Difford's own brother included, that it can make them weep on demand.

"It ['Electric Trains'] is in some ways quite a deeper lyric [than 'Third Rail'] because it's more about what childhood means, for most men anyway," says Difford. "When I look back on my childhood, my memories are stretched over a real fascination for trains, and in my day it was still steam trains. My family used to go on steam train holidays every year. We would get the sleeper train up to Scotland, and the power of being in a station full of steam trains was unbelievable. It was like 'This is what men do – they drive trains'. It was a proper job, one you would aspire to as a young boy in short trousers. They were important, the big ones and the model ones under the bed."

The Train Kept A-Rollin'

Difford now regards *Some Fantastic Place* and the period encompassing late 1992 and 1993 as the pinnacle of his career as a lyricist, which is saying something for a man with an awful lot of arrows in his musical armoury. Forging songs such as "Third Rail" and "Electric Trains" proved to be a hugely cathartic experience. They also demonstrated, much to his relief, that he could produce work of the highest quality while sober. Neither sold as well as, say, Squeeze's 1979 UK number two hit "Up The Junction" (not strictly a train song despite being about a girl from Clapham, London's Clapham Junction station being the busiest in the country), but they remain two of the most finely crafted singles to have come out of 1990s Britain.

▨▨▨▨▨▨▨▨▨▨▨

The cathartic release afforded by trains, model ones or otherwise, and the colourful world they inhabit, had been brought home to another of Britain's great post-war pop lyricists while convalescing inside St Thomas' Hospital in London as a teenage tracheotomy patient. The sights and sounds emanating from the River Thames on one side of the hospital and Waterloo railway station on the other helped sustain Ray Davies throughout his recovery, as already touched on in Chapter 5. That had been in 1957.

Fast forward almost 47 years. On 5 January 2004, Davies was walking through the French Quarter of New Orleans with his girlfriend Suzanne Despies when a car pulled up alongside them. A young man got out and demanded her purse, which Despies handed over without any resistance. Davies, however, was having none of it and started chasing the thief who turned and shot him in the leg. Fortunately the injury wasn't life threatening, but the whole unfortunate incident left a psychological as well as a physical scar on Davies. Not only that, but history started repeating itself.

"That [the shooting and what happened next] was a very life changing experience," says Davies. "I got wounded in New Orleans and afterwards I recuperated for a while in a place called Bay St. Louis in Mississippi. They call it the 'redneck riviera'. I stayed in a little bed and breakfast in Bay St. Louis next to where the freight trains cross the river. There you are – the trains and the river all over again. That's when it came to me. I lay there thinking about the lonesome train, the trains that have driven me all my life, right back to when I was a kid growing up in Finchley near the Underground station. It was like they were taking me home, the chickens coming home to roost. I was re-evaluating my life, and they [trains] symbolise a lot in one's life."

138

The "it" Davies refers to is "The Getaway (Lonesome Train)" from his 2006 solo album *Other People's Lives*. The sound of the trains crossing the Bay St. Louis railroad bridge, which like so much of the area's infrastructure was subsequently destroyed by Hurricane Katrina in August 2005, caused him to reflect both on his own situation and other people out there itching to change their surroundings. That train sound is the signal for them to drop everything and walk after weeks, months or even years spent plotting their getaway. As Davies says, "To me, trains represent a way of escape, a means of going to a better place. Not many people write songs about buses or jets. They write songs about people escaping on trains."

For the record, Davies' alleged assailant, Kawan Johnson, was never brought to trial (the case was twice dismissed because, Davies claims, he was only notified of the trial dates days beforehand leaving him little time to make the trip from London). The crass insensitivity and lack of professionalism displayed by some law enforcement and medical professionals following the shooting still leaves him aghast. "I'm sorry for what happened but Mr. Davies showed poor judgement in running after the individuals," was the terse response from police chief Eddie Compass while answering questions from reporters. A radiologist even asked Davies for an autograph having just shown him an x-ray of his injured leg.

If Status Quo were after a similarly cathartic train experience while touring Australia in 2000, then they were to be left disappointed. Exactly whose idea it was to have the band performing on top of a railway wagon in the scorching Queensland heat has gone unrecorded. Maybe it was one of those things that seemed like a good idea at the time inside an air-conditioned office. Quo, to be fair, could have said no but we are talking about a band that enjoys a bit of horseplay.

"Ever since the Spice Girls came along everything [in the music business] has become increasingly about marketing," says Francis Rossi. "It isn't necessarily about the content and music anymore. It's the marketing. And because record sales are depleting more and more there are people out there who are always coming up with some angle about how to promote you. So there we were in Australia, on tour, and someone's thinking about how to raise our profile. I don't know if they knew we'd done a few train songs or whatever, but we find ourselves on this train a bit like the 'Orient Express' which was nice. That took us to this peculiar stop in the middle of fucking nowhere where we played to about half-a-dozen people on the back of a flatbed railway truck... in 30 to 40 degree heat! Was that a sensible thing to do? Probably not. And it raises the old question about whether you're actually prostituting yourselves. We've been around so long that we've pretty much seen it all, but you do start to ask yourself 'How far is too far?' But it raises the profile and that's what it's all about. I'd like it to be solely about the music, but it isn't."

Status Quo's Australian tour of 2000 proved to be a huge success in what had previously been a backwater for the band, the rewards of which they continued to reap for years. In 2012, their song "Down Down" became the soundtrack to an advertising campaign by the Aussie supermarket firm Coles, with Quo going so far as tweaking the lyrics to suit the brief (*"Down Down, prices are down"*). Reviled by some, the accompanying commercial featuring the group performing the song became the most Googled advertisement of the year in Australia. "All of which goes to show that playing flatbed trucks in the middle of the fucking Outback does in fact pay off in the long run," laughs Rossi.

tᴜᴜᴜᴜᴜᴜᴜᴜᴜᴜᴜᴜᴜᴜ

"The freight trains continue to roll but the stations are awfully lonesome." So said Johnny Cash in 1974 while addressing the state of the USA's railroads, in particular the decline in passenger traffic which had started with the arrival of jet airliners and continued apace once the Interstate highway system began spreading its wings. And yet the pull of the railroads remained strong in American musical circles as Dennis Locorriere would discover while attending his Nashville songwriting nights, the ones where "every-fucking body had a train song." Some even had two, among them the rockabilly revivalist Brian Setzer who included "Trouble Train" ("about that down-bound one, you know, that's going to hell") on his *Songs From Lonely Avenue* album with the Brian Setzer Orchestra, while also finding time to pen "Mystery Train Kept A-Rollin" ("you see what we did there?") for the Stray Cats. The latter is a homage to his beloved Sun Records in which "everyone's got a job on a train: Johnny [Cash] shovelling coal; Jerry Lee [Lewis] is the brakeman; Carl Perkins is punching the tickets, and so on."

However, in Britain exactly the opposite was starting to happen. The UK's decline as an industrial power meant fewer freight trains rolling around the country. The flip side of the coin was a burgeoning white collar army ready and willing to ride passenger trains to work. People in positions of power decreed that anything which didn't fit in with their vision of this new service sector railway should be done away with. And so out went:

- long established and romantic sounding named trains such as The Devonian, the Pines Express and The Talisman
- trains with drop-dead gorgeous old style Pullman cars like the Manchester Pullman and the Yorkshire Pullman
- milk trains and overnight passenger services aimed at society's night owls
- bustling freight yards full of battered wagons and busy shunting engines
- railway coaches with tables you could sit around and talk, ditched in favour of new anti-social "airline" style seating plans
- railway coaches with individual compartments that were ideal for socialising, steamy encounters or making a racket with a guitar
- dining cars on virtually all passenger trains except long distance expresses running into and out of London
- engine sheds rammed with locomotives waiting their next turn of duty
- quirky little independent shops on railway station concourses
- rails that went clickety-clack when you went over them
- trains that actually looked like trains

By the turn of the century, so much of what had made Britain's railways interesting and seductive was gone, replaced by an anodyne corporate culture (overseen increasingly by foreign-based companies) driven by targets and profits. It all seemed horribly clean, tame and contrived, qualities the majority of musicians pride themselves on not being. Small wonder that the UK's well of train songs, brimming since the 1950s, began drying up as the 20th century drew to a close. There was little left to bewitch the new breed of British singers, musicians and songwriters coming through.

"Trains are a bit shit now, aren't they?" says the singer La Roux with a sigh. "I got on a Virgin train the other day and it's not very inspiring. It does what it's supposed to do, sure, but it doesn't make you want to sit down and write a song about a journey to Leeds. I'm too young to remember the old magic when expresses had names and there was this romanticism about them, but I do get the feeling that I really missed out on something, that there was this entire world of characters out there and experiences you could have."

"Modern designs of trains, it seems to me, are just buses on rails," adds Ian Anderson. "They don't have anything aesthetically attractive about their construction or appearance. They're just purely functional. It's hard to get excited about the trains that take you to the various satellites at London Heathrow Terminal 5. They're almost like the trains you'll find on the Long Island Rail Road, glorified tube trains really doing a specialised job of short-haul functional routes transporting as many people as quickly as possible."

Despite his passion for the big blue Deltic diesel, Andy McCluskey believes the beginning of the end of Britain's absolute love affair with the railways – and, thus, the first cloud on the horizon for the train song in the UK – can be pinpointed to the demise of steam locomotives. "It's much easier to wax lyrical about antique machinery because it had a brutal simplicity of form that I think people understood. You know that if you boil water then it creates steam, the force of the steam pushes the valves which moves the pistons, which turns the wheels, and that's how it moves. And you actually hear it move – chuff, chuff, chuff. That sense of sound being connected to the actual movement gives it real meaning. It's an organic, easily understandable machine, whereas of course now everything is dominated by electricity. People don't really understand how electricity works – how it's generated, how it's used on a railway line, how the motor and dynamos on a train work to generate the power. They don't understand electricity nearly as much as they understand steam engines. Everything has been fine-tuned to the point where most people don't even understand how things work."

That said, Britain's train song reserves didn't completely run dry. Written by Elton John and Bernie Taupin, "This Train Don't Stop There Anymore" from 2001 saw the former reflecting on his career while contemplating a future without, so the lyrics appear to suggest, having to depend on drugs for creativity and stimulation. David Bowie's "5.15 The Angels Have Gone" from the following year was similarly enigmatic, detailing a series of train journeys to no particular destination. Is it about someone escaping from a relationship? Does it address loss of faith? Or is it really just the tale of a man hanging around cold stations waiting for late running trains? With Bowie, you never could tell.

Recalling on German television how he came to write the 2005 worldwide hit "You're Beautiful", former soldier turned singer James Blunt said, "It was about a moment when I saw my ex-girlfriend on the

Underground in London and she was with her new boyfriend, who I didn't know existed. She and I caught eyes and lived a lifetime in that very small space of time, in a millisecond. We wondered if time and space had been different what might have happened, but we didn't do anything and I haven't seen her since."

They, however, were the precious few. Besides the occasional album track such as "The Getaway (Lonesome Train)" and Joe Strummer's posthumously released "Long Shadow", written by the former Clash frontman during April 2002 specifically for Johnny Cash (who turned it down), Britain went mighty quiet on the train song front for several years.

As still and hushed, you could say, as the country's railway stations had become.

||||||||||||||||||

But then, from out of nowhere, something strange happened. Heading into the second decade of the 21st century, the UK suddenly awoke from its train song slumber. And it wasn't the present that drove this unexpected renaissance but a love, understanding and appreciation of the past, back when the railways had charisma.

Andy McCluskey's train song mojo suddenly returned one day between business meetings with a lawyer and an accountant in London. "I was actually in Covent Garden which is where the London Transport Museum is, so I decided to have a look around while I had time to kill. Standing inside the museum, I see a poster for 'Metroland'. And immediately I'm thinking 'Oh that's a title, that's a great title'. During the early part of the 20th century the Metropolitan Line (which connects central London with its north west suburbs) decided that they needed to advertise for more passengers, so they came up with this slogan 'Come and live in Metroland', i.e. move out to the suburbs and commute to town. You don't have to live in the filth of the city centre – come and live in the green fields. And that, I think, was very much the sort of attitude that people had back then between the First and the Second World Wars.

"Technology and transportation was going to offer a new utopian vision. And of course the reality was that the Metropolitan Line, along with all the other suburban railway lines, became victims of their own success. The more people who came to live in the leafy fields meant that the leafy fields were submerged under mass swathes of suburban building. The very act of reaching out to their future paradise destroyed it, which

I rather like as an idea. That fitted into the broader theme of the *English Electric* album we were working on. This utopian vision of science and medicine and technology offering solutions to all mankind's ills wasn't the panacea people thought it was going to be. It actually created its own problems."

"Metroland", with its accompanying animated video of a commuter train journeying through a green and pleasant land which steadily morphs into an urban nightmare, subsequently became OMD's first single from *English Electric* released in 2013. "Paul Humphries [the band's keyboard player] came up with the sequencer sound and the melody," says McCluskey. "There was a hint in both our minds of Kraftwerk sequencers from the *Trans-Europe Express* album and 'Europe Endless'. We didn't want to pastiche or copy it, but we felt there was an essence of it there. I'm very fond of it ['Metroland'] because it ticks a lot of my boxes, like antique machinery and the way in which society has changed. It's looking back in time, but it feels very relevant."

▥▥▥▥▥▥▥▥

Ralph McTell barely had to step outside his west of England front door to find the material for another new train song, perhaps the most poignant of many he has written. "Just across the road from where I live now in Cornwall is a river, and on the other side of the river was a narrow gauge railway line. The steam trains used to roll out of St Austell carrying clay – china clay, which is white – and take it down to the harbour at Pentewan where it was shipped off all over the world. Legend has it that during the First World War they took the tracks up and sent them, and the train, to the front line to ship young soldiers up to be slaughtered. It occurred to me that in the Bible it says that man was made out of clay. These young men who often died without graves were buried in fields and became clay. There was this cycle."

McTell discovered that one of the little trains which had worked on the line was called Canopus, a saddle tank engine (so called because the water tank sat on top of the boiler, much like a saddle sits on a horse) built in 1901 by steam locomotive manufacturers Manning Wardle of Leeds, Yorkshire. Besides china clay, Canopus – which ended its days not in Cornwall, nor in France, but working at a factory near the present day site of London's Heathrow Airport – also took children on Sunday school outings to the sea at Pentewan.

144

"There's one picture of all the trucks loaded up with kids," says McTell who, in 2014, wrote a song called "Canopus" for inclusion on an EP called *The Unknown Soldier* commemorating 100 years since the outbreak of the First World War. "It was a really good metaphor for the way man can use a machine for peaceful means and then for war. It makes a statement, this little train. Whether it's totally accurate matters not because the clay and the soldiers really did become one."

As a young man, songs and films featuring trains had often inspired Bryan Ferry, in particular those originating from the USA which seemed a million light years away from the industrial terrain of his native north east England. Hardly renowned as a singer of train songs, in 2014 the Roxy Music frontman put that right with "Midnight Train" from his solo album *Avonmore*, a "vehicle for a feeling" about lost love, lost hope and lost dreams.

"So many blues songs weave in and around train mythology, Howlin' Wolf being a particular favourite of mine who captures the bleakness of the lonesome railroad very well," says Ferry. "The railroad provided much inspiration for blues artists in the vast American landscape, all that waiting and hoping, loved ones coming and going, and the final inevitability of what is gone is gone... in a puff of smoke. I listened to a lot of these songs when I was young. Lead Belly's 'Rock Island Line' and [Chas] McDevitt and [Nancy] Whiskey's 'Freight Train' were two records that particularly resonated with me at the time.

"Also, so many great movies featured key scenes on trains which fired my imagination – *Strangers On A Train*, *The 39 Steps*, *Some Like It Hot*, *From Russia With Love* etc. There's something compelling about high drama in a confined space with the outside world rushing by as a backdrop. Sadly, much of the mystique and glamour and romance has gone, but I still travel by train when I can. A little imagination goes a long way."

Graham Parker, a Brit now living in New York State, went one step further by condensing the entire history of the American railroads into a four minute pop song, something Johnny Cash hadn't even dared to attempt.

"There are various entrances off Route 209 near where I live to what's known as the O&W Trail," says Parker. "That's Ontario & Western. Just like in the UK, canals were important business routes for moving goods around the country, followed by the train lines which put canal travel out of business. My son and I are often to be found walking the 'rail trail' which has about 27 miles of negotiable and well cared for stretches. It's like a long thin park with lots of nature including a prehistoric looking pond crawling with snakes, turtles and beaver lodges. The rails themselves are gone, but chunks of ancient woodwork and old metal plates are off to the side of the trail and railroad spikes (designed to keep rails firmly in place) are often found if you keep your eyes peeled in the dead leaves on the edge of the trail. We collect them and have around a dozen or so. They are just like snowflakes, all unique. Every one of them was hand-forged and beaten into shape in the late 1800s and early 1900s. As we were scouting for them one day, my son challenged me to write a song called 'Railroad Spikes', so I did."

Released in 2015, on the Graham Parker And The Rumour album *Mystery Glue*, "Railroad Spikes" is probably the closest thing you will ever find in song to an A to Z history of the railways; that initial railroad boom of the 19th century, the way it provided employment, the navvies, the death of the canals, the greed associated with many of the early railroad entrepreneurs (*"Exploit the world to get what you need"*), Pullman cars, how the metal that went into laying the railroads was channelled instead into boats, planes and bullets during the Second World War, all culminating in the automobile doing for the railroads what the railroads had done for the canals.

"We went to the Delaware and Hudson Canal Museum in nearby High Falls and I did some reading," adds Parker. "It was quite sad when I got near the end of the song when Henry Ford rears his head. I rarely write a song as specific as this, but the groove alone convinced me it was album-worthy. Close your eyes and you're on that train with all its history, majesty and human progress, hurtling across America at impossible speed."

It wasn't just the older generation of British singers and songwriters who suddenly seemed to catch the train bug. While visiting the Bodmin And Wenford heritage railway in Cornwall, barely a dozen miles from Ralph McTell's home, the folk singer and musician Seth Lakeman got talking to a volunteer train driver by the name of Tony Hallworth from the nearby village of St Mabyn. Hallworth told Lakeman all about working on the iron road, a career that had started with British Railways in 1960 when he was 17 years old, and was continuing even in retirement. Suitably impressed, Lakeman went away and wrote "Last Rider" about Hallworth, a song that with its shuffling train-like beat owed a big debt of gratitude to the skifflers of the 1950s. Somewhat bemused by his 15 minutes of fame, Hallworth told the *Cornish Guardian* "To me, working with locomotives has always been a vocation. It's all I ever wanted to do. It's in the blood."

And then there was the train song unlike any other train song ever recorded.

14

NIGHT MAIL.

In 1934 the General Post Office, established in 1660 by King Charles II to distribute items of mail initially just around England, commissioned the toy manufacturing company Bassett-Lowke to produce a model of one of its Travelling Post Offices for display at exhibitions. Travelling Post Offices, known as TPOs for short, were fast trains on which teams of workers sorted mail in transit with letters being collected and dropped off at various points along a network of routes. Bassett-Lowke's model version proved to be hugely popular with the public, something that gave the GPO an idea.

Why not make a film about a real life TPO and the people who work on it?

The GPO was a massive organisation in the 1930s, so large that it even had a film unit (set up in 1933) to make documentaries showcasing its broad range of work through the relatively new medium of cinema. Established by the pioneering Scottish filmmaker John Grierson, the unit ran on pennies as much as pounds relying on the youthful vigour of young men (often with left-wing sympathies) eager to gain experience or raise their profile as writers, producers, directors, musicians and even poets. Until then, documentary films had tended to be regarded as rather dull filler material screened prior to the real entertainment of a Hollywood movie. The GPO's film unit with its increasingly innovative and daring use of sound, visual style, narrative and editing changed that. And nothing the unit ever produced topped *Night Mail*, the 24-minute story of the 8.30 p.m. weekdays and Sundays TPO from London's Euston station bound for Glasgow, Edinburgh and Aberdeen.

Directed in black and white by Harry Watt and Basil Wright, *Night Mail* relies heavily on statistics. A 340-tonne train made up of 12 coaches pulled by a Class 6 engine, manned by 40 post office workers handling half a million letters to be picked up, dropped off or taken on for morning delivery in Scotland. Trains from Lincolnshire and Derbyshire connect at Tamworth. Trains from Warwickshire and Leicestershire connect at Rugby. And so on. It could so easily have been dull in the extreme.

But it wasn't.

Alongside the barrage of statistics were shots of pistons pumping furiously, levers being pulled by busy signalmen, the driver and fireman breaking their backs to keep time, mail bags in leather pouches being whisked off into trackside nets as the train travels full pelt, the often comedic interaction between the sorters ("Take it away sonny boy", "Right-o handsome"). It showcased a previously unseen world where the proletariat grafted while the bourgeoisie slept soundly in their beds, working class men communicating through slang and regional accents. Informative, entertaining and realistic – that's *Night Mail*, even if some of the action from inside the sorting vans was in fact filmed on a set at the film unit's studio in Blackheath, south east London, using real post office workers (rather than actors) encouraged to sway on their feet as if riding a real train. Not that you would notice, such was the careful attention to detail of the unit's production team.

Among those on the unit's payroll in 1936, the year *Night Mail* was made, was the composer Benjamin Britten (then just 22 years old) and poet W. H. Auden who at £3 per week was earning less at the GPO than he had working as a schoolteacher. It was Grierson who commissioned the pair for *Night Mail*, Britten to write the music and Auden to undertake some assistant directorial duties. "Now I don't want any bloody highbrow stuff," Harry Watt told Britten, demanding that the music be jazzy. Britten wasn't a jazz man but he liked trains and knew all about the rhythms they created. As did Auden, which helped when Grierson and Basil Wright, having seen a rough cut of the documentary and deciding something was missing, asked him to produce a poem for an alternative ending. Auden wrote the words while watching a new cut, recalling that he timed "the spoken verse with a stopwatch in order to fit it exactly to the shot on which it commented."

The finished article, combined with Britten's music, was and indeed remains masterful ("rap before rap" according to the University of York academic Derek Attridge, who produced an essay on the similarities between Auden's poem and its delivery with Ice T's "The Coldest Rap"). As the train begins its steady ascent into Scotland over the formidable Beattock Summit, so begins Auden's now famous poem: "*This is the Night Mail crossing the border*".

The section of *Night Mail* featuring Auden's poem in its entirety (narrated by unit assistant Pat Jackson, later to become a film director in his own right) barely lasted three minutes, yet it's still the most memorable part of a remarkable piece of cinematic work. "The final sequences as the train drives at dawn through the northern moors, the sheep dog racing the train and the rabbits scurrying to cover, set to the simple visual verses of Mr Auden, are extraordinary exciting," wrote the novelist and author Graham Greene reviewing *Night Mail* in *The Spectator* magazine. Premiered at the Arts Theatre in Cambridge, the documentary went on to become the GPO film unit's biggest box-office success as well as a major influence on other movie makers and, in the case of Auden's poem, a regular fixture in modern day English school classrooms. Screened during 1936 and 1937, *Night Mail*'s appeal meant it was repeated in cinemas for years afterwards. One of those who remembered watching it was a young Bruce Reynolds, born in 1931 and raised in south west London around the Clapham Junction area.

"That was my big scene at the time, the cinema," Reynolds told me when I interviewed him in 2003 for a project unconnected with this book. "Back then you always had a two film show, with one film preceding the main picture. You could go to one cinema and see two films, go to another and see two films, and so on. At that age in particular you are stimulated by what you see and a lot of what I saw was trains, or films that had trains in them. You know, [Alfred] Hitchcock's *The Lady Vanishes*, *Shanghai Express*, *Brief Encounter*, all the westerns, and of course *Night Mail*."

Twenty seven years after *Night Mail* was released Reynolds, who died in 2013, would mastermind an audacious heist targeting a southbound TPO travelling from Scotland to London Euston, escaping with almost £2.7 million in notes (the equivalent of around £51.5 million in 2016) being transferred from Scottish banks to head offices in London. The Great Train Robbery, as it became known, made him one of the most wanted men on the planet. And 42 years after that, in 2005, Reynolds' son Nick and his band Alabama 3 recorded "Have You Seen Bruce Richard Reynolds?'" written by folklorist Jim O'Connor and originally cut in 1967 by the singer Nigel Denver, one of several songs inspired by the robbery (including Paul Hardcastle's "Just For Money" and "No One Is Innocent" by the Sex Pistols).

But I'm digressing. Back to *Night Mail* and the train song billed at the end of Chapter 13 as being unlike any other train song ever recorded.

Formed in London during 2009 by J. Willgoose, Esq (guitars, keyboards, banjo) and Wigglesworth (drums, alto saxophone), Public Service Broadcasting are an instrumental group that take samples from old public information films, archive footage and propaganda material and set them to music. Their intention, so Willgoose says with tongue firmly in cheek, is "to teach the lessons of the past through the music of the future." On CD, vinyl or whatever your format of choice the group are both stimulating and refreshing but it's live, when the duo play in front of visuals projected onto screens, where they really come into their element. Imagine Winston Churchill, Morrissey, Depeche Mode, a roll of black and white film, Neil Armstrong, Big Audio Dynamite, Noel Coward, Orbital, David Niven and Kraftwerk thrown together in a blender on full power for three minutes. That's PSB.

The band released their debut album, *Inform – Educate – Entertain*, in 2013 to widespread acclaim. Among the 11 track listing was "Night Mail", PSB's attempt at setting some of the dialogue and poetry from the film to music. The effect was sublime, arts writer Thomas H Green calling it "a thing of techno beauty," and the song rapidly became a high point in their live shows (along with "Spitfire" from the same album containing samples from the 1942 movie *The First Of The Few*). Just as well really, considering the torment Willgoose went through while attempting to bring all the various strands together.

"The idea for the rhythm, that drum beat that kicks in from the start, had been present for about a year and it came from me being mildly obsessed with 'Running Up That Hill' by Kate Bush which has a similar but different drum beat driving all the way through it," says Willgoose. "I wanted to take that and go somewhere else with it. I just didn't know where. Then it occurred to me that it had a similar rhythm to a train, that de-dum, de-dum, de-dum. I was simultaneously aware of *Night Mail*, the film by Harry Watt and Basil Wright, and at some point it dawned on me that they sort of went together. I was kind of in there with the BFI [the British Film Institute, which held *Night Mail* in its archive] so getting hold of it for our use was relatively straight forward. That was it – 'Let's do it!' And then I actually tried to write the song..."

Which was when the headaches began.

"The whole process turned out to be immensely frustrating and quite painful. We had to speed the poetry up to fit in with our tempo, which was a slightly different approach to a lot of the spoken word stuff we had done. I was certainly very daunted about tackling it because, in terms

151

of material, it was by far and away the most famous thing we had ever used. There's always a risk that you're going to balls it up. You don't want to do that when you're talking about a piece of work that involved W. H. Auden and Benjamin Britten, something that's regarded almost as a national treasure. So we set to work and the results are what you hear. Live, it's definitely one that gets a good response. It fits into our set extremely well and is certainly one of our stronger songs, I'd say. There was always something that was there to be had and I think I got it, but I almost feel that something got away. 'Spitfire' and 'Everest' (also from *Inform – Educate – Entertain*, using samples from the 1953 documentary *The Conquest Of Everest*) I'm much more at peace with."

If that wasn't enough, PSB then ran into a spot of bother with the video for "Night Mail", shot at night on an English heritage railway and showing the band pretending to play their instruments surrounded by stationary trains parked in darkened sidings. "We got an angry letter sent in to the *Yorkshire Post* newspaper saying 'What are they doing standing around on railway lines? They're trespassing on national rail property. It's a terrible example for children'. Never mind that it was a private railway in Essex. So we got into trouble for that. People don't like you standing on railway lines for artistic purposes, even when they're not being used. We found that out the hard way. When we released it I said where it was filmed and got told off by the railway manager because I don't think they wanted people to know that they'd let us film there. So, a railway museum in Essex. There you go."

Which just might have been the Mangapps Railway Museum near the town of Burnham-on-Crouch. But I didn't tell you that. And neither, honest mister railway manager, did J. Willgoose, Esq.

▦▦▦▦▦▦▦▦

"If it's about folk, then it's folk," the late singer and songwriter Ian Dury once remarked. Taken in that context, "Night Mail" is as much a folk song as Ewan MacColl's "Dirty Old Town", a slice of social history documenting a way of life that no longer exists. In 2003, the Royal Mail, which had assumed responsibility for the TPOs following the GPO's abolition in 1969, decided to do away with them and transport post by road and air instead. The final trains ran in January of the following year, a handful being retained for emergency purposes and to deal with heavy Christmas loads. Travelling Post Offices, so the Royal Mail insisted, had been a Victorian solution to a Victorian problem of moving post around the country before the invention of motorways and aircraft. "Like mail coaches before them, TPOs are now part of the Royal Mail's history, not its future," said a company spokesman citing savings of £10 million per year. Trade unions, unsurprisingly, strongly disagreed with the decision along with several pressure groups which raised questions over road safety and pollution. Down came the curtain on 165 years of service.

"It is much more than a job, it is a lifestyle," said Steve Griffiths, a manager on board one of the doomed TPOs, at the time. Their demise, Griffiths added, would be a shock to the system for workers whose "whole lives from Monday lunchtime until Saturday morning are organised for them" around the trains. Some were redeployed. Some took voluntary redundancy. Others left the Royal Mail altogether for a new challenge, which is easier said than done when you've been part of a dedicated team for years. In an age when a machine can sort 30,000 letters in an hour compared to 3,000 by hand on a train, the decision was a logical one in a business sense. Romantically, it had all the heart of a jellyfish.

And so another slice of the UK's once colourful railway scene disappeared. Thankfully we have *Night Mail* the documentary, *Night Mail* the poem and "Night Mail" the song through which to remember Britain's postal trains and the immense social and economic role they fulfilled. Public Service Broadcasting's "to teach the lessons of the past through the music of the future" manifesto may have been delivered through an irony-laden grin, but with "Night Mail" they came darned close to pulling it off.

15

DON'T STOP BELIEVIN'

It is a warm Saturday evening in the summer of 2015. The Midland Hotel pub in the Yorkshire town of Normanton is bouncing on its foundations to the sound of chatter vying for airspace with a steady stream of karaoke singers, the vast majority of them female. A tall blonde haired woman, merry rather than drunk, teeters to the microphone and awaits her cue. The music begins, an introductory keyboard riff that rises and falls for around 20 seconds, and then she's away. The song is "Don't Stop Believin'" by the band Journey, the story of a small town girl and a city boy who take midnight trains going anywhere in a bid to break their chains and live a little. She gives it her best shot, veering in and out of tune, and the pub joins in *en masse* with the fist-pumping finale. Job done, the woman acknowledges the smattering of applause with an unsteady curtsy and returns to her table of friends.

Back in the Victorian era, Normanton was one of the most important railway centres in Britain. It was here that a succession of lines running from east to west and north to south met above rich seams of coal buried deep beneath the ground. On being brought to the surface, the coal needed trucks in which to be transported, the trucks needed steam locomotives to be pulled by, the steam locomotives needed men to operate and maintain them, and Normanton grew rapidly from a farming community into a railway mecca. The people who lived there needed a station to use which expanded to such an extent that it boasted, at 520 feet, one of the longest railway platforms in the world. At that time trains didn't have dining cars, stopping instead for refreshment breaks at key stations on route. Normanton's location at the bullseye of Britain's rail network, roughly halfway between London and Scotland on the Midland Railway and England's east and west coastlines, meant it became the Grand Central station of the north, with passengers alighting from trains to devour food and drink before boarding them again bound for destinations as far afield as Liverpool, Glasgow and Bristol. Queen Victoria was a frequent visitor and, word has it, at least two American presidents also broke their journeys at Normanton during visits to Britain. By 1890, more than 700 local people were employed on the railways with nearly a million passengers a year using the station.

Come 1990, the number of employees had fallen to zero. The introduction of dining cars meant trains stopped calling at Normanton for refreshments. Gradually the mines closed down. With them went the trucks, the locomotives, the engine sheds, the sidings and eventually the station buildings themselves, demolished in the late 1980s having become unsafe. All that remains now of Normanton's once proud railway heritage is an unmanned halt served by an hourly stopping service shuffling its way between Sheffield and Leeds. Oh, and a slightly tipsy woman in the Midland Hotel singing about midnight trains going anywhere.

So is Normanton a metaphor for the train song within the modern day music scene, not just in Britain but other parts of Europe and North America as well? Don Brewer of Grand Funk Railroad believes it is. "I don't think trains are as mystical or as romantic as they used to be. I think trains always used to have all this imagery, that sense of wanderlust where people imagine getting on a train and going across the country from north to south or whatever. I don't think it's like that anymore. Are there that many songs being written about trains now? I hear all the old ones, but I'm not hearing anything new. Maybe I'm just listening in the wrong places."

Likewise Chris Difford. "I don't think trains are as important to kids and young people today, so it stands to reason that you probably won't get as many songs about trains from younger artists who are coming through. I think trains have lost their identity in the same way that cars have. Cars aren't quite as shapely or as beautifully made as they once were. I was very lucky to have been brought up in an age when there was beauty in power. I'm constantly disappointed by train journeys in a way that I never used to be. It used to be a real passion of mine, but there you go. That's progress, I guess."

But then there are many singers, songwriters and musicians who reckon otherwise. "Modern songwriters are very aware of what has come before them, and it's impossible to ignore the allure of trains," says Eric Bibb. "There's just so much great music around from so many genres with trains in it. I think a lot of that allure is actually still there. Take all of those grand old train stations. Some have gone, yeah, but there are plenty still around. When someone like Alison Krauss names her group Union Station you know it's impossible to remove the imagery of railroads and trains from songwriting."

"Have you seen a book called *Steam, Steel And Stars*?" asks Brian Setzer. "If not, then you need to. It's a book of photographs taken during the 1950s by a guy [Ogle Winston Link] who took really artistic shots of locomotives rolling through towns. You see this big old locomotive rolling by right next to a drive-in movie at night, and he actually lit the whole place just as he wanted it. I saw it years ago and it's stayed with me, those images. Trains go back to the American west where they were the lifeline. They brought goods, they brought people to new lives, and when you saw something like that rolling through a prairie it must have been like looking at a beast, the biggest mightiest thing you'd ever seen. I think it's endured because of that romantic vision of what it was. It's such a romantic and symbolic figure, a big locomotive rolling through your town. If people don't see it anymore, it very well could go by the wayside. But you can still see them rumbling through. Flying in an aeroplane isn't as romantic. It doesn't do it. The train kept a-rollin' because there's so much history."

"There's a song on my latest album [*A Secret Game*] called 'Brief Encounter' inspired by the film *Brief Encounter* which was of course set around trains and the comings and goings at a railway station," adds the singer and songwriter Billy Nicholls. "It's one of my favourite films, a bit of a weepy. At the very end there's this bit where Celia Johnson has had her affair with Trevor Howard and they've parted at the station. She goes back to her husband who's reading his newspaper in front of the fire, and he says 'You've been away a long time. Thank you for coming back to me'. And it breaks your heart. It's like he knew all along what was going on. That song is inspired by the whole ending to the film of which the trains are a central part."

"It'll never go out of style because someone out there is always going to be hurt." So says Valerie Simpson about "Destination Anywhere" and lost-love songs of a similar nature featuring trains – Dolly Parton's "Blue Smoke" (in which a heartbroken woman heads for the train depot to buy a one-way ticket out of town) keeping the flame burning well into the second decade of the 21st century. Then again "Destination Anywhere", written in 1968 by Simpson and Nickolas Ashford, failed to find an audience until 1990 when it featured in *The Commitments*, an absurdity that laughs in the face of any debate over whether music is time sensitive.

"I'm going to carry it on anyway, as 'Railroad Spikes' suggests," adds Graham Parker of the train song tradition. "I don't think the evocative idea of train travel will die any time soon. I'm quite often on trains in the UK and there's a great relief in not being on the clogged roads and still a certain beauty to the scenery through the window, whether it be the tangle of train lines as you exit or enter a major station or the sight of the countryside hurtling by. Trains will pop up in songs well into the future."

Francis Rossi agrees with Parker, especially now mankind's love affair with other forms of transportation seems to have waned. "We built the roads and the motorways and now they are all full up. You used to see people tinkering with their cars on a Sunday. No one does that anymore because we don't understand how they work. Then you've got the airports. 'Have you got a bomb in your shoe? Take your fucking shoe off'. Leave me alone! We [Status Quo] still get that on private jets. Do you think we're going to get on our own plane and blow ourselves up? But there's still something about the railroads that I don't think has gone. There's still this romance in a train. There's nothing that would make me want to sing a song about fucking airports, but I'd still want to sing a song about taking a train ride."

"They may not be the iconic [train] songs of previous generations, but then how many truly iconic songs get written today?" says Andy McCluskey sounding a note of caution affecting the music industry in general. "It's never been easier for musicians to make music and get it out there through modern technology, but the sheer volume of it all and the here today, gone tomorrow nature of the music business means it has never been harder to get the music heard by the kind of audiences that enable you to make a proper living from it. People will continue to write and record train songs. Whether you get to hear them though is another matter."

Besides Yorkshire karaoke singers, Alison Krauss' backing band, 1950s photographs, *Brief Encounter*, abandoned railroad spikes found on American nature trails and Francis Rossi's airport check-in nightmares, there is something else that just might sustain the train song for many years to come.

God.

‖‖‖‖‖‖‖‖‖‖‖‖‖

In November 1978, Bob Dylan was staying at a hotel in Tucson, Arizona, when he felt what he later described as "a presence in the room that could only be Jesus." Dylan had been going through tough times. A combination of drugs, drink and a bitter divorce that forced him back on the road for a nine-month slog across 10 countries (dubbed the "Alimony Tour") had arguably left him open to some kind of lifestyle conversion. Then again, his band at the time featured several musicians, among them guitarists Steven Soles and T Bone Burnett plus multi-instrumentalist David Mansfield, who were open about their Christianity. Whatever the reason behind his sudden conversion, Dylan accepted Jesus (in contradiction to the Jewish faith in which he was raised) and committed himself to 14 weeks of intense Bible studies with an evangelical group called the Vineyard Christian Fellowship Church based in southern California. He emerged consumed by the idea of a returning Messiah, convinced that the apocalypse was inevitable (and could only be survived by the righteous, as predicted in the Book Of Revelation) and having written a batch of songs about his new found beliefs. Those songs found their way onto the first of three back-to-back Christian rock albums by Dylan that would, as Allan Jones later wrote in *Uncut* magazine, "test to the point of estrangement his relationship with his audience". That album would be called *Slow Train Coming*.

Recorded at Muscle Shoals Sound Studio in Sheffield, Alabama, under the auspices of producer Jerry Wexler and with a band featuring talents such as Mark Knopfler (who when hired was unaware of the religious nature of Dylan's material), *Slow Train Coming* sold well on the back of its excellent production quality and the single "Gotta Serve Somebody" which won a Grammy for Best Rock Vocal performance of the year. There were, however, many who found the album to be one almighty chore underpinned by Dylan's harsh sermonising. The critics, by and large, loved the music, hated the lyrics. But what exactly did the three words on the front cover mean? Dylan characteristically refused to expand, preferring to let the record do his talking, but there would appear to be two viable interpretations – the slow train coming is either a sign of the impending apocalypse or a symbol of deliverance, the latter echoing the recurring theme of salvation, unity and brotherly love addressed by others such as Lead Belly ("Midnight Special"), Curtis Mayfield ("People Get Ready"), Bob Marley ("Zion Train") and Eric Bibb ("Get On Board").

That, in itself, begs another question. Did Dylan, a white man, get an especially raw deal from the critics, most of who were white, for daring to tackle what had traditionally been seen as a black man's preserve?

The train has always been a complicated social symbol for African Americans, something to be celebrated and feared in equal measure. On the one hand, it is a physical object which played a pivotal role in the emancipation of the southern slaves, a way for them to move on and better themselves. On the other, it assisted in breaking up families by taking people to far off parts of the country, leaving loved ones behind. As far as blues musicians were concerned, trains provided material and rhythms for their songs while acting as a strong sexual metaphor. In the gospel tradition, the train also meant death. When you died, it was the train which carried your spirit from this earth.

Up until *Slow Train Coming* no white musician with a mainstream appeal equal to that of Dylan had written God-fearing lyrics of such an earnest nature, not even Johnny Cash who was traditionally regarded more as a country artist. If Dylan was guilty of anything, it was perhaps the self-righteous, lecturing quality of the songs on *Slow Train Coming* which lacked the warmth of "People Get Ready" or "This Train Is Bound for Glory". He didn't exactly help his cause either by refusing to play anything released pre-1979 while on tour promoting the album. Maybe the critics were overly harsh, but when you set your standards as high as Dylan had during the 1960s and most of the 1970s, then any *volte-face* is likely to be a risky manoeuvre.

Despite the premature passing of Marley and Mayfield, not to mention Dylan's rough ride during what became known as his "Jesus years", the spiritual train song has continued to flourish among black and white singers, songwriters and musicians. "It's still there, that train that's going to come and take you home, the analogy that's been drawn so often," says Valerie Simpson, acknowledging the continual role of the train in gospel music. One such song, dubbed "pure secular gospel" by the magazine *Entertainment Weekly*, came from the somewhat unlikely source of Bruce Springsteen who took elements of "People Get Ready" and "This Train Is Bound For Glory" for his own "Land Of Hope And Dreams" from the 2012 album *Wrecking Ball*. This time, unlike the version of "This Train Is Bound For Glory" that Woody Guthrie describes singing to a boxcar full of men in his autobiography *Bound For Glory*, it is not just for the righteous, but is all inclusive from sinners to saints and everything in between. Featuring the New Jersey-based Victorious Gospel Choir, "Land Of Hope And Dreams" has been seen as the rousing moment when Springsteen traded in the motorbike of his youth and hitched a ride instead on the gospel train that has been rolling through American music since the late 19th century.

There is also, as Nick Cave points out, "a bit of gospel singing" in "O Children" from 2004's *Abattoir Blues/The Lyre Of Orpheus*, albeit gospel of a far darker nature than that of "Land Of Hope And Dreams". Cave describes the train that comes and takes the children away as a "symbol of deliverance" but listening to the song it could, like Dylan's *Slow Train Coming,* just as easily be interpreted as the impending apocalypse rolling down the track towards its unsuspecting victims. Ironically, Cave has gone on record declaring *Slow Train Coming* to be his all-time favourite album, one he described to *Mojo* magazine in January 1997 as being "full of mean spirited spirituality" and "a genuinely nasty record." As long as there are musicians around like (or being influenced by) Dylan, Cave, Springsteen and Eric Bibb then train songs featuring God, religion or faith of some kind will almost certainly continue to be written.

Don't stop believin' indeed.

Ever since the first spikes on the Baltimore & Ohio Railroad were driven into the ground back in 1828, so the railways have been there providing the musically minded with fuel for their creativity, a vehicle literally to tell stories and engineer sounds. Trains became the soundtrack to the soundtrack of our lives, evoking in particular the spirit of rock'n'roll, folk, country, the blues and skiffle. There was a time, when trains of a certain style and vintage ploughed across the land, when railways and music didn't just go well together but were joined at the hip. The heyday of the train song may have left the station, but the countless tracks that were recorded, including some of the most instantly recognisable sounds in our music collections, bear testimony to the fact that the late Carl Perkins was spot on in his assessment that "everyone loves a train." Except perhaps, as Robert Johnson might argue from beyond the grave, when it is spiriting someone you hold dear away, possibly forever. And all your love is in vain.

Picture the world heavyweight boxing champion Sonny Liston listening repeatedly to "Night Train" performed by tenor saxophonist and fellow St. Louis resident Jimmy Forrest while preparing for fights, as he would at home and in the gym.

Think about the young Chester Arthur Burnett, aka Howlin' Wolf, sat outside at night watching steam locomotives thundering through White Station, Mississippi, sparks flashing from their smokestacks like lightning bolts.

Remember Johnny B. Goode sat beneath the tree beside the railroad tracks, strumming his guitar to the rhythm that the train drivers made.

Imagine sitting alongside Steve Goodman as he rides on board the City Of New Orleans from Chicago to New Orleans, observing everything that is magical about train travel yet being consumed by melancholy over why this particular "*native son*" of the USA seems to have no future.

Laugh at the surreal if entertaining spectacle of TV Smith launching into his apocalyptic song "Runaway Train Driver" and immediately being surrounded by congas of jubilant people moving their arms in a circular piston-like motion while making loud train noises.

Sit back and listen to *Live At Shea Stadium* by The Clash as drummer Terry Chimes kicks into "Train In Vain", Joe Strummer mimicking the gung-ho energy of a steam engine with his 'Whoo hoo!' howls into the New York City night.

Some 23 years after performing at Shea Stadium, and a little over two years following Strummer's premature death at the age of just 50, a group of people gathered at Bristol Temple Meads railway station to witness his widow, Lucinda, name one of the few remaining British 1960s class 47 diesel locomotives after her late husband. The gesture was a fitting tribute to an inspirational man, one Strummer would no doubt have appreciated given his far-reaching knowledge of musical influences and genres. That evening inside Bristol's Colston Hall the singer and songwriter Elvis Costello acknowledged the day's events by performing "Mystery Train", the track Junior Parker had wanted to make 50 coaches long but which Sam Phillips insisted on keeping at 16. "That was for Joe Strummer," remarked Costello at the song's close.

"There are so many train songs," says Jeremy Spencer. "But do you know what? I'm a little bit surprised that there aren't even more. Think about it. An awful lot of musicians write their songs on guitars. What does the fretboard on a guitar look like? Train tracks stretching away into the distance. If you play guitar, then they are always going to be there in front of you, this subliminal reminder of a way to another place. It's like in America where those train tracks stretch away into the distance over the horizon to who knows where? People with guitars were always going to write songs about trains. I would imagine as long as train tracks and fretboards are shaped the way they are, then they probably always will."

POSTSCRIPT

We're back at Widnes station where yet another plaque commemorating Paul Simon's composing of "Homeward Bound" has been erected, this one on the wall right next to the ticket office on platform two. It is supposedly thief-proof. When the ticket office shuts at night, so the station house in which it is located gets locked up. Any attempt at stealing the plaque would therefore have to be made during business hours in full view of the station staff.

To quote the ticket man on duty the last time I passed by, "That isn't going anywhere."

THE TRACKS
OF THEIR YEARS

While researching this book I asked the majority of the musicians, singers and songwriters that I interviewed if they had a favourite train song, one written or recorded by somebody other than themselves. You will have encountered many of their answers on the preceding pages. A few more are listed here:

Ian Anderson (musician, songwriter and vocalist with Jethro Tull)
"I've always really liked 'Click Clack' by Captain Beefheart which is driven by those rather complex rhythms you get when a train's wheels are crossing over the joins in the rails. But I think my favourite has got to be 'Last Train To San Fernando' by Johnny Duncan And The Blue Grass Boys, the first gramophone record I ever owned, bought from Woolworths at the end of Princes Street in Edinburgh. That's where it all started for me both musically and in terms of trains because they've continued to fascinate me as a means of transport ever since."

Eric Bibb (musician, singer and songwriter)
"There's a song called 'This Train Is Bound For Glory' which is an old folk song, probably more gospel. That's a song that I grew up with. It's part of my DNA. That's probably my pick. Randy Newman has also written any number of great train songs. There's one called 'Dixie Flyer' about a legendary train that runs down to New Orleans. But they [trains] are all over the place for me. There's not a blues singer anywhere that doesn't have a train in their repertoire. And you can't forget 'People Get Ready' by Curtis Mayfield where the train is a metaphor for people coming together with a common purpose. That's one of my absolute favourites."

Don Brewer (drummer and co-lead singer with Grand Funk Railroad)
"Besides Grand Funk Railroad, I also tour with a band called Bob Seger And The Silver Bullet Band, and occasionally Bob throws in this song called 'Long Twin Silver Line'. It's a great railroad song, a rockin' song, all high energy about a train coming through going to Colorado and California. There's these diesel engines and they're pulling ninety-something freight cars down the 'Long Twin Silver Line' and it ain't gonna stop for no one."

Pete Brown (beat poet, musician and songwriter)
"I do like 'Night Train'. There are various versions of that but one of the best is by James Brown. It's a song that everybody seemed to play in jazz clubs back in the sixties and you used to get all sorts of funky versions which were terrific. 'How Long Blues' has got to be in there which I think goes back to the twenties, and 'Choo Choo Ch'Boogie' by Louis Jordan, and 'Southbound Train' which Big Bill Broonzy wrote and Muddy Waters sang. I could go on and on, there are just so many."

Nick Cave (musician, singer and songwriter)
"Johnny Cash's 'Folsom Prison Blues' is the one for me. What a powerful song."

Ray Davies (musician, songwriter and lead singer of The Kinks)
"There are just so many train songs. It could be anything from the fifties, sixties, or even further back. It might even be the theme tune to the *Six-Five Special*. '*Over the points, over the points, over the points, the Six-Five Special's steaming down the line, the Six-Five Special's right on time...* it's time to jive on the old Six-Five!' I think that's how it went."

Chris Difford (musician, singer, songwriter and co-founder of the group Squeeze)
"I like 'Girl On The Train' by Pete Atkin. It's brilliant."

Bryan Ferry (musician, songwriter and vocalist with Roxy Music)
"I guess I'd have to say 'Freight Train' by Chas McDevitt and Nancy Whiskey which I listened to so much when I was young and which really resonated with me at that time."

Nigel Fletcher (founder member of the group Lieutenant Pigeon and former railway signalman)
"My favourite train song is 'Freight Train' as performed by Chas McDevitt and Nancy Whiskey. I loved it then and I still love it now, not just because it's about trains but because of the way it is performed. It has got that simple yet infectious skiffle beat that gets you every time."

Dave Goulder (former steam locomotive cleaner turned folk musician)
"It would probably have to be Ewan MacColl's 'Song Of The Iron Road'. It's the essence of a really good moving-along train song and I love the visuals in it. There's also a song by the famous folk singer Cyril Tawney called 'In The Sidings' which is about an old guy who has been pensioned off. It's very poignant. Whenever anyone plays it on the radio it's nearly always my recording of it rather than Cyril's which is a shame because Cyril was a much better singer than me. That would run 'Song Of The Iron Road' a very close second."

Graham Gouldman (musician, singer, songwriter and co-founder member of 10cc)
"My favourite train song, although it's not strictly just about trains, is 'Trains And Boats And Planes' by Burt Bacharach and Hal David, as sung by Dionne Warwick. It's just a beautiful, melancholic song."

Robyn Hitchcock (musician, singer and songwriter)
"My favourite is Bob Dylan's 'It Takes A Lot To Laugh, It Takes A Train To Cry' which is a fascinating song. It contains a mixture of lines from old folk songs with new stuff added on top. You can picture the singer staring out of the window, worrying, thinking, smoking, not going to sleep. I love it."

Chas Hodges (singer, songwriter, former session musician and one half of Chas & Dave)
"Obviously the first one that comes to mind is 'Rock Island Line' by Lonnie [Donegan] which I think he may even have got off Lead Belly. 'Midnight Special' has got to be in there which everyone's done, much like 'Wabash Cannonball' which is another belter from way back. We do a Chuck Berry one, 'Rockin' On The Railroad', in some of our shows. There are so many, but those stand out for me."

Jimmy "Duck" Holmes (blues musician and owner of the celebrated Blue Front Café in Bentonia, Mississippi)
"It's what I call 'Train Train' but it's known by lots of different names because several artists have done versions of it – '*Train I ride, 16 coaches long, that long black train got my girl and gone*'. And it goes on to say '*Train train coming on down the track, I wonder if that train is bringing my baby back*'. That's one of those songs that has just grown and changed as different people have sung it, but 'Train Train' is the title as I know it."

John Illsley (musician, songwriter and co-founder member of Dire Straits)
"For me it's 'Mystery Train' by Elvis, which I discovered on *The Sun Sessions* album which was released in 1976, even though it was recorded in the fifties. I love those Sun recordings with Scotty Moore on guitar. They sound so basic and stark yet so marvellous, and 'Mystery Train' stands out as the pick of the bunch."

Matt Johnson (musician, singer, songwriter and founder member of The The)
"Hank Williams uses railway imagery in quite a few of his songs, and there are plenty of contenders. But I'll go with '(I Heard That) Lonesome Whistle', a melancholy little tale."

Tom Johnston (musician, songwriter, co-founder member and lead singer with The Doobie Brothers)
"I think it's got to be 'Midnight Special' by Lead Belly, one of the very first songs of his that I ever heard. I loved his version of the blues and that song really stands out. Blues just sort of lends itself to railroads. That would come top closely followed by 'Love In Vain' by The Rolling Stones which has that sad, mournful train taking off from the station."

Elly Jackson (songwriter and vocalist with La Roux)
"It depends on what kind of train song you mean. If it's using trains as a metaphor, then for me it's 'Right Down The Line' [by Gerry Rafferty]. If you're talking about songs that sound like trains then it's 'Moskow Diskow' [by the Belgium group Telex] which is a real train electronica track in a similar kind of style to Kraftwerk, taking the sound of a train and making the beats danceable. And 'Johnny B. Goode' [by Chuck Berry]. That was a huge track for me as a kid which really got me into music. There's that image in there of him sitting beneath the trees by the railroad

track. 'Right Down The Line' is my favourite song of all time, but all of those are great train songs."

Dennis Locorriere (*musician, songwriter and former lead singer with Dr. Hook And The Medicine Show*)
"The one that springs immediately to mind is Paul Simon's 'Train In The Distance'. It's not even really about trains. It's about life. Wherever you are, that train means there's somewhere else. If you're not happy here, well, there's that train in the distance which represents hope. It can even take you there. I also really like 'Duquesne Whistle' by Bob Dylan."

Chas McDevitt (*musician and leading light in the British skiffle phenomenon of the 1950s*)
"My favourite train song is 'City Of New Orleans' written by the late Steve Goodman. It was made famous by Arlo Guthrie and Willie Nelson, but Goodman's version is my favourite because of its simplicity and sincerity. His guitar playing is precise and the performance is delicately understated. Sadly, he died young and never really reaped the benefits of his talents. The song evokes a picture of rural America and the destination is forever my land of dreams!"

Andy McCluskey (*musician, songwriter, vocalist and co-founder member of Orchestral Manoeuvres In The Dark*)
"Although 'Europe Endless' is my favourite Kraftwerk song it doesn't actually mention trains in the lyrics, even though I always assume that the endless journey in question is by train. So I'm going to go for 'Trans-Europe Express' [also by Kraftwerk]. It's an electric tone-poem, trying to recreate the rhythms of the steel and generate music out of the sounds of trains and railway travel. It's scary to think how influential that song is. In fact I'd go as far as saying it is probably one of the most important songs of all time."

Ralph McTell (*musician, singer and songwriter*)
"There's so many to choose from, but 'Working On The Railroad' by Jesse Fuller is one that I recorded on an album called *Blue Skies Black Heroes* which is a proper railroad work song. It had a huge influence on me, the 12-string guitar that he [Fuller] uses and his one-man band approach. It's a song about the mechanics of laying track, getting paid off and the familiar things that underline so many blues songs. It's all there for me,

some of the most joyful and wonderfully inventive music that I've ever heard. I fell in love with the 12-string guitar as a result of him [Fuller], then found Blind Willie McTell from whom I took my name, so you could say I owe a lot to that song!"

Sarah Jane Morris (singer, songwriter and former member of The Communards)
"My favourite train song would have to be 'Coal Train' by Hugh Masekela but Laura Nyro's 'Been On A Train' is a close second. She [Nyro] was around at the same time as Carole King, Carly Simon and Joni Mitchell and had one of those voices which is absolutely haunting. It's a song about her friend who has more tracks on his arm through taking drugs than there are on a railway track. She's basically watching him inject. That song moves me."

Billy Nicholls (singer, songwriter and producer)
"The track I would choose is a song called 'Someday My Love May Grow' by a band called Mother Earth featuring the singer Tracy Nelson who had a fantastic voice. It's a song about leaving on a train which really affected me. It's the classic case of someone being jilted. The original version was by the songwriter Eric Kaz but Tracy Nelson's voice makes this one of the best cover versions I have ever heard."

Graham Parker (singer, songwriter and backed for many years by The Rumour)
"I suppose 'Love In Vain' by Robert Johnson would be at the top of my list closely followed by 'City Of New Orleans' either by Steve Goodman, who wrote it, or Arlo Guthrie who first covered it. 'Love In Vain' is a lost love song and you can feel that train pulling out of the station with all your hopes riding away with it. 'City Of New Orleans' is the name of an actual train and in Goodman's lyrics and brilliant chord progressions you can't help but feel as though you're sitting next to him, going along for the ride."

Dave Pirner (musician, songwriter and lead vocalist with the group Soul Asylum)
"I would pick two songs. There's 'City Of New Orleans' because it's just one of the best songs ever written. And then there's the theme tune to *Casey Jones*. I know there's been lots of different versions of the song but

the one I'm on about is the theme to the TV show that I loved as a kid. *'Casey Jones, steamin' and a rollin', Casey Jones...'* and so on. That just takes me back. Simple times man, simple times."

Francis Rossi (musician, singer, songwriter and co-founder of Status Quo)
"Definitely 'Freight Train'. It was Nancy Whiskey and Chas McDevitt who did it when I was a kid, but we were doing a show in Copenhagen once and there was a band on before us called Big Fat Snake who had a singer called Peter Viskinde. They were great and did the most fantastic version of 'Freight Train' that I've ever heard. I had to get the track off him and had it on my phone and iPad and so on. Such a beautiful version."

Jack Wesley Routh (musician, singer, songwriter and producer)
"There's 'Folsom Prison Blues', 'Hey Porter', 'City Of New Orleans', 'This Train' and so many, many more."

Peggy Seeger (singer, songwriter, activist, half-sister of Pete Seeger, married to Ewan MacColl until his death in 1989)
"One I really like is 'Danville Girl' which lots of different people have sung, among them Woody [Guthrie]. *'My pocket book was empty, my heart was full of pain, ten thousand miles away from home, bumming the railroad train, I was standing on the platform, smoking a big cigar, waiting for the next freight train to carry an empty car, I got off at Danville, fell in with a Danville Girl, you bet she was a pretty one too, she wore those Danville curls, she took me into her kitchen, she treated me nice and fine, she got me in the notion of bumming all the time, she wore her hat on the back of her head like high-toned people all do, but the very next train come down the line I bid that girl adieu, I pulled my cap down over my eyes, walked down to the railroad track, then I bummed the next freight train and never did look back'.* It's a sweet tune, one that to me really, really expresses the size of America, because the railroad tracks in the United States literally disappear into the distance."

Brian Setzer (musician, songwriter and lead vocalist in Stray Cats and the Brian Setzer Orchestra)
"It's got to be 'Mystery Train', the Elvis version, because that's the song that started the whole thing for me and lots of other people. When Elvis played that, it was something so brand new. The guitar had never been played like that. The base had never been slapped like that. And of course

Elvis singing just brought it into the stratosphere. And it's so simple. It didn't take much. But sometimes it's the simple things that are the most difficult to do. You can picture them all sitting in the studio, Elvis going 'Now Scotty, we need something that sounds like a train'. And Scotty goes 'Well, how about this?' It's just a bunch of guys sitting around who are friends, going 'What do you think about this?' That's where all the sparks fly, when you get buddies sitting around in a room with the same idea."

Paul Simmonds *(musician, songwriter and co-founder member of folk punk group The Men They Couldn't Hang)*
"For me it's Woody Guthrie and 'This Train Is Bound For Glory' because it's about the emancipation of the people. The train is opening the country up, moving people around, making them free. What can possibly be better than that?"

TV Smith *(musician, songwriter and former lead vocalist in punk group The Adverts)*
"One of the first albums I was really interested in was *Johnny Cash At San Quentin* which had 'I Walk The Line' on it, so that would have to be up there. I know it's not really about trains, more using them as a metaphor, but I like it. There are so many Johnny Cash songs about trains though. Take your pick from any one of them!"

Jeremy Spencer *(musician, singer, songwriter and part of the original Fleetwood Mac line-up)*
"It would be 'Freight Train', definitely. The whole thing about travelling and moving has been my life so there's something in that song that really gets to me. I must have been about 7 years old when it [the Chas McDevitt and Nancy Whiskey version] came out and I was completely mesmerised. Even now, whenever I hear it, it's like 'Wow!' It can't fail to move you."

Jim Weatherly *(songwriter)*
"I've always loved 'Mystery Train' by Elvis. That's the one for me."

J. Willgoose, Esq. *(songwriter and arranger with the group Public Service Broadcasting)*
"If I had to choose one it would be Johnny Cash and 'Folsom Prison Blues' which a lot of people might forget is actually about a train. The train represents freedom and excitement which the guy in prison doesn't

have. He longs to travel and take the train but can't because he's stuck behind bars. It's an incredibly powerful song."

DIXIE FLYERS

Here follows a chronological list of what might be defined as the 100 best known or most influential songs featuring trains and railways:

1. "John Henry" by various artists (traditional, exact year of origin unknown)
2. "I've Been Working On The Railroad" by various artists (traditional, exact year of origin unknown)
3. "Life's Railway To Heaven" by various artists (written by M E Abbey and Charles Davis Tillman, published in 1893)
4. "Casey Jones" by various artists (copyright Eddie Newton and T Lawrence Seibert, originally attributed to Wallace Saunders, exact year of origin unknown, sometimes known as "The Ballad Of Casey Jones")
5. "Wreck Of The Old 97" by various artists (original writer or writers unknown, exact year of origin unknown)
6. "Man Of Constant Sorrow" by various artists (written by Sheldon Beverly, published in 1913 by Dick Burnett)
7. "Midnight Special" by various artists (traditional, exact year of origin unknown)
8. "Wabash Cannonball" by various artists (traditional, exact year of origin unknown)
9. "How Long, How Long Blues" by Leroy Carr (recorded in 1928, written by Leroy Carr)
10. "Waiting For A Train" by Jimmie Rodgers (recorded in 1928, written by Jimmie Rodgers)
11. "Hobo Bill's Last Ride" by Jimmie Rodgers (published in 1929, written by Waldo O'Neal)
12. "Brother, Can You Spare A Dime?" by various artists (written in 1930 by Edgar Yipsel "Yip" Harburg)

13. "This Train Is Bound For Glory" by various artists (traditional, exact year of origin unknown, sometimes known as "This Train")
14. "Mr Conductor Man" by Big Bill Broonzy (recorded in 1932, written by Big Bill Broonzy)
15. "Hobo's Lullaby" by various artists (written in 1934 by Goebel Reeves)
16. "Night Mail" (from the 1936 film *Night Mail*, words by W. H. Auden, music by Benjamin Britten, narrated by Pat Jackson)
17. "Love In Vain" by Robert Johnson (recorded in 1937, written by Robert Johnson)
18. "Orange Blossom Special" by various artists (written in 1938 by Ervin T. Rouse)
19. "Coronation Scot" (composed in 1938 by Vivian Ellis, performed ever since by orchestras worldwide)
20. "Take The 'A' Train" by Duke Ellington (first recorded in 1941, composed in 1939 by Billy Strayhorn)
21. "Chattanooga Choo Choo" by Glenn Miller And His Orchestra (recorded in 1941, written by Mack Gordon and Harry Warren)
22. "Choo Choo Ch'Boogie" by Louis Jordan And His Tympany Five (released in 1946, written by Denver Darling, Milt Gabler and Vaughn Horton)
23. "Nine Pound Hammer" by Merle Travis (from the 1947 album *Folk Songs Of The Hills*, a traditional song adapted by Merle Travis)
24. "Dirty Old Town" by various artists (written in 1949 by Ewan MacColl)
25. "(I Heard That) Lonesome Whistle" by Hank Williams (released as a single in 1951, written by Hank Williams and Jimmie Davis)
26. "Night Train" by Jimmy Forrest (an instrumental first released in 1952 and since adapted by others including Duke Ellington – who recorded it as "Happy-Go-Lucky Local" – and James Brown, originally written by Jimmy Forrest, Lewis Simpkins and Oscar Washington)
27. "Mystery Train" by Elvis Presley (released as a single in 1955, originally written and recorded in 1953 by Junior Parker and Sam Phillips)
28. "Hey Porter" by Johnny Cash (released as a single in 1955, written by Johnny Cash)
29. "Rock Island Line" by Lonnie Donegan (released as a single in 1955, original writer unknown)

30. "Folsom Prison Blues" by Johnny Cash (originally released as a single in 1956, subsequently released in 1968 as a single from Cash's live album *At Folsom Prison*, written by Johnny Cash)

31. "The Train Kept A-Rollin'" by Johnny Burnette (released as a single in 1956, first recorded in 1951 by Tiny Bradshaw who co-wrote the song with Syd Nathan)

32. "Smokestack Lightning" by Howlin' Wolf (released as a single in 1956 having been written by Wolf – real name Chester Arthur Burnett – several years previously and recorded in 1951 as 'Crying At Daybreak')

33. "All Aboard" by Muddy Waters (first recorded in 1956, later included on the 1969 album *Fathers And Sons*, written by Muddy Waters)

34. Theme song to *Six-Five Special* BBC television show (as screened from February 1957 until December 1958, performed by Don Lang And His Frantic Five)

35. "Last Train To San Fernando" by Johnny Duncan And The Blue Grass Boys (released as a single in 1957, written by Bob Devere)

36. "Freight Train" by Chas McDevitt and Nancy Whiskey (released as a single in 1957, interpreted from the original version written and performed by Elizabeth Cotten)

37. "Johnny B. Goode" by Chuck Berry (released as a single in 1958 and included on the *Chuck Berry Is On Top* album of the following year, written by Chuck Berry)

38. 'The Iron Road' by Ewan MacColl featuring Peggy Seeger (from the 1958 album *Second Shift*, written by Ewan MacColl, sometimes known as "Song Of The Iron Road")

39. "Let It Rock" by Chuck Berry (released as a single in 1960 from the album *Rockin' At The Hops*, written by Chuck Berry, sometimes known as "Rockin' On The Railroad")

40. "The Loco-Motion" by Little Eva (released as a single in 1962, written by Gerry Goffin and Carole King)

41. "King Of The Road" by Roger Miller (released as a single in 1964 from the album *The Return Of Roger Miller*, written by Roger Miller)

42. "Uptight (Everything's Alright)" by Stevie Wonder (released as a single in 1965 from the album *Up-Tight*, written by Stevie Wonder, Sylvia May and Henry Cosby)

43. "A Well Respected Man" by The Kinks (released as a single in 1965, written by Ray Davies)

44. "People Get Ready" by The Impressions (released as a single in 1965 from the album *People Get Ready*, written by Curtis Mayfield)

45. "Look Through Any Window" by The Hollies (released in the UK as a single during 1965 and in the USA the following year, written by Graham Gouldman and Charles Silverman)

46. "It Takes A Lot To Laugh, It Takes a Train to Cry" by Bob Dylan (from the 1965 album *Highway 61 Revisited*, written by Bob Dylan)

47. "Last Train To Clarksville" by The Monkees (released as a single in the USA during 1966 and in the UK the following year, written by Tommy Boyce and Bobby Hart)

48. "Homeward Bound" by Simon & Garfunkel (released as a single in 1966 from the *Parsley, Sage, Rosemary And Thyme* album of the same year, written by Paul Simon)

49. "Green, Green Grass Of Home" by Tom Jones (released as a single in 1966 and included on the *Green, Green Grass Of Home* album of the following year, written by Claude "Curly" Putman Jr.)

50. "Waterloo Sunset" by The Kinks (released as a single in 1967 from the *Something Else By The Kinks* album, written by Ray Davies)

51. "Train To Skaville" by The Ethiopians (released as a single in 1967, written by Leonard Dillon under the name Jack Sparrow)

52. "White Room" by Cream (released as a single in 1968, written by Jack Bruce and Pete Brown)

53. "Destination Anywhere" by The Marvelettes (released as a single in the USA in 1968, written by Nickolas Ashford and Valerie Simpson)

54. "Hear My Train A Comin'" by Jimi Hendrix (frequently played live by Hendrix between 1967 and 1970, finally released in 1973 on the soundtrack to the film *Jimi Hendrix*)

55. "Love In Vain" by The Rolling Stones (from the 1969 album *Let It Bleed*, a live version of which was also included on the following year's long player *Get Yer Ya-Ya's Out*, written by Robert Johnson)

56. "Marrakesh Express" by Crosby, Stills and Nash (released as a single in 1969 from the album *Crosby, Stills & Nash*, written by Graham Nash)

57. "The Night They Drove Old Dixie Down" by The Band (from the 1969 album *The Band*, written by Robbie Robertson)

58. "Station Man" by Fleetwood Mac (from the 1970 album *Kiln House*, written by Jeremy Spencer, Danny Kirwan and John McVie)

59. "Me And Bobby McGee" by Janis Joplin (released as a single in 1971 from the album *Pearl*, originally recorded by Roger Miller, written by Kris Kristofferson and Fred Foster)

60. "Locomotive Breath" by Jethro Tull (from the 1971 album *Aqualung*, written by Ian Anderson)

61. "Main Theme – Carter Takes A Train" by Roy Budd (main theme tune to the 1971 film *Get Carter*, written by Roy Budd)

62. "American Pie" by Don McLean (first released as a single in 1971 from the album *American Pie*, written by Don McLean)

63. "City Of New Orleans" by Steve Goodman (released as a single in 1971 from the album *Steve Goodman*, written by Steve Goodman)

64. "Sylvia's Mother" by Dr. Hook And The Medicine Show (released as a single in 1972 from the 1971 album *Doctor Hook*, written by Shel Silverstein)

65. "Love Train" by The O'Jays (released as a single in 1972 from the album *Back Stabbers*, written by Kenny Gamble and Leon Huff)

66. "Long Train Runnin'" by The Doobie Brothers (released as a single in the USA in 1973 from the band's *The Captain And Me* album, written by Tom Johnston)

67. "Westbound Train" by Dennis Brown (first released as a single in Jamaica in 1973, since included on several compilation albums, written by Dennis Brown sampling elements of Al Green's song "Love And Happiness")

68. "Midnight Train To Georgia" by Gladys Knight And The Pips (released as a single in the USA in 1973 and in the UK three years later, taken from the 1973 album *Imagination*, written by Jim Weatherly)

69. "5.15" by The Who (released as a single in 1973 from the album *Quadrophenia*, written by Pete Townshend)

70. "Crystal Chandeliers And Burgundy" by Johnny Cash (from the 1974 album *The Junkie And The Juicehead Minus Me*, written by Jack Wesley Routh)

71. "Stimela (Coal Train)" by Hugh Masekela (from the 1974 album *I Am Not Afraid*, written by Hugh Masekela)

72. "The Loco-Motion" by Grand Funk Railroad (released as a single in 1974 from the album *Shinin' On*, a reworking of the 1962 Little Eva recording written by Gerry Goffin and Carole King)

73. "Train Kept A-Rollin'" by Aerosmith (released as a single in 1974 from the album *Get Your Wings*, a reworking on the song written in 1951 by Tiny Bradshaw and Syd Nathan)

74. "Trans-Europe Express" by Kraftwerk (released as a single in 1977 from the album *Trans-Europe Express*, written by Ralf Hütter, Florian Schneider and Emil Schult)

75. "Right Down The Line" by Gerry Rafferty (from the 1978 album *City To City*, written by Gerry Rafferty)

76. "City To City" by Gerry Rafferty (from the 1978 album *City To City*, written by Gerry Rafferty)

77. "The Gambler" by Kenny Rogers (released as a single in 1978 from the album *The Gambler*, written by Don Schlitz)

78. "Down In The Tube Station At Midnight" by The Jam (released as a single in 1978 from the album *All Mod Cons*, written by Paul Weller)

79. "Slow Train" by Bob Dylan (released as a single in 1979 from the album *Slow Train Coming*, written by Bob Dylan)

80. "Train In Vain" by The Clash (from the 1979 album *London Calling*, written by Joe Strummer and Mick Jones)

81. "Zion Train" by Bob Marley And The Wailers (from the 1980 album *Uprising*, written by Bob Marley)

82. "Modern Girl" by Sheena Easton (released as a single in 1980 from the album *Take My Time*, written by Chris Neil)

83. "9 To 5" by Sheena Easton (released as a single in 1980, called "Morning Train (Nine to Five)" in the USA, from the album *Take My Time*, written by Chris Neil)

84. "Don't Stop Believin'" by Journey (released as a single in 1981 from the album *Escape*, written by Jonathan Cain, Steve Perry and Neal Schon)

85. "Train In The Distance" by Paul Simon (from the 1983 album *Hearts And Bones*, written by Paul Simon)

86. "Sledgehammer" by Peter Gabriel (released as a single in 1986 from the album *So*, written by Peter Gabriel)

87. "Slow Train To Dawn" by The The (released as a single in 1987 from the album *Infected*, written by Matt Johnson)

88. "London" by The Smiths (a B-side to the 12-inch format of the 1987 single "Shoplifters Of The World Unite", and also released on the band's *The World Won't Listen* album of the same year)

89. "Dixie Flyer" by Randy Newman (from the 1988 album *Land Of Dreams*, written by Randy Newman)

90. "Downtown Train" by Rod Stewart (released as a single in 1989 and included on *The Best Of Rod Stewart* album from the same year, written by Tom Waits)

91. "Runaway Train" by Soul Asylum (released as a single in 1993 from the 1992 album *Grave Dancers Union*, written by Dave Pirner)

92. "Trains" by Al Stewart (from the 1993 album *Famous Last Words*, written by Al Stewart)

93. "Missing" by Everything But The Girl (first released as a single in 1994 from the album *Amplified Heart*, remixed and reissued as a single in 1995)

94. "Electric Trains" by Squeeze (released as a single in 1995 from the album *Ridiculous*, written by Chris Difford and Glenn Tilbrook)

95. "This Train Don't Stop There Anymore" by Elton John (released as a single in 2001 from the album *Songs From The West Coast*, written by Elton John and Bernie Taupin)

96. "O Children" by Nick Cave And The Bad Seeds (from the 2004 album *Abattoir Blues/The Lyre Of Orpheus*, written by Nick Cave)

97. "You're Beautiful" by James Blunt (released as a single in 2005 from the album *Back To Bedlam*, written by James Blunt, Sacha Skarbek and Amanda Ghost)

98. "Rock 'N' Roll Train" by AC/DC (released as a single in 2008 from the album *Black Ice*, written by Angus Young and Malcolm Young)

99. "Land Of Hope And Dreams" by Bruce Springsteen (from the 2012 album *Wrecking Ball*, written by Bruce Springsteen and featuring elements of "People Get Ready" by Curtis Mayfield)

100. "Night Mail" by Public Service Broadcasting (from the 2013 album *Inform – Educate – Entertain*, written by J. Willgoose, Esq)

SLOW BURNING COMPANIONS

... and here are another 100 songs featuring trains and railways that may have escaped your attention which are, in the opinion of this author, well worth investigating:

1. "Promised Land" by Chuck Berry (released as a single in 1965 from the album *St. Louis To Liverpool*, written by Chuck Berry using the melody from "Wabash Cannonball")
2. "Back Up Train" by Al Green (from the 1967 album *Back Up Train*, written by Curtis Rodgers and Palmer E. James)
3. "Canadian Railroad Trilogy" by Gordon Lightfoot (from the 1967 album *The Way I Feel*, re-recorded in 1975 for the album *Gord's Gold*)
4. "Last Of The Steam-Powered Trains" by The Kinks (from the 1968 album *The Kinks Are The Village Green Preservation Society*, written by Ray Davies)
5. "Train Song" by The Pentangle (from the 1969 album *Basket Of Light*, written by Bert Jansch, John Renbourn, Danny Thompson, Terry Cox and Jacqui McShee)
6. "Train To Nowhere" by Savoy Brown (released as a single in 1969 from the album *Blue Matter*, written by Chris Youlden and Kim Simmonds)
7. "Graveyard Train" by Creedence Clearwater Revival (from the 1969 album *Revival*, written by John Fogerty)
8. "Last Train And Ride" by Ralph McTell (from the 1969 album *Spiral Staircase*, written by Ralph McTell)
9. "Terminus" by Ralph McTell (from the 1969 album *Spiral Staircase*, written by Ralph McTell)
10. "One After 909" by The Beatles (from the 1970 album *Let It Be*, written by John Lennon and Paul McCartney)

11. "Been On A Train" by Laura Nyro (from the 1970 album *Christmas And The Beads Of Sweat*, written by Laura Nyro)

12. "Mean Old Fireman" by Fleetwood Mac (from the 1971 album *The Original Fleetwood Mac*, written by Arthur Crudup)

13. "I'm The Man Who Put The Engine In The Chip Shop" by Dave Goulder (released on the 1971 album of the same name, written by Dave Goulder)

14. "Railroad" by Status Quo (from the 1971 album *Dog Of Two Head*, written by Francis Rossi and Bob Young)

15. "In the Sidings" by Cyril Tawney (originally from the 1972 album *In Port*, re-released in 2013 on the album *Man Of Honour*)

16. "Someday My Love May Grow" by Mother Earth featuring Tracy Nelson (from the 1972 album *Tracy Nelson/Mother Earth*, written by Eric Kaz)

17. "Click Clack" by Captain Beefheart (from the 1972 album *The Spotlight Kid*, written by Captain Beefheart under his real name Don Van Vliet)

18. "Stop That Train" by Bob Marley And The Wailers (from the 1973 album *Catch A Fire*, written by Peter Tosh)

19. "Subway Train" by the New York Dolls (from the 1973 album *New York Dolls*, written by David Johansen and Johnny Thunders)

20. "These Foolish Things" by Bryan Ferry (from the 1973 album *These Foolish Things*, written by Eric Maschwitz and Jack Strachey)

21. "Slow Train" by Status Quo (from the 1974 album *Quo*, written by Francis Rossi and Bob Young)

22. "Rudy" by Supertramp (from the 1974 album *Crime Of The Century*, written by Rick Davies and Roger Hodgson)

23. "Railroad Song" by Lynyrd Skynyrd (from the 1975 album *Nuthin' Fancy*, written by Ed King and Ronnie Van Zant)

24. "Slow Burning Companion" by Ralph McTell (from the 1976 album *Right Side Up*, written by Ralph McTell)

25. "A Passage To Bangkok" by Rush (released as a single from the 1976 album *2112*, written by Neil Peart, Geddy Lee and Alex Lifeson)

26. "Watch The Moon Come Down" by Graham Parker And The Rumour (from the 1977 album *Stick To Me*, written by Graham Parker)

27. "Nighttime In the Switching Yard" by Warren Zevon (from the 1978 album *Excitable Boy*, written by Warren Zevon, Jorge Calderon, David Lindell and Waddy Wachtel)

28. "I Can't Stop Lovin' You (Though I Try)" by Leo Sayer (released as a single in 1978 from the album *Leo Sayer*, written by Billy Nicholls)
29. "Last Train To London" by the Electric Light Orchestra (released as a single in 1979 from the album *Discovery*, written by Jeff Lynne)
30. "Deltics" by Chris Rea (from the 1979 album *Deltics*, written by Chris Rea)
31. "Moskow Diskow" by Telex (released as a single in 1979 from the album *Looking For St Tropez*, written by Telex)
32. "Whatever You Want" by Status Quo (released as a single in 1979 from the album *Whatever You Want*, written by Rick Parfitt and Andy Bown)
33. "Long Twin Silver Line" by Bob Seger And The Silver Bullet Band (from the 1980 album *Against The Wind*, written by Bob Seger)
34. "The Royal Mile" by Gerry Rafferty (released as a single in 1980 from the album *Snakes And Ladders*, written by Gerry Rafferty)
35. "Crazy Train" by Ozzy Osbourne (released as a single in 1980 from the album *Blizzard Of Ozz*, written by Ozzy Osbourne, Randy Rhoads and Bob Daisley)
36. "Fade To Grey" by Visage (released as a single in 1980 from the album *Visage*, written by Billy Currie, Chris Payne and Midge Ure)
37. "Under Your Thumb" by Godley & Creme (released as a single in 1981 from the album *Ismism*, written by Godley & Creme)
38. "The Things That Dreams Are Made Of" by The Human League (from the 1981 album *Dare*, written by Philip Oakey and Philip Adrian Wright)
39. "Southern Pacific" by Neil Young And Crazy Horse (from the 1981 album *Re-ac-tor*, written by Neil Young)
40. "I.G.Y (What A Beautiful World)" by Donald Fagen (released as a single in 1982 from the album *The Nightfly*, written by Donald Fagen)
41. "Waiting For A Train" by Flash And The Pan (released as a single in 1983 from the album *Headlines*, written by Harry Vanda and George Young)
42. "Trains" by Ian Anderson (from the 1983 album *Walk Into Light*, written by Ian Anderson)
43. "Some Of My Best Friends Are Trains" by The Waterboys (originally recorded in 1983, included on the 2002 reissue of the album *A Pagan Place*, written by Mike Scott)

44. "I Often Dream Of Trains" by Robyn Hitchcock (from the 1984 album *I Often Dream Of Trains*, written by Robyn Hitchcock)

45. "All The Way Home" by Spinal Tap (from the 1984 film *This Is Spinal Tap*, "written" by David St Hubbins and Nigel Tufnel)

46. "Locomotion" by Orchestral Manoeuvres In The Dark (released as a single in 1984 from the album *Junk Culture*, written by Orchestral Manoeuvres In The Dark)

47. "Smalltown Boy" by Bronski Beat (released as a single in 1984 from the album *The Age Of Consent*, written by Bronski Beat)

48. "Train Running Low On Soul Coal" by XTC (from the 1984 album *The Big Express*, written by Andy Partridge)

49. "Downbound Train" by Bruce Springsteen (from the 1984 album *Born In The USA*, written by Bruce Springsteen)

50. "Poor Paddy" by The Pogues (from the 1984 album *Red Roses For Me*, a reworking of the traditional song "Poor Paddy Works On The Railway")

51. "Train Long Suffering" by Nick Cave And The Bad Seeds (from the 1985 album *The Firstborn Is Dead*, written by Nick Cave)

52. "Driver 8" by REM (released as a single from the 1985 album *Fables Of The Reconstruction*, written by REM)

53. "Manic Monday" by The Bangles (released as a single from the 1986 album *Different Light*, written by Prince)

54. "(Waiting For) The Ghost Train" by Madness (released as a single in 1986, written by Graham McPherson)

55. "Hobo's Meditation" by Dolly Parton, Emmylou Harris and Linda Ronstadt (from the 1987 album *Trio*, written by Jimmie Rodgers)

56. "Kings Cross" by Pet Shop Boys (from the 1987 album *Actually*, written by Chris Lowe and Neil Tennant)

57. "Midnight Train" by The Men They Couldn't Hang (from the 1988 album *Waiting For Bonaparte*, written by Paul Simmonds)

58. "If Love Was A Train" by Michelle Shocked (from the 1988 album *Short Sharp Shocked*, written by Michelle Shocked)

59. "End Of The Line" by the Traveling Wilburys (released as a single in 1989 from the album *Traveling Wilburys Volume 1*, written by Bob Dylan, Jeff Lynne, Tom Petty, George Harrison and Roy Orbison)

60. "Over The Hillside" by The Blue Nile (from the 1989 album *Hats*, written by Paul Buchanan)

61. "From A Late Night Train" by The Blue Nile (from the 1989 album *Hats*, written by Paul Buchanan)

62. "Rain, Steam & Speed" by The Men They Couldn't Hang (released as a single in 1989 from the album *Silver Town*, written by Paul Simmonds)

63. "Night Train To Lorca" by The Pogues (from the 1989 album *Peace And Love*, written by Jem Finer)

64. "Driving The Last Spike" by Genesis (from the 1991 album *We Can't Dance*, written by Tony Banks, Phil Collins and Mike Rutherford)

65. "Zoo Station" by U2 (from the 1991 album *Achtung Baby*, lyrics by Bono, music by U2)

66. "Last Train To Trancentral" by The KLF (released as a single in 1991, written by The KLF)

67. "Trains Of No Return" by Ofra Haza (from the 1992 album *Kirya*, written by Ofra Haza and Bezalel Aloni)

68. "That Train Don't Stop Here" by Los Lobos (from the 1992 album *Kiko*, written by Cesar Rosas and Leroy Preston)

69. "Runaway Train Driver" by TV Smith (from the 1992 album *March Of The Giants*, written by TV Smith)

70. "Secret World" by Peter Gabriel (from the 1992 album *Secret World*, written by Peter Gabriel)

71. "Third Rail" by Squeeze (released as a single in 1993 from the album *Some Fantastic Place*, written by Chris Difford and Glenn Tilbrook)

72. "Signalman White" by Blyth Power (from the 1995 album *Paradise Razed*, written by Joseph Porter)

73. "Stanley Road" by Paul Weller (from the 1995 album *Stanley Road*, written by Paul Weller)

74. "The Day We Caught The Train" by Ocean Colour Scene (released as a single in 1996 from the album *Moseley Shoals*, written by Ocean Colour Scene)

75. "Long Dead Train" by Hugh Cornwell (from the 1997 album *Guilty*, written by Hugh Cornwell)

76. "Blue Train" by Robert Plant and Jimmy Page (from the 1998 album *Walking Into Clarksdale*, written by Robert Plant and Jimmy Page)

77. "5.15 The Angels Have Gone" by David Bowie (from the 2002 album *Heathen*, written by David Bowie)

78. "Long Shadow" by Joe Strummer And The Mescaleros (from the 2003 album *Streetcore*, written by Joe Strummer and Smokey Hormel)

79. "Mystery Train Kept A-Rollin'" by the Stray Cats (a studio track taken from the otherwise live album *Rumble In Brixton*, released as a single in 2004, written by the Stray Cats)

80. "Have You Seen Bruce Richard Reynolds?" by Alabama 3 (from the 2005 album *Outlaw*, written by Jim O'Connor)

81. "Black Cowboys" by Bruce Springsteen (from the 2005 album *Devils & Dust*, written by Bruce Springsteen)

82. "The Getaway (Lonesome Train)" by Ray Davies (from the 2006 album *Other People's Lives*, written by Ray Davies)

83. "Slow Moving Train" by Eric Burdon (from the 2006 album *Soul Of A Man*, written by John Keller)

84. "Get On Board" by Eric Bibb (from the 2008 album *Get On Board*, written by Eric Bibb)

85. "Trouble Train" by The Brian Setzer Orchestra (from the 2009 album *Songs From Lonely Avenue*, written by Brian Setzer)

86. "Oil Tanker Train" by Merle Haggard (from the 2010 album *I Am What I Am*, written by Merle Haggard)

87. "The Sound Of A Train" by Dennis Locorriere (from the 2010 album *Post Cool*, written by Dennis Locorriere)

88. "Duquesne Whistle" by Bob Dylan (from the 2012 album *Tempest*, written by Bob Dylan and Robert Hunter)

89. "Metroland" by Orchestral Manoeuvres In The Dark (released as a single in 2013 from the album *English Electric*, written by OMD)

90. "Stimela (Coal Train)" by Sarah Jane Morris (from the 2013 album *Bloody Rain*, a reworking of Hugh Masekela's 1974 song, written by Hugh Masekela)

91. "Graffiti On The Train" by Stereophonics (from the 2013 album *Graffiti On The Train*, written by Kelly Jones)

92. "Old Toy Trains" by Nick Lowe (from the 2013 album *Quality Street*, written by Roger Miller)

93. "Blue Smoke" by Dolly Parton (released as a single in 2014 from the album *Blue Smoke*, written by Dolly Parton)

94. "Last Rider" by Seth Lakeman (from the 2014 album *Word Of Mouth*, written by Seth Lakeman)

95. "Canopus" by Ralph McTell (from the 2014 EP *The Unknown Soldier*, written by Ralph McTell)

96. "Railway Tracks" by John Illsley (from the 2014 album *Testing The Water*, written by John Illsley)

97. "Midnight Train" by Bryan Ferry (released as a single in 2015 from the album *Avonmore*, written by Bryan Ferry)

98. "Railroad Spikes" by Graham Parker And The Rumour (from the 2015 album *Mystery Glue*, written by Graham Parker)

99. "Taking That Damn Train Again" by The Everlasting Yeah (from the 2015 album *Anima Rising*, written by Raymond Gorman, Ciaran McLaughlin, Brendan Kelly and Damian O'Neill)

100. "Brief Encounter" by Billy Nicholls (from the 2016 album *A Secret Game*, written by Billy Nicholls).

ACKNOWLEDGEMENTS

My sincere thanks to the many singers, songwriters and musicians who shared their memories, thoughts and opinions with me over the two years that it took to research and write this book. Talking to you was supposed to be work, but it certainly didn't feel like it.

Several other "mere mortals" went above and beyond in their efforts to put me in touch with those who I sought to interview. I duly tip my hat to Sadaf Ahmed, John Baine (aka "Attila The Stockbroker"), Sari Matinlassi-Bibb, June Bickford, Caroline Boyce, Beryl Brockman, Kristen Carranza, Dave Clarke, Sarah-Clare Conlon, Suzi Goodrich, Susan Holder, Jeff Konkel, Lee Kavanagh, Anne Leighton, Juliet Sharman Matthews, Chris Metzler, Alistair Norbury, Bob Pitt, Ilona Sawicka, Margrit Seyffer and Caroline Stegner.

Jack Bruce, who sadly passed away in 2014, steadfastly refused to be interviewed during the early stages of my research insisting that his long-time songwriting partner and friend Pete Brown take centre stage. That didn't stop him from pointing me in the right direction on several occasions while I dug for material. Thank you Jack, wherever you are.

Transport writer David Brown, former press officer at the Charisma record label, deserves a pint or two for providing early encouragement while CP Lee, Brian Smith and Geoff Speed were invaluable sources of information regarding the music scene in north west England during the 1960s. Derek Attridge, Paul Gribble, Jenny Gribble, Mike Hodges, Bernard Rose and Matt Biffa generously shed light on the ties that bind trains and songs with paintings, poetry, film and music videos. As for Martin Lawrence, well, I could have listened to him reminiscing about London's Waterloo station circa 1967 for days.

For sourcing and supplying photographs I am indebted to Jennie Clayton, Mary Ann Clayton, Steve Dix, Trevor Ermel, Russ Harrington, Dan Kendall, Bethany Marsh, Rob O'Connor and Jamie Parker.

Acknowledgements

Soundcheck Books have been a joy to work with from the off. Creative, encouraging, honest, knowledgeable, like-minded, patient, supportive – everything an author could wish for.

Thank you to my long suffering partner Jane for daring to share her life with the working patterns, mood swings and precarious bank balance of a freelance writer, and to my children Rhiannon and Luca for tolerating my absences while the book came together.

Last but not least thanks to the late, great Carl Perkins who set the train a-rollin' in the first place.

Spencer Vignes
Cardiff, UK
August 2016

BIBLIOGRAPHY

Ackroyd, Peter: *London, The Biography* (Vintage, 2001)

Adebayo, Dotun: obituary from *The Guardian* on Dennis Brown (1999)

Aitken, Ian: article from the *Screenonline.org* website on *Night Mail* (2014)

Bedford, David: *Liddypool, Birthplace Of The Beatles* (Dalton Watson Fine Books, 2011)

Black, Johnny: article from *Q* magazine on the Mississippi Delta and its musical connections (1995)

Bradshaw, George: *Bradshaw's Handbook* (Collins, 2014)

Buckley, David: *Kraftwerk: Publikation* (Omnibus Press, 2012)

Cash, Johnny: *Cash: The Autobiography Of Johnny Cash* (Harper, 1997)

Celmins, Martin: sleeve notes taken from *The Vaudeville Years Of Fleetwood Mac* (Receiver Records, 1998)

Drury, Jim with Chris Difford & Glenn Tilbrook: *Squeeze, Song By Song* (Sanctuary, 2004)

Fletcher, Nigel and Woodward, Rob: *When Show Business Is No Business* (Ranwell Press, 2000)

Goddard, Simon: *The Smiths: Songs That Saved Your Life* (Reynolds & Hearn Ltd, 2002)

Gordon, S P: *Trains: An Illustrated History Of Locomotive Development* (Cathay Books Ltd, 1976)

Guralnick, Peter: *Last Train To Memphis: The Rise Of Elvis Presley* (Abacus, 1995)

Guthrie, Woody: *Bound For Glory* (Penguin Books, 2004)

Hynde, Chrissie: *Reckless* (Ebury Press, 2015)

Johnson, Peter: *An Illustrated History Of The Travelling Post Office* (OPC, 2009)

Jones, Allan and Love, Damien: article from *Uncut* magazine on Bob Dylan's career in the 1980s (2014)

Bibliography

Martens, Todd: article from the *Los Angeles Times* about the use of music in the film *Harry Potter And The Deathly Hallows: Part 1* (2010)

Marx, Klaus: article from *Railway World* magazine on Waterloo station (1977)

Miles, Barry: *Many Years From Now* (Vintage, 1998)

Morrison, Blake: article from *The Guardian* newspaper on the making of the film *Night Mail* (2007)

Murray, Charles Shaar: article from *Q* magazine on Robert Johnson (1990)

Myers, Marc: article from *The Wall Street Journal* on "Midnight Train To Georgia" (2013)

Palm, Carl Magnus: *Bright Lights, Dark Shadows: The Real Story Of Abba* (Omnibus Press, 2001)

Porterfield, Nolan: *Jimmie Rodgers: The Life And Times Of America's Blue Yodeler* (University Press of Mississippi, 2007)

Rockett, Ron: *Normanton: A Railway History* (Normanton Library, 1998)

Salewicz, Chris: *Redemption Song: The Definitive Biography Of Joe Strummer* (HarperCollins, 2006)

Snow, Mat: article from *Q* magazine on Led Zeppelin (1990)

Stewart, Rod: *Rod, The Autobiography* (Century, 2012)

Townshend, Pete: *Who I Am* (HarperCollins, 2012)

Wald, Elijah: *Escaping The Delta: Robert Johnson And The Invention Of The Blues* (Amistad/HarperCollins, 2005)

INDEX

ABOUT THE AUTHOR

Spencer Vignes is a freelance writer who lives in Cardiff, Wales. He has contributed to over 100 newspapers, magazines and agencies across the world and is the author of six books including *The Server*, nominated for the 2003 William Hill Sports Book of the Year Award. Raised on the post-punk music scene of the late seventies and early eighties, he's been a lover of trains since childhood. Follow him @SpencerVignes or visit www.spencervignes.co.uk for more information.